QUAINT, EXQUISITE

04/19/19

My beloved, Daniel,

I wished for the first book
I signed to be yours - I don't
know how much of this you will enjoy,
and how much find pedantic, hysterical,
or shrill, but anyway, it is yours,
all of it, for you,
with my love,
with all my love,
Grace
xoxo

Quaint, Exquisite

VICTORIAN AESTHETICS AND THE IDEA OF JAPAN

GRACE E. LAVERY

PRINCETON UNIVERSITY PRESS
PRINCETON & OXFORD

Published by Princeton University Press
41 William Street, Princeton, New Jersey 08540
6 Oxford Street, Woodstock, Oxfordshire OX20 1TR

press.princeton.edu

LCCN 2018959174
ISBN 9780691183626

British Library Cataloging-in-Publication Data is available

Editorial: Anne Savarese and Thalia Leaf
Production Editorial: Debbie Tegarden
Jacket/Cover Design: Chris Ferrante
Jacket/Cover Credit: *Portrait of Emily Caroline Massingberd*, by John Collingham Moore (1829–1880). Detail. Gunby Hall, Lincolnshire, UK National Trust Photographic Library / Bridgeman
Production: Jacquie Poirier
Publicity: Jodi Price
Copyeditor: Brittany Micka-Foos

This book has been composed in Arno Pro

Printed on acid-free paper. ∞

Printed in the United States of America

10 9 8 7 6 5 4 3 2 1

I think that if I were Japanese I would dislike most of the things that non-Japanese people write about Japan.

—PIERRE BOURDIEU, "SOCIAL SPACE AND SYMBOLIC SPACE" (1991)

CONTENTS

PREFACE

ANOTHER EMPIRE: VICTORIAN JAPAN

THIS BOOK CONCERNS A COMPLEX IDEA about Japan that developed in the English-speaking world in the second half of the nineteenth century. That idea comprised a number of apparent oppositions: Japan was perceived as beautiful but dangerous; as ultramodern or postcapitalist, but nonetheless stilly immersed within the cocoon of tradition; as Westernized, but still as the most un-Western place conceivable. Though an "idea"—an imaginary phenomenon—this set of associations developed for real historical reasons: this book will therefore move, sometimes quickly, across the boundary that conventionally separates claims about real historical objects from claims about psychic or ideological phenomena. And although the idea developed in the nineteenth century, the distinctive rhetorical function with which Japan has been endowed persists to this day, and vestiges of the tendency of non-Japanese people to treat the idea of Japan as an exceptional Oriental subject can be observed in, for example, the Hokusai "Great Wave" Unicode emoji (one of only two emoji depicting a recognizable art-image), the ASMR-inflected art-pop of the YouTube artist Poppy; and the marketing copy of upscale knifeware. So, in order to understand the essential character of the idea, this book will occasionally grapple with such contemporary objects.

Although this version of Japan was and remains an Orientalist idea, it is not merely false. So this book does not seek to debunk it. Indeed, some of the non-Japanese writers most keen to perform that particular interpretive act—the debunking of Western Japanophilia is as old as Western Japanophilia itself—have been motivated by their own kind of bad faith. Likewise, though it was often promoted by Western writers with an incomplete understanding of their topic, it has also frequently been promoted by Japanese people themselves. It has been leveraged in the service of Japanese cultural projects at a range of scales, from individual artists petitioning for legitimacy and cultural access in the West, to the curatorial rhetoric deployed by the Japanese state to justify its imperial ambition in East Asia, an alibi that important literary figures like Yone Noguchi and Okakura Kakuzo were pressed to formulate. So although, in this book, the idea of Japan is described relatively independent of the distinctive history of the Japanese state, it does not follow that the Japan that appears here is merely a semiotic "system" that exists, ineffably, "faraway" from the observer.[1] Rather, like other ideas, the idea of Japan tilts towards an object possibly knowable, but actually unknown, or not fully known. Orientalists writing about Japan have been, generically, quick to proclaim that they know *nothing* about Japan, a hyperbolic defense presumably erected to protect against the more troubling acknowledgement that they simply *do not know enough*. Yet that condition—the felt inadequacy of a knowledge-practice straining to do some kind of justice to a complex object—is at the root of the idea of Japan, as it is at the root of the particular *kind* of thinking that that idea has continually prompted, and with which it is (this book will argue) indissociably linked: aesthetic judgment in general, and what Kant calls the "subjective universal" character of the judgment of taste in particular.

Because writers in the nineteenth century did, I call the aesthetic category into which the idea of Japan has been placed "the exquisite." The exquisite is the point at which converge an *insuperable* beauty and an *irresistible* violence, both of which Victorians relentlessly ascribed to their idea of Japan. My book attempts to answer three questions about this aesthetic category. One: how did an Orientalist understanding of Japanese culture, derived through contemplation of a range of practices and objects like the haiku, the tea ceremony, and the art of the samurai sword, come to signal to Western observers an aesthetic universality—the feeling that *everybody in the world* should and would find this object beautiful—far more powerfully than any other cultural practices, whether Orientalist, primitivist, or Euro-American? Two: how did Asian Anglophone writers of the late nineteenth and early twentieth centuries come to market their privileged access to Orientalized aesthetic immediacy, and to what political, psychic, and cultural ends? Three: which aspects of this theoretical association between the idea of Japan and aesthetic immediacy have endured (and which not) the long history of relations between Japan and the West that now distances us from the 1850s, where this book's historical argument begins? As I answer those questions through close readings of a range of objects—musical, visual, textual, material, cinematic, performative—I rely on the following argument, prosecuted in historical terms in the book's introduction: the construction of Japan as an aestheticized exception to various taxonomies of race, gender, nation, ethnicity, modernity, and culture was possible *because* Japan confronted the West as an Other Empire; and, as a result, the aesthetic paradigm of the Other Empire has retained, in the intervening period, an immanent formal and thematic connection with Japan.

By this latter, I mean that, even now, representations of Japan compel Western writers and artists to confront the limits of their narcissism, in ways that other Orientalisms do not—and because I am using a psychoanalytic framework to understand narcissism, I capitalize "Other" to indicate a psychic relation. In a 2016 interview the film director Quentin Tarantino said, with what passes for affection, "in the last 25 years, when it comes to industrial societies, hands down the most violent cinema that exists in any one country is Japan. Sometimes grotesquely so. And as we all know, they have the least violent society of all."[2] I take it that Tarantino believed himself to be reciting some version of a psychoanalytic argument about the ethics of sublimation: the subject called "Japan" has successfully offloaded its demons into aesthetic representations, and by prettifying representations of violence, Japan has abolished the real thing. But Tarantino only very barely conceals his own delight in representations of violence for their own sake: as an *aesthetic*, rather than an ethical, good. Japan is not merely the object of Tarantino's (psycho)analysis, then, but the American director's own *sujet supposé savoir*, a subject that has already achieved that which he aspires to achieve. Japan therefore serves Tarantino as both an inspiration *and* a rival that he can never defeat. Different versions of this paradigm will be found throughout this study, in Gilbert and Sullivan, J.A.M. Whistler, Oscar Wilde, and W. B. Yeats; and negotiations with it will be found, in turn, by the Asian Anglophone authors this study reads in detail: Yone Noguchi, Onoto Watanna, and Mikimoto Ryuzo.

Cultural historians argue that something called "history"—whatever its ontological status—produces the rhetorical and aesthetic forms that give cultural objects their shapes. This book takes that principle more literally than cultural historians generally do, by assigning relatively ornate aesthetic forms to relatively contingent, even sometimes unremarkable historical events. The event of Japanese modernization is not, any longer, held to be among the major metanarratives of Western modernity, and so, unlike the *capitalism* that structures the aesthetic categories of zany, cute, and interesting in Sianne Ngai's book *Our Aesthetic Categories*, the *late capitalism* that performs a similar role for Fredric Jameson's account of postmodernism, or the *counterculture of modernity* that organizes the Black aesthetic tradition for Paul Gilroy, the particular history I will be narrating sometimes seems obscure next to the corresponding developments in the aesthetic domain. That a diplomatic expedition to London conducted by a Japanese prince in 1905 could reorganize—in aesthetically and politically measurable terms—the hermeneutics of Orientalism in the United Kingdom: the alignment seems suspiciously neat, oddly fitting, merely *clever*. Yet this claim, which I lay out in the book's first chapter, is nothing more than a historical argument holding itself accountable to a historical archive, at a more granular scale than literary historicism generally attempts to access. When I talk about history shaping ideology, then, I am referring to very discrete histories, like Sadanaru's mission, that sometimes feel orthogonal to or even remote from the historical metanarratives that occupied the same space and time as the stories I relate here.

This play of major and minor characterizes a historiographical method I have come to think of as *quaint*. Like "exquisite," "quaint" was a word Victorians attributed, with a vagueness entirely compatible with obsessiveness, to Japanese culture. (Both also had other functions, too.)[3] It referred to an oblique, slippery relation to history, a distinctive mode of passing into the past. Nothing is quaint from the get-go; an object, text, body, or event acquires the quality of quaintness as it becomes historical—or, more precisely, as it *fails* to become historical. My method of reading and describing cultural objects, I hope, responds to the affective texture of quaintness and to some degree reproduces it: it is the history of the *otaku* ("nerd") or the "Victorianist"; and, even more so, my quaint historiography is inspired by the queer historiographies of, among others, Ann Cvetkovich, Carolyn Dinshaw, and Heather Love. Like queerness, quaintness blurs the line between observing historian-subject and observed historical-object; describing or otherwise dwelling with the queeny, chintzy, and merely ornamental flotsam of history inevitably imparts to the observer the stale perfume of irrelevance. Yet quaint is not (simply) queer, and although many of the figures whose bodies, lives, and works conceptualized the exquisite were figures touched by queerness, what finally defines the quaint is its irretrievability by *any* major history, including the histories of repression and emergence, sociability and privation, love and violence that detain queer theory. Not only most of the texts, but also the genres for which those texts are taken as exemplary, seem today at best adorably irrelevant, and at worst queasy and cringey: *The Mikado* / light opera; "The Little White Girl" / sentimental portraiture; "My love's lengthened hair . . ." / Anglophone haiku; *What Is Ruskin in Japan?* / Japanese Victoriana; *Madame Butterfly* / sentimental romance. Like the rose petals of Heliogabalus, quaintness first prettifies, then submerges, and finally smothers all with which it comes into contact. If a little history turns one away from aesthetic immediacy, a lot brings one back to it. Related to which, I feel compelled to protest—this is the most embarrassing sentence that I have ever written—that the *style* of this book, which gazes too long into its own reflection, is, to the slim degree it makes sense to refer to style as intentional, an attempt to animate the queer-and-quaintness of my objects, the exquisite quality that lingers around them, unless and until they are put to work in the service of historical metanarrative.

There exists a substantial body of scholarly work exploring the historical and aesthetic attachment often felt by white Western queers to Japanese aesthetics, to which the present work is immensely indebted.[4] Unlike those who treat that association as a historical contingency, however, I argue that the particular affinity between queers and Japanese aesthetics is a logical consequence of the composition of aesthetic experience in the modern period. Since the author's own (subjective, albeit universal) experiences will form an important source of evidence, it seems reasonable to admit that my own relation to Japanese aesthetics derives from an early Stephin Merritt song named "How to Get Laid in Japanese," a Future Bible Heroes composition from their first EP, *Lonely Days* (1997).[5] It is the loneliest of the songs on that collection, one of the loneliest in Merritt's extremely lonely oeuvre. In his mordant baritone, Merritt intones a set of casually heartbreaking pick-up lines in Japanese: *asu-o shinji ni ikimasen ka,* don't you live for tomorrow? He does not pronounce these words with any care. He stumbles from one question to the next—*tabako wa ikaga desu-ka? / Dare ka ga o machi desu-ka?*—without receiving answers. He recites a musical phrasebook, frantically but ineffectively memorized before a night out in Shinjuku Ni-chome. Underneath, synth strings highlight cheaply suspended sevenths, cheesy and cruisey, and the melody reverbs as though being absorbed by the chrome of an elevator, as you stand in silence, going up. Getting laid in Japanese conceptualized as sex without togetherness, bright surfaces gliding over each other. Even if the primary aesthetic characteristic of such elevatorish music is derivativeness—"going through the motions," maybe—it does not follow that it is therefore blunt or inefficacious. Quite the opposite; the affective manipulations of "How to Get Laid in Japanese" are no less brutally effective for being banal; the song's banality is central to its erotic appeal. There is an exquisite obliquity to a song that knows how to touch you, and therefore exhibits for you your degraded objecthood, the fact that you are merely the latest in an infinitely extensive series of touched, touchable things. The exquisite, Stephin Merritt reassures you, *works,* whether or not you will it, whether or not you wish it did.

I cannot neglect to point out, however, that the finished object I contemplate in 2018 is being given to a world quite unlike the one that gave it to me. Ours has become a newly ghastly cosmos, in which the *Japoniste* hypercapitalist dystopias of 1980s and 1990s pop culture (Blur's "Yuko and Hiro" is another one) feel like mere discomforts, devoutly to be wished. In 2016, the already dominant force of white ethnonationalism dramatically extended its political power in the two places where I have spent most of my life, the United Kingdom and the United States. These events and their analogues elsewhere may be signs that the transnational affective flows that I describe in detail in this book are to be curtailed. Perhaps they have already ended. If that is true, then of course it goes without saying—or, I hope it does—that, once cut off, such flows will not be missed, nor should they be mourned. In at least one sense, however, there would be some grounds for seeing continuity between the world of this book and that of our broken present, since even the macrohistory

FIGURE 0.1. Gabe from *The Office.*

of American ethnonationalism—whose primary narratives are those of white supremacy, imperialism, settler colonialism, and white ethnic nativism: the major themes, that is, of modernity itself—cannot be told without the aesthetic exceptionalization of Japan by white people. The white *otaku* trolls on the 4chan *pol* thread, the online forum in which the insurgent white nationalist movement established its political priorities and cultural protocols, were mostly young men; and 4chan itself was initially convened to discuss, as the domain name suggests, a stylized Japanese aesthetic they accessed through *anime* and *manga,* through pornography, and through "transracial" fantasizing. So we will note the strange recurrence of the Western fascination with Japanese art in a number of politically consequential scenes—and also that the figure of the young man, peculiarly obsessed with Japanese art, Japanese sex, and Japanese violence has mutated, however, from the revolutionary prison abolitionist Oscar Wilde to the jobsworthy fuccboi Gabe from *The Office,* who proudly displays his *katana* when his coworkers visit his man cave. For such latter-day *japonistes,* an Other Empire was already within reach.

I would like to acknowledge with deep gratitude the engagement of my colleagues, who have stimulated, challenged, delighted, supported, and provoked me at every turn. Some have even gone to the trouble of reading the whole thing! To those people I am especially indebted: James Eli Adams, Anne Cheng, Eric Falci, Catherine Gallagher, Joshua Gang, Margreta de Grazia,

Daniel Hack, David Kurnick, Cliff Mak (who also helped me unfutz my paratext), Kent Puckett, Paul Saint-Amour, Katie Snyder, Elisa Tamarkin, and Carolyn Williams. I am thankful for the judicious encouragement of Anne Savarese, the editor who commissioned this project for Princeton University Press, who has had an enormously salutary effect on its composition. I was a graduate student at the University of Pennsylvania during an extraordinary time, and am grateful for the sustained and scrupulous attention of my dissertation committee: Paul Saint-Amour, Josephine Nock-Hee Park (in whose graduate class, "Modernism and the Orient," the idea for this project came about), and Jed Esty, many of whose marks are incorporated herein. And to the other faculty at Penn whose engagements with my work were frequent, freely given, and capacious: Nancy Bentley, Max Cavitch, Jim English, Suvir Kaul, David Kazanjian, Ania Loomba, and Heather Love. The three research assistants with whom I have worked, Alexandra Dumont (UC Berkeley), Eleanor Rowe (Brown University), and Mary Mussman (UC Berkeley) did, in truth, more than assist in research: they shared their ideas and pushed back against mine, and they found things.

I am also grateful for the engagements, in prose, in person, over the phone, and in quick-fire email exchanges, to all of the following interlocutors, who have helped the project grow over the last decade. This book is stronger thanks to the careful labor of: • *colleagues within UC Berkeley*: Elizabeth Abel, Charles Altieri, Stephen Best, C. D. Blanton, Églantine Colon, Ian Duncan, Nadia Ellis, Anne-Lise François, Catherine Flynn, Mark Goble, Steven Goldsmith, Lyn Hejinian (who is the *Greatest of All Time*), Michelle Koerner, Celeste Langan, Steven Lee, Colleen Lye, David Marno, D. A. Miller, Poulomi Saha, Namwali Serpell, Emily Thornberry, Winnie Wong, Dora Zhang. • *colleagues working at other institutions*: Zarena Aslami, S. Pearl Brilmyer, Christopher Bush, James Buzard, Natalia Cecire, Alicia Christoff, David Coombs, Michelle Decker, Jonathan Farina, Renee Fox, Amanpal Garcha, Lauren Goodlad, Devin Griffiths, Eric Hayot, Nathan Hensley, Claire Jarvis, Anna Kornbluh, Sebastian Lecourt, Allen MacDuffie, Cliff Mak, Benjamin Morgan, Nasser Mufti, Mat Paskins, Jessica Rosenberg, Jesse Rosenthal, Zach Samalin, Rachel Teukolsky, Michael Tondre, Marlene Tromp, Ross Wilson, Alex Woloch, Danny Wright, Robert Young. • *groups that have invited me to share research from this book*: the UC Berkeley English department nineteenth-century reading group; graduate students in the Spring 2014, Fall 2015, and Spring 2018 classes; readings groups at the University of Oxford (thanks especially to Ankhi Mukherjee, David Russell, and Helen Small); the University of California, Los Angeles (thanks especially to Michael Cohen, Jonathan Grossman, Anne Mellor, and Anahid Nersessian); Osaka University (thanks especially to Gerry Yokoda); and the University of York (thanks especially to John Bowen, Matt Campbell, and James Williams). • *and non-academic readers who have brought other expertise to bear on my work*: Julie Rose Bower, Seiriol Davies, Kate Genevieve, Helena Goundry Butler, Samuel Goundry Butler, and Alexander Page. • *in a category of his own, in every sense, but especially in having expanded my sense of what it means to be read*: Daniel Alexander Mallory Ortberg.

This book is dedicated to my families, plural.

Grace Elisabeth Lavery
Oakland, CA
September 2018

QUAINT, EXQUISITE

INTRODUCTION

Analytic of the Exquisite

Too much philosophy had been written in Europe; everything from the most commonplace to the most sublime, had been collected, catalogued, commented upon, raked up merely for the sake of raking up barren knowledge. It now became necessary to remove the dust and the cobwebs that had settled upon it, and infuse new life by purifying, remodeling, and developing that heap of knowledge. And what could accomplish this better than Japanese art? Its influence was everywhere felt. It called forth, for instance, the short story literature, in which Anderson, Turgenjew, Verga, and the modern French and Scandinavian writers are masters—a tendency towards brevity and conciseness of expression, which suggests a good deal more than it actually tells. Its law of repetition with slight variation, we can trace in Poe's poems, the work of the French symbolists, and, above all else, in the writings of Maurice Maeterlinck, that quaint combination of Greek, medieval, and Japanese art reminiscences.

—SADAKICHI HARTMANN, *JAPANESE ART* (1903)[1]

Gone were but the Winter,
Come were but the Spring,
I would go to a covert
Where the birds sing;

Where in the whitethorn
Singeth a thrush,
And a robin sings
In the holly-bush.

Full of fresh scents
Are the budding boughs
Arching high over
A cool green house:

Full of sweet scents,
And whispering air

Which sayeth softly:
"We spread no snare;

"Here dwell in safety,
Here dwell alone,
With a clear stream
And a mossy stone.

"Here the sun shineth
Most shadily;
Here is heard an echo
Of the far sea,
Though far off it be."

—CHRISTINA ROSSETTI,
"GONE WERE BUT THE WINTER" (1866)

I. More than Unsatisfying, Less than Incomplete

Of the descriptions given by the unnamed readers of Christina Rossetti's poem "Gone Were but the Winter" whose responses I. A. Richards gathered in the second chapter of *Practical Criticism* (1929), his groundbreaking study of the interpretative strategies and presuppositions of Cambridge undergraduates in the 1920s, one of the more sympathetic responses is marked 2.71, and reads "In its own rather tiny way, it is quite exquisite."[2] Richards was scrupulous in refraining from diagnosis of student motivations, yet this sentence, along with a concluding description of Rossetti's phrase "mossy stone" as evoking "the intended atmosphere of quietness and uninterrupted peace," provokes an uncharacteristic intervention from Richards: "In the last reading a reminiscence of the principles of Japanese gardening might be respected. 'Its own rather tiny way' supplements the impression" (40). Neither the student nor the poem has mentioned Japan in any way, but the calmness of the mossy stone—in which Richards might be expected to have seen an allusion to Wordsworth's "violet by a mossy stone / half hidden from the eye"—instead suggests to him an Orientalized form of landscape gardening.

What accounts for this association?

Japanese gardening had, prior to 1929, attracted a good deal of interest from Western horticulturalists. In 1894, San Francisco hosted the *California Midwinter International Exposition,* for which was constructed a Japanese Tea Garden in Golden Gate Park, the first of dozens in the United States. Travelers to the park often had recourse to literary tropes in narrating their experiences: "to feel truly Brobdignagian, one should visit the Japanese tea garden," wrote the correspondent for *Overland Monthly*; where "the dainty Yum-Yum" (a reference to the female lead of *The Mikado*) spends her time.[3] But of particular interest to the *Overland* correspondent was the "very fascinating [twist]" that governed Japanese design in general: "their peculiar ideas of proportion. No doubt the fact that the trunks and branches of their stunted pine tree are a miniature copy of the natural tree, while the leaves are of almost normal size, does not in the least interfere with their idea of the beauty of the whole." British gardeners were also fascinated by these "dwarf trees" (now called bonsai) and the miniature gardens into which they were compiled with "scrupulous exactness": "dwarf" here indicated not merely a pleasing *miniaturization*, but a potentially disturbing compression/distention of proper proportion in individual parts. The *1900 Supplement to the Dictionary of Gardening*, for example, admitted that "when correctly treated, these trees are properly proportioned as regards trunk and branch, leaf and flower, and not mere outrages upon Nature."[4] The most assiduous promoter of bonsai gardening in London at the turn of the century was a Japanese commercial trader named Toichi Tsumura, who delivered a paper entitled "Dwarf Trees" at the London Japan Society in 1902, in which, like the author of the *Overland* article, explained Japan by reference to *Gulliver's Travels*, but in this case describing the plants as "Lilliputian specimens."[5] Tsumura insisted further that, although Japanese art in general preferred to miniaturize its subjects than to magnify them, it did not follow that "their work is apt to be more often pretty and fascinating than dignified and imposing" (5).

Richards's student may not have known any of this, of course. But he was tapping into an aspect of aesthetic discourse whose effects have been, like Wordsworth's stone and Sadakichi Hartmann's Japan in the epigraph above, "everywhere felt" since the mid-nineteenth century: the *exquisite*. It is a term ubiquitous in the literature of the British aesthetics, though its meanings are grasped only obliquely: it was a word, so to speak, always written in italics. An exquisite object is *extremely* beautiful; it is also *weirdly* incomplete. It is also, as often as not, able to hurt its consumer or contemplator: "a cigarette is the perfect type of a perfect pleasure," Lord Henry Wotton tells Dorian Gray, because "it is exquisite, and it leaves one unsatisfied."[6] *It leaves one*: after having marked you with its sharp point, the cigarette departs like a lover in a taxi, leaving behind a cloud and a cough.[7] Yet "exquisite" was more than a synonym for "unsatisfying"; Lord Henry's "and" (as well as Wilde's performatively exquisite comma) distinguishes between the two ideas even while it conjoins them. The cigarette is its own effect, complete in itself, without either a half-life or much of a consequence: for all the intensity of the exquisite (and, in certain respects, there is no louder word in nineteenth-century aesthetics) it remains in another sense muted, familiar, a current easily tapped within the broader flow of consumer goods. The first paradox of the exquisite: it is both high-intensity and low-intensity, unspeakably alien and unremarkably familiar, intensely-to-be-desired and easily-to-be-obtained.

The association Richards made between Japanese cultural practices and a Victorian lyric poem was not, obviously, correct, but neither was it simply wrong. By the end of the nineteenth century, a set of ideas, forms, and feelings associated with Japanese art were thereby *also* associated with great achievements in the arts—particularly the literary and visual arts, and particular instances within one of those two media that referenced the other (paintings inscribed with poems; poems especially attentive to typographical composition). By the 1870s, Japan appeared to have outstripped Western cultures in its production of objects universally recognizable as beautiful. According to some of the strongest formulations of that position, Japan had not merely approached but already attained the position of universal aesthetic legibility—a development that threatened Euro-American cultural power. "Japanese art is not merely the incomparable achievement of certain harmonies in colour," wrote the Victorian poet A. C. Swinburne, "*it is the negation, the immolation, the annihilation of everything else.*"[8] The principle of aesthetic universality that underpinned Swinburne's assessment of Japan distinguished his interest in Japan both from earlier and contemporary Orientalisms. An appreciation of Japanese art did not mean mystified genuflection towards the latent creativity of the Other—this was not the kind of condescension that, in Edward Said's influential account of Orientalism, formalized the logic of imperialism for the written word.[9] Rather, Japanese art appeared as a force already manifested, a creativity already cultured: an *other*, in other words, whose claims to aesthetic universality had already gained priority over the Western *self*. Japan's ontological priority conditioned for Victorians—and, this book will argue, continues to condition—a wide range of aesthetic, historical, political, and cultural fantasies, both populating and sharply delimiting the imaginative field of the modern world.

The late-Victorian tendency to represent Japan as an exception to various rules was also relatively discontinuous from the attitudes towards Japan that preceded it. In his important 1856 book *The Grammar of Ornament*, the architect Owen Jones constructed a detailed comparative history of ornamental representational practices, written towards the Arnoldian aim of improving contemporary art by furnishing artists with a better critical vocabulary. His book ranges from the ornamental practices of "savage tribes," among whom, he notes, "there is scarcely a people, in however early a stage of civilization, with whom the desire for ornament is not a strong instinct" (13). He follows ornamental forms through the Asian and European stages of his contemporary historiography, and derives from his narrative thirty-seven normative propositions, printed at the book's opening, which treat Oriental ornament as illustrative of the principles of natural law. According to Proposition 12, for example, "All junctions of curved lines with curved or of straight lines with straight should be tangential to each other. *Natural law. Oriental practice in accordance with it*" (6). That neither Japan nor Japanese ornamentation appears in *The Grammar of Ornament* is only somewhat surprising: it was published only three years after Commodore Matthew Perry arrived in Japan, and it was written in part as a record of the Great Exhibition of 1851 for which Jones had served as interior designer.[10] Yet the absence of Japanese art from one of the midcentury's major accounts of comparative aesthetic theory points to a larger truth of the period: that, as a rapidly modernizing and militarizing empire, Japan could not easily be forced to conform to the earlier Victorians' teleological histories of culture, narratives which tended to culminate in a celebration of European cultural supremacy.

As Richards's editorial comment suggests, "exquisite" was indeed the later Victorian period's favorite word for Japanese culture. It appears everywhere in writing on Japan from the 1860s onwards, and will be encountered throughout this book to describe the smallness of a tree, the sadness of a poet, and the effect of a sword slicing through flesh. Laurence Oliphant's *Narrative of the Earl of Elgin's Mission to China and Japan* (1860) mentioned the "exquisite taste displayed in the gardens and cottages upon the roadside" in Edo suburbs.[11] In *Tales of Old Japan* (1871) A. B. Mitford talked excitedly of the "exquisite designs, harmonious colouring, rich gilding" of the same city.[12] Isabella Bird's popular *Unbeaten Tracks in Japan* (1880) uses the word sixteen times to describe a parade of Japanese objects: a *kakemono*; a piece of moss; a number of silk scarves; a small wooden Buddha; a basket; a small but comfortable bedroom ("I almost wish the rooms were a little *less* exquisite"); "Japanese agriculture"; a piece of hemp.[13] Further examples, in their dozens, will be forthcoming. These associations did not derive from Japanese writers or artists themselves, but from the Orientalists: they nonetheless furnished such writers, when they approached the English language, with a set of stereotypes and associations with which they were compelled to grapple. Those associations are quite clear: Japan is elegant, but perhaps excessively so; its decorative arts exhibit an economy of arrangement, which is perhaps indicative of parsimony; the price of Japanese supremacy in the aesthetic realm is an indefinite, but persistent, discomfort.

An Oriental imaginary in which a tasteful formal arrangement is distinctively associated with an experience of some kind of pain: such is, indeed, the oldest version of "exquisite" that obtains in the English language, at least according to the *Oxford English Dictionary*. The word's very etymology, exquisite, indicates an object that has been "sought out," whose preciousness is dependent upon the distance one has traveled to obtain it. It is found in the early histories of Oriental adeptness in the arts of torture: Richard Knolles's *General Historie of the Turkes* (1603) dwelt salaciously on the "exquisite torture" (704) and "most exquisite torments" (770) enacted in the Constantinople of Suleiman the Magnificent.[14] And "exquisite" has become, in the past century, an almost (but still not entirely) schlocky term to describe the copresence of erotic desire and unsublimated violence: "Dear Miss Steele, you are quite simply exquisite," writes Dorian's near-namesake Christian, initiating another interminable series of emails.[15] There is a formal similarity between Knolles's torture and Bird's slightly cramped bedroom, despite the difference of degree, and though we will certainly find "exquisite" deployed to describe moments of powerful *thematic* violence (in, for example, critics' abundant use of the term to describe the gorier moments of Quentin Tarantino's movies), such thematic discomfort is logically secondary to, and (I will argue) a symptom of, the *conceptual* disfiguration within the formulation of the exquisite.

Conceptual disfiguration—a representation premised on the failure of representation; an attempt to sublimate into form the *fundamental* incongruity of the represented object—undergirds a range of Western aesthetic constructions of Japan, which have been, from the outset, particularly moved to explore the violence implicit in beauty. Ruth Benedict's widely read popular ethnography, *The Chrysanthemum and the Sword* (1946), describes Japanese culture's central contradiction as between "militaristic and aesthetic" characteristics, the bipolarity of which gives her study its title. Both her claim that beauty and violence were twinned, and her sense that "shame" was the primary conceptual framework through which that contradiction was managed, were aimed with ethnographic brio at Japanese "culture," but succeeded instead in describing the Western theory of the aesthetic *itself*. The "annihilation of everything else" that Swinburne imagines as the cost of Japanese achievement in color expresses, to be sure, an anxiety about Japanese cultural influence that recurs in a more extreme form in various invasion narratives (such as H. G. Wells's *The War in the Air*) or the period's various "yellow peril" novels. But that is only an extreme example of the general case. In the depictions of hyper-aestheticized Japanese womanhood common to the *Madame Chrysanthème* genre (a central focus of this book's fifth chapter), the beauty inheres in suicide considered as one of the fine arts. As the *Madame Chrysanthème* genre attests, the emblematic suggestiveness of the katana—a symbol that limns intense beauty to unbearable violence—that is, in a sense, *already both chrysanthemum and sword*—both predated and has outlasted Benedict's analysis of Japanese culture. The "shame" associated with Japanese aesthetics, though it is understood differently between and among Victorian Orientalists and Japanese émigrés, reverberates through the Savoy Opera *The Mikado,* (which depicts a world in which flirtatious speech is punishable by death), the Japanese-inflected writings of W. B. Yeats (for whom the Japanese and the Irish were similar castes of aristocrats, humiliated by their more vulgar neighbors), and perhaps most poignantly of all in the writings of the Japanese Ruskin enthusiast Mikimoto Ryuzo, who wrote copious notes detailing his desire to be closer to his (long dead) mentor.

Let me construct an imaginary reading of the Rossetti poem—a reading that, quite possibly, has never occurred to a reader before, certainly did not occur to Rossetti, and may not even have occurred to Richards's misguided student. "Gone Were but the Winter" *is,* after all, about Japan—or rather, it is about the aesthetic formation that became, by the end of the nineteenth century, unthinkable without Japan. The poem's meter, which begins in sententious coupleting, gradually loosens to the point of exhibiting, in its final five-line stanza, something like a *tanka,* which unspools over five plain lines a pair of gnomic contradictions. The first asserts that the sun, impossibly, "shineth / most shadily," a presentation that prepares the reader for another, less resolved contradiction: "here," in an English "covert," or thicket, the poet recounts hearing "an echo / of the far sea / though far off it be." Audibly virtual, the echo does not bring the sea closer, but it does make it more *present*—the "far off" location rendered by poetry, and absent as place. This poem expresses the ambivalent optimism, tempered by responsibility, of an enormous distance breached by form and representation, and its effect is somber, sober, and powerful. These effects, indeed, are not mitigated by the poem's evident silliness: its talking air, and its awkward—but precise—repetitions of "sing," "scents," and "dwell." (This latter, incidentally, is proof positive that the poem is about Japan, because how could it not be a reference to Yone Noguchi's lines "I dwell alone / Like one-eyed star, / In frightened, darksome willow threads"?) There is more to be said, to be sure—my eye is especially drawn to the unusual use of the noun "covert," which surely calls to be read not merely as a noun but, punning, as an adjective, and indicating, in a poem concerned with duty, protection, and freedom, an indirect relation to legal *coverture.* But given its ambient poignancy, animistic sense of responsibility, and domesticated exoticism—especially notwithstanding that this poem is, in the very same ways, rather trivial, tedious, and cringeworthy—I, at least, can hardly disagree that it is *quite* exquisite. At least a world within a misreading of Rossetti. But where did it come from?

II. The Melancholic Condition of the Subjective Universal

So, by the end of the nineteenth century, "Japan" had come to signify an affective conundrum that had been discovered by the Western discourse of aesthetics. It was, in that sense, the name for a *problematic* within aesthetics: a term that Michel Foucault uses to designate the moment when an old idea is felt to be newly in need of a solution, to be "take[n] care of"; or when a certain logical or rhetorical premise is newly unsettled and challenged.[16] That problem was nothing less than the entire project of aesthetics as such—of describing or justifying the apparent existence of a judgment devoid of both moral value and logical necessity, but possessed of the same kind of universal ambition as a moral or mathematical claim. The condition that became problematic in this sense was powerfully and famously described by Immanuel Kant, whose theory of aesthetic judgment was undergirded and suffused by a melancholic dimension that has been palpable to many of his readers. Not least to Thomas De Quincey, whose comic essay "On Murder Considered as One of the Fine Arts" not only appears in the *OED* as the first text to contain the word "*aesthetically*," but which satirizes Kantian thinking on morality and aesthetics as tending to produce split subjects and moral panics.[17] Kant's first approaches to the emergent branch of philosophy called, by Alexander Baumgarten, "aesthetik," (1750) are contained within his early book *Observations on the Feeling of the Beautiful and Sublime* (1764), which contains prefigurative elements of the systematic theory of aesthetics outlined in the *Critique of Judgment*.[18] Kant's early enthusiasm for the science of aesthetics, as Baumgarten had laid it out, is visible in many of his earlier works: as early as 1771, he wrote to his student Marcus Herz that he wanted to write a foundationalist philosophical treatise establishing, among other things, "the theory of taste."[19] That neither the *Observations*, nor the occasional dismissive references to Baumgarten in the *Critique of Pure Reason* (1781), accomplished that task did not dissuade Kant from trying again almost decade later; the *Critique of Judgment* was published in 1790, and at last established, to its author's satisfaction, the existence of a priori principles governing aesthetic judgment.

The earlier text can appear quite "un-Kantian" at times, since it is temperamentally inductive, and not yet committed to the "critical" position with which Kant's three *Critiques* are associated: "sublime" and "beautiful" are terms the philosopher uses to aggregate quite diverse phenomena, both objective (a flower is beautiful) and subjective (taste for the beautiful can, in men, degenerate into foppishness). The relative weakness, indeed contingency, of the bonds grouping these uses of the term together becomes clearest in the fourth and last of the book's four sections, in which Kant comes to consider "national characteristics, so far as they depend upon the distinct feeling of the beautiful and sublime." The "national characteristic," as Kant adduces it here, is necessarily both subjective (it is felt by individuals) and objective (it is recognizable as an empirical datum in the world), and its origins needn't brook too much inquiry: whether "these national differences are contingent and depend upon the times and the type of government, or are bound by a certain necessity to the climate, I do not here inquire."[20]

The title of the book, *Beobachtungen über das Gefühl des Schönen und Erhabenen,* differs in a couple of interesting respects from that of Edmund Burke's 1757 book on the same topic: *A Philosophical Enquiry* (rather than Kant's mere "observations") *into the Origins of Our Ideas* (in Kant, no origins, no "us," and no ideas) *of the Sublime and the Beautiful.*[21] In the "First Introduction" to the *Critique of Judgment,* Kant laid the (reasonable) charge against Burke that the latter's *Philosophical Enquiry* was merely inductive in its logic, and therefore incapable of sustaining a properly *philosophical inquiry* into the a priori nature of aesthetic judgment. In place of "origins," then, Kant had developed an extraordinary geographical analogy, which connects European national differences to counterparts in Asia: Arabs are the "Spaniards of the orient"; the Persians are like the French ("good poets, courteous, and of fairly fine taste"), and

> the Japanese could in a way be regarded as the Englishmen of this part of the world, but hardly in any other quality than their resoluteness—which degenerates into the utmost stubbornness—their valor, and disdain of death.[22]

The Japanese and the British: death cultists. Versions of this analogy will recur throughout this book—to take two examples: in the association between the death penalty in Japan and domestic British satire in *The Mikado,* and in the poet Yone Noguchi's melancholic relation to a Victorian poem about death in his own haiku—but Kant's analogy entails the bold claim that aesthetic taste as an index of racial essence.

This aspect of Kantian aesthetics is, of course, less than central to Kant's more famous formulations. But a sense of cultural belonging as logical grounds for the transcendental aesthetic never disappears entirely. In the *Critique of Judgment,* Kant sets out to ground a transcendental account of aesthetics in a circuit of perception and cognition called "reflective judgment," of which he admits four species: the agreeable, the good, the beautiful, and the sublime. The latter two are aesthetic judgments, "by which is understood one whose determining ground cannot be other than subjective."[23] Yet although grounded in the subject herself, aesthetic judgment calls out to the world of objects for consent and agreement: "we allow no one to be of a different opinion, without, however, grounding our judgment on concepts, but only on our feeling, which we therefore make our ground not as a private feeling, but a common one."[24] This is the melancholic condition of the "subjective universal": we demand that everybody feel the same way about a beautiful object as we do, even as we know that not everybody will. "[Common sense] does not say that everyone *will* concur with our judgment but that everyone *should*" (§22). The *Critique of Judgment* offers an array of such unmet demands: "when we call something beautiful, the pleasure that we feel is expected of everyone else, just as if it were to be regarded as a property of the object . . . but beauty is nothing by itself, without relation to the feeling of the subject." This "feeling" is not "emotion," a term that Kant aligns with "charm" to designate the pathological modality of interested judgment. (I mention this observation, which I take from Jean-François Lyotard's work on the Kantian sublime, in order to differentiate the position I have called "melancholia" from "feeling" as the term is sometimes used, to designate particular emotional states, oriented to and in some sense determined by, objective conditions. The absence that I have been describing as constitutive of Kantian judgment preexists the pleasure that may follow from the successful *completion* of the judgment of the beautiful—or, for that matter, that may be incurred in the final movement of the judgment of the sublime.)[25]

Nor is the satisfaction the Kantian subject receives from the judgment of the beautiful reducible to conscience, or the usual meaning of "common sense."[26] In an essay glossing Hannah Arendt's foundational rereading of Kant, Ronald Beiner usefully distinguishes between four distinct kinds of reasoning, which might otherwise be conventionally lumped together as "common sense." The first, which he does indeed call (1) "common sense," is the "ideal norm" that, in aesthetic judgments, everybody ought to agree with me. Common sense thus immediately postulates another form of agreement, which Arendt calls (2) "consensus"—but this kind of reasoning is merely posited, and neither logically nor empirically consequent from the first kind. At a still further degree of reflective remove from the initial judgment "this object is beautiful," a subject may be able to estimate whether or not that judgment *will indeed* meet with general assent—that is, whether or not the object thought beautiful will be held so by others. This form of reasoning, which Beiner calls (3) "*sensus communis,* or "public sense," seeks to determine whether or not one's judgment conforms to "good taste"—with the caveat (I would add) that, in the case that it does not, it is rather too late in the process of reflection to do anything about it. A quite distinct notion of common sense, which Beiner imports from Kant's essay "What Is Enlightenment?," is (4) the "public use of one's reason," which she takes to argue that "thinking *in public* can be constitutive of thinking *as such*." By placing Kant's explicitly political essay into a series of notions of publicness that she derives from his account of aesthetic judgment, Beiner argues, Arendt articulates a powerful case for the *Critique of Judgment* as an implicitly political book concerned with using reason to modulate between the cognitive lives of individuals and the social demands with which they must negotiate.

The subjective universal character of the judgment of taste is its flaw, a crack between the bounded exocentric position of the subject and the regime of objects (here including, indeed primarily comprising, other people) to which that subject appeals for concurrence and affirmation. It is in this sense the subjective counterpart of the exquisite objects I have been describing, which nestles between their beauty and their capacity to harm. The "harm" implied by subjective universality is, as Lyotard reminds us, never actually incurred by the melancholy subject—because the *ascription* of assent is sufficient for Kant's judgment of taste to be enjoyable, whatever anybody else thinks—but the position of the subject fantasizing reciprocity for his own affective investments in objects is, in the real world, a highly precarious one.[27] It implies a very fragile social relation between the aesthetic observer and the Other with whom he shares a "common [feeling]," who is thereby positioned as the phantasmatic guarantor of his own judgment—which then the Other may fail or refuse to ratify. Such failures and refusals constitute the central part of the history of cultural engagement between Japan and Britain: in Whistler's rejection of Mortimer Menpes after the latter's trip to Japan; in Yone Noguchi's plagiaristic relation to Victorian verse; in Mikimoto Ryuzo's intolerable distance from his beloved John Ruskin. These are stories about the inherent defectiveness of subjective universality—stories in which people *believe* that they can experience a "common feeling" with another human being through an aesthetic medium, and find that belief cruelly rebuffed. To be sure, the connection "Japan/the West" holds no necessary logical relation to these aspects of Kantian aesthetics. But, for historical reasons that the philosopher could hardly have seen coming, Japan became, in the nineteenth century, a highly privileged site for testing philosophical "universals" of a number of kinds, and in the aesthetic domain above all.

The word "melancholy" has a number of distinct resonances in psychoanalytical discourse relevant to the reading of Kant I have outlined, centrally the foundational paradox as Freud describes it: "the analogy with mourning led us to conclude that [the melancholic] had suffered a loss in regard to an object; what he tells us points to a loss in regard to his ego."[28] The problematic *location* of absence that a melancholic may exhibit as self-censure or self-hatred, following the loss (through death or departure, for example) of a loved one, can be resolved, Freud thinks, if one observes that what appear to be self-censures on the part of the melancholic are, more authentically, reproaches directed at the loved object that, by virtue of being lost, can no longer receive them. Thus the melancholic directs at herself an animus originally destined for another. Kant's view of the judgment of the beautiful is likewise predicated on a fuzziness concerning subject and object—we are wont to describe an object as beautiful, he argues, whereas in fact "the beautiful" more properly names a subjective procedure of perception and judgment. This much is well understood. The part that, in my view, has been missed by most readers of Kant, is that, on the grounds of that subject/object confusion, the *ascription* of object-like qualities to "the beautiful" inscribes an absence into the scene of a cognitive judgment that should, by rights, be experienced as pure self-presence. Aesthetic judgment persuades an observer that his judgment is objective, whereas in fact it is only universal and not objective at all, so that the appeals an observer makes to the "common sense" of others rests on shaky grounds.

Certain scholars of Kant have already found ways to explore the melancholic dimension of his thinking, so it is worth distinguishing between the Freudian account of melancholy I offer here to the Lacanian version articulated by Roberto Esposito in *Terms of the Political: Community, Immunity, Biopolitics*.[29] Esposito understands Kantian phenomenology, his famous bracketing of the *ding an sich*, as a melancholy self-exclusion from the narcissistic fantasy of self-presence in line with Lacan's famous barring of consciousness from the world of "the Real." The ethical dimension of Kantian thinking, Esposito argues, derives from Kant's experimental approach to freedom in the absence of the *ding an sich*: "Kant's melancholic man knows that community as such is unrealizable, that the *munus* of our *communitas* is the law that prohibits its perfect fulfillment. Yet perhaps Kant's melancholic man is also the first to know that *munus* is also a gift, that that impossibility which reminds men of their finitude also endows them with the freedom to choose that it may become its necessary opposite" (34). Esposito is arguing towards a different *telos* than the present work: he wonders what use Kant might be in establishing political communities in the present and future, while I am charting how Kant has helped to construct and deconstruct aesthetic communities in the present and past. But that is not the only difference between us: my (more pessimistic) view is that the subjective universal character of the judgment of taste is not, for Kant, an enabler of freedom, but rather the origin of a deep dysfunction within subject/object relations, one that, like narcissism (Freud's analogy, p. 249), ensures the fundamental severance of any *subjective* practice of freedom from any *objective* relation of community.

In this sense, my own position vis-à-vis Kant coheres perhaps surprisingly with the reading of the *Third Critique* offered in a spirit of criticism towards the end of Pierre Bourdieu's *Distinction*. Bourdieu, as is well known, sets out to prove that the supposedly "pure" nature of the judgment of taste reflects nothing more than "the universalization of the dispositions associated with a particular social and economic condition" (495). Yet, though his work has doubtless been vulgarized into a churlish debunking of the kind he struggles, at all turns, to resist, *Distinction* refuses to allow its reader the satisfaction of concluding that sociology will provide, since aesthetics cannot, a firm ground for the objective analysis of taste.

> Since we know that the very principle of the symbolic efficacy of philosophical discourse lies in the play between two structures of discourse which the work of formalization seeks to integrate without entirely succeeding, it would be naïve to reduce the truth of this double-discourse to a subterranean discourse in which the Kantian ideology of the beautiful is expressed and which analysis reconstitutes by reconnecting the web of notations blurred by the interferences of the structures. The *social categories of aesthetic judgment* can only function, for Kant himself and for his readers, in the form of highly sublimated categories, such as the oppositions between beauty and charm, pleasure and enjoyment of culture or civilization, euphemisms which, without any conscious intention of dissimulating, enable social oppositions to be expressed and experienced in a form conforming to the norms of expression of a specific field. What is hidden, that is, the double social relationship—to the court (the site of civilization as opposed to culture) and to the people (the site of nature and sense)—is both present and absent; it presents itself in such a guise that one can in all good faith not see it there and that the naively reductive reading, which would reduce Kant's text to the social relationship that is disguised and transfigured within it, would be no less false than the ordinary reading which would reduce it to the phenomenal truth in which it appears only in disguise. (495–96)

Bourdieu has been generally understood as a mere adversary of Kant, but in this context he appears rather as an eminent chronicler of the social causes and effects of Kantian aesthetic judgment, which were understood as dialectical not merely by the Marxian sociologist, but by the Prussian transcendentalist who, we have seen, installed the phantom community at the center of his account of aesthetics. That melancholy dimension of the subjective universal judgment makes itself felt as a series of apparent contradictions within the exquisite object: the exquisite can be (too) small, but it can also be (too) grand; (too) sublime or (too) beautiful; (too) close or (too) far away; (too) sadistic or (too) masochistic—it can be *too too*, as the late-Victorian period's mercurial pleonasm has it. These distortions can be dwelt with in theoretical and critical terms—and they will be, over the course of this book. They are not, however, merely historical data—surplus evidence that, when people talk about aesthetics, they frequently say things that are inconsistent or nonsensical—but evidence of the difficulty of *gathering* historical data about aesthetic experiences. Treated as historical phenomena, in other words, these conceptual distortions seem less like mere eccentricities, and more like the staging of "mere eccentricity" as a historical problem.

III. The Ethnic Eccentric

Simply because Victorians granted to Japan the ambiguous privilege of being the Other Empire, does not mean that Japan indeed modernized the way that Victorians thought they did—or, indeed, that Victorians knew much about the subject at all. Whether Japan really was that kind of historical exception—the world's first non-Western modernity—is a matter of deep and ongoing controversy among scholars in East Asian studies: there are, to be sure, good reasons to treat the notion with deep suspicion. The difficulty is well framed by Tani Barlow in her introduction to the collection *Formations of Colonial Modernity in East Asia*. "A binary [of Self and Other] disciplined the discourses of modernization in Japan because lacking a homogenous 'Japanese' self, the heterogeneity that had been the enabling condition of life in the archipelago before would reassert itself, and the project of colonial modernity—the formation of the Japanese nation-state through the colonization of Asia—might have foundered, as state-making ventures foundered in China before 1949. The colonial modernist binary worked both ways, however. It required constant efforts at consolidation to maintain a seamless, unperturbed homogenous self, but the effort rested on recruiting (or, more crudely put, in incorporating) compliant others. Japanese imperialism established the conditions for always complicit others—[Alan S.] Christy's example is Okinawan elites—to desire their own ethnicization and embrace their diminished status as "not yet modern" (under Japanese inscription) or as 'modernizing' (in the U.S. cold war lexicon)" (12). Christy's essay explores the distinctive position of Okinawa in the construction of a Japanese mythology of modernity, and in particular argues that the "assimilative slant" of the Japanese national project depended on a complex negotiation between Japanese state officials and Okinawan cultural workers.[30] Yanagi Soetsu, the central figure of the *Mingei* ("arts and crafts") movement within Japanese modernism, exemplifies Christy's sense of this complexity. In the "debate on dialects" of 1940, Yanagi spoke passionately in favor of maintaining Okinawan dialects. He did so, however, not in order to resist the ethnicizing project of the Japanese state, but to dispute its methods, and to commend the value of indigenous culture as a secondary practice of modernizing Japanese citizens. Later, the story coming full circle, Yanagi was "adapted" into English by the potter Bernard Leach and enjoyed a brief spell of popularity as "The Japanese William Morris."[31]

Christy's understanding of the role of both "indigenous" and "Japanese" cultural practices in establishing a modern concept of the nation-state in Japan is extended and amplified in a number of different domains; the question is summarized by Dipesh Chakrabarty, in the afterward to another collection of essays.[32] These essays, in various forms, assert connections between the auto-aestheticization of the Japanese modernist project, and the political formations of capitalism and the nation-state. But Chakrabarty, by analogy with the modernization of South Asia, pressurizes what sometimes seems to him an unduly teleological connection between the two notions: "I know from the Indian examples of Gandhi and Tagore that there is no inexorable logic or process of historical inevitability that must always, anywhere and everywhere, lead romantic/aesthetic nationalism into statist and fascist jingoism. This happened in Japan, and happened in particular instances in Indian history, but these were instances in which, in my terms, the state was able to assimilate to its own ends the much richer, older, and more complex histories of the training of the senses that the subject of modernity embodied. How this happened, and where, is for the historian to explain" (296). Terse as Chakrabarty sounds here, he acknowledges that he writes as a nonspecialist; the difficulty he faces is in encountering a scholarly field in which aesthetics, as such, often seems inextricably linked with social and political metanarratives from which, in other contexts, aesthetic thinking is either forcefully distinguished, or actively antagonistic.[33] Japanese exceptionalist ideology was licensed in the period of imperial expansion by theories of national and racial consolidation—many of which, such as Kuki Shuzo's influential account of *iki*—were founded explicitly on aesthetic thinking.[34] Even more pertinently, Okakura Kakuzo's *Ideals of the East*, a foundational text of Japanese art historiography, was written by an imperial bureaucrat towards the goal of promoting Japanese power in Taiwan and Korea, and was mobilized by Japanese imperialists to justify the annexation of those territories and the confiscation of Taiwanese and Korean cultural treasures. Such Japanese texts in English are, obviously, important documents for charting the modernization and cultural hybridity of East Asia: they are also, I claim, important documents for examining the meanings of aesthetics, Victorianness, and the English language in the same period. (It is *solely* this latter importance on which I will place any argumentative pressure: I am *not* a scholar of East Asia, and I do not read Japanese.) These texts intervened in English literary culture in different ways, and with different tactical and strategic objectives, and differences between these writers abound in both their accounts of Japanese aesthetics and their methods of promoting it:

Noguchi's history of the haiku treats it as a portable kind of "effect," Hartmann constructs it as a discrete and regulated genre. They did so while loudly rebutting the mystifications of Western "Japonisme," as both an inhibitor and a perversion of what Okakura calls "any history of Japanese art-ideals" (*Ideals*, 4). Some, like the modernist novelist Soseki Natsume, traveled to the West to promote Japanese literature, and to learn the British canon, with material support from the Japanese government; others, like Hartmann, traveled alone, as bohemian outsiders scraping a living from criticism, poetry, and performance. Some (notably Noguchi) revised their positions as the Japanese Empire collapsed from the fraught liberalism of the Meiji and early Taisho periods into the militarist nationalism of the Showa era. But each of these writers, in different ways, sought to draw connections between the vitality of Japanese aesthetics and the promise of a Japanese national future, both thematically and formally.

As I hope is already clear, this book is less concerned with litigating this historiographical problem than with exploring the imaginary ramifications of exceptionalist ideology for British and Japanese Anglophone writers and artists. There is a complexity here, however. Merely by opening the *question* of whether Japan was an exceptionally modern place that would not, perforce, fall under the British imperial gaze, Victorians *already* placed Japan as an exception to the general principle of Orientalism: that East is East and West is West and never the twain shall meet. This second-order exceptionalism, an exceptionalism that operates at the level of aesthetic ideology but *not* at the level of macrohistorical narrative, was sublimated into the idea of "eccentricity."[35]

In the British Orientalist imaginary, Japan passed quickly from obscurity into eccentric modernity. Prior to the arrival of the American Commodore Perry's ships in Edo harbor in July 1853, British readers knew little of Japanese culture and history, and that which was known had been filtered through Dutch travelers, who alone among European powers had maintained a trade relationship with Japan through the two-and-a-half centuries of Japanese isolationism. Japan was remote enough that it may as well have been fictional: it almost appeared so, when Lemuel Gulliver arrived there in 1709, and found that, more foreign than even Luggnagg or Laputa, Japan was so inaccessible as to be basically without interest.[36] In 1841, John Murray published an anonymous author's *Manners and Customs of the Japanese in the Nineteenth Century, from Recent Dutch Visitors of Japan, and the German of Dr. Ph. Fr. von Siebold*, which formalized a vocabulary that would outlast the relative ignorance that produced it: customs are "strange," "curious," and "eccentric," rather than barbarous or savage. "We smile at such strange views," wrote one of the book's many reviewers.[37] There are exceptions to this general rule: frequently the Japanese form of government is described as "iron despotism," but even this is not evidence of a vestigial or premodern mode political system. Indeed, Perry's mission to Japan was conducted not in order to civilize a backward nation, but in order that the United States might be the *first* Western power to snag a new trade relationship with a nation whose fitness for global trade was assumed by all parties.[38]

Perry's was a trade mission freighted with cultural ambitions, inaugurating, on both sides of the Atlantic, a surge in interest in the literary and aesthetic possibilities afforded by the normalization of diplomatic relations with the Japanese Empire—with Perry himself among the first to exploit them. On his return to Europe in 1854, Perry stopped by Liverpool to ask the novelist Nathaniel Hawthorne, who was serving as American consul there, to suggest somebody to write up a report of his travels for Congress and the general public. Hawthorne suggested Herman Melville, among others, and wrote in his journal that the task "would be a very desirable labor for a young literary man, or, for that matter, an old one: for the world can scarcely have in reserve a less hackneyed theme than Japan."[39] Perry chose instead to commission an Episcopal minister named Francis Lister Hawks to write the *Narrative of the Expedition*, published in 1856, yet the title page of commercial publication places Perry's own name in a more prominent spot, as though his command of the "American Squadron" were the more salient factor in the text's publications, Hawks being cast as the mere amanuensis of a more appropriately epochal form of authorship.

In one important respect, the *Narrative* exceeded even Hawthorne's enthusiastic assessment of the literary potential of Japan for literary writing. While the novelist had written excitedly about the novelty of the "theme" of Japan, Hawks and Perry produce an account of American diplomacy touched, too, by what they took to be Japanese *form*. At various points in both Perry's transcribed notes and Hawks's editorial interventions, the authors become aware that the Commodore's demeanor and method of negotiation might seem arrogant or high-handed. That, the reader is assured, was an important dimension of Perry's "policy," and was predicated on an intuition that the Japanese would respond to theatrical performances of pomp, given the very theatricality of the courtly culture he encountered. "In a country like Japan, so governed by ceremonials of all kinds, it was necessary to guard with the strictest etiquette even the forms of speech; and it was found that by a diligent attention to the minutest and apparently most insignificant details of word and action, the desired impression was made upon Japanese diplomacy; which, as a smooth surface requires one equally smooth to touch it at every point, can only be fully reached and met by the nicest adjustment of the most polished formality" (238). Form, then, appeared to Perry as both ethnically particular (it is Japanese) and as functionally universal (an American can learn it). And

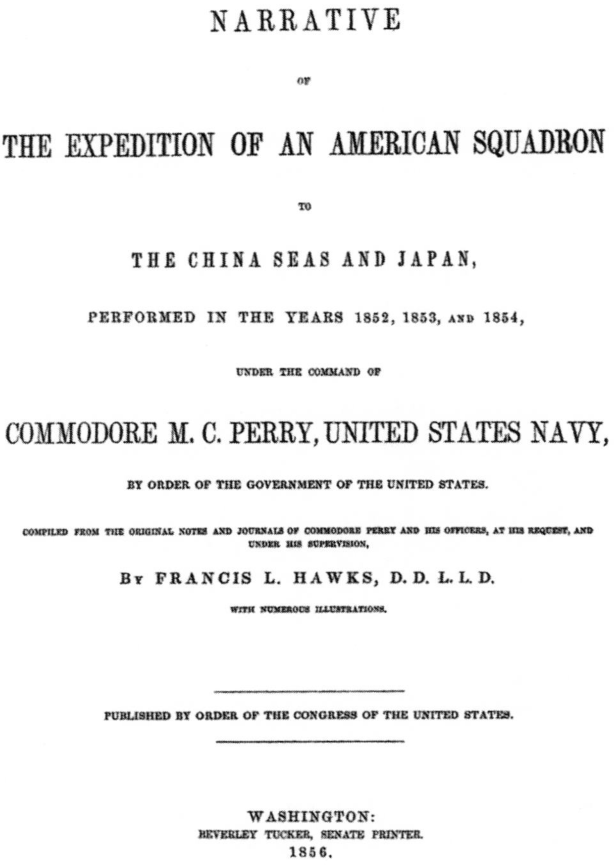

NARRATIVE

OF

THE EXPEDITION OF AN AMERICAN SQUADRON

TO

THE CHINA SEAS AND JAPAN,

PERFORMED IN THE YEARS 1852, 1853, AND 1854,

UNDER THE COMMAND OF

COMMODORE M. C. PERRY, UNITED STATES NAVY,

BY ORDER OF THE GOVERNMENT OF THE UNITED STATES.

COMPILED FROM THE ORIGINAL NOTES AND JOURNALS OF COMMODORE PERRY AND HIS OFFICERS, AT HIS REQUEST, AND UNDER HIS SUPERVISION,

BY FRANCIS L. HAWKS, D. D. L. L. D.

WITH NUMEROUS ILLUSTRATIONS.

PUBLISHED BY ORDER OF THE CONGRESS OF THE UNITED STATES.

WASHINGTON:
BEVERLEY TUCKER, SENATE PRINTER.
1856.

FIGURE 0.2. Title page, Francis L. Hawks, *Narrative of the Expedition of an American Squadron* (1856).

in his startlingly erotic simile, he begins to imagine the absolute proximity that form alone can provide: the infinite proximity of two smooth outlines brought to occupy the same space, but only after each has been sanded down to an absolute degree. The aesthetic ramifications of Perry's theatrical formalism echoed throughout Victorian aesthetic controversies in which the impact of Japanese modernization could be felt only remotely: in the debates around the "finished" work of art, for example, that animated much of the antagonism between J.A.M. Whistler and John Ruskin, for example, and in the evocative treatments of the samurai sword as an eroticized outline. For now, however, I simply want to note that Perry's diplomatic mission did not merely provide writers with new things to express, but both enabled and necessitated new modes of expression, modes both charged with the affective turbulence of a newly globalized world, and tasked with resolving that turbulence.

Many readers of *Moby-Dick*, published in 1851 in the midst of an American debate about the best methods of opening trade relations with Japan, have seen the tale of a monomaniacal sea captain bent on netting the big fish as, in some sense, an allegory for the American pursuit of Japanese trade.[40] A couple of years after Melville's novel, the Scottish writer Charles Macfarlane published a new account of Japanese history and culture, in which he offered pointers to the American delegation: "Should force be resorted to, the best means of proceeding would probably be to take possession of one of the smaller islands, or of some peninsula or promontory" (104).[41] Yet even in the midst of that bloodthirsty passage, Macfarlane is careful to note that the Americans should not imagine themselves to be *bringing*, but to be *safeguarding*, Japanese modernity: "Should our very enterprising and energetic breathren begin with a too free use of Bowie-knives and Colt's revolvers, . . . slaughters and atrocities will be committed, and an interesting people will be plunged back into complete barbarity" (104). On the other hand, as the *Spectator* pointed out in a review of Murray's *Manners and Customs*, "we dare say the system also "works well," as Canning said of the Unreformed Parliaments."[42] Strange, ornamental, lovable, charming, pretty, clever: this was an Orientalism constructed not to prove the backwardness of the Other, but to demonstrate its eccentricity. How to do so?

IV. Biographies of Unusual Men

Historians and critics of the cultural relations between Japan and Britain at the fin de siècle have often seized on the theme of eccentricity as a vehicle for detailing, and occasionally sensationalizing, the lives of individual migrant Japanese writers. The title of Christopher Benfey's book *The Great Wave: Gilded Age Misfits, Japanese Eccentrics, and the Opening of Old Japan* (2004), for example, postulates two implicit analogies: first, between cultural mobility (the referent of the Hokusai reference) and a weirdness inscribed on the bodies of Japanese migrants as biographical eccentricity.[43] And, second, between the (American) "misfits" and their Japanese counterparts, who are alike only in their unlikeness from some broadly construed notion of modern (or modern*ist*) norms. Benfey's book is hardly alone in these respects. The Japan Society, founded in 1891 by the decidedly eccentric dandy and son of Hungarian émigrés Arthur Diosy, continues to publish *Biographical Portraits* of British and Japanese personages.[44] These thumbnail sketches by both British and Japanese writers usually focus on diplomats, military personnel, and missionaries, rather than on writers and artists, but among the jingoistic celebrations of their subjects' manly virtues, there is a recurring investment in their individual weirdness, an embodied minorness that gently works to undermine the major histories of which, nonetheless, they are taken to constitute vital parts.

Among the generic problematics of biography is that by narrating an individual's life and career it thereby isolates that individual, potentially pathetically; the biographical critic reproduces the loneliness of the historical subject. "Loneliness" being one of the aesthetic effects associated with the disfiguration of the subjective universal, nobody is lonelier than the subject of a biography. Nonetheless, both Japanese and British people involved in developing the inter-imperial relationship themselves loudly asserted their own eccentricity too. The poet John Todhunter was, in 1892, the secretary of a literary club named "the Sette of Odd Volumes," and recorded in light verse the "Japanese Night" held there on the 3rd of June:

Again the ODD VOLUMES assembled
  Correctly got up to a man,
Prepared to discuss, with *hors d'oeuvres*
  THE ART OF OLD JAPAN
We drank to the Queen; we boasted
  What wonderful Guests we had got:
And then in a batch they were toasted,
  And served up, hot and hot.
    O, the Inros of Old Japan!
    Kakimonos of Old Japan!
How instructive to hear the ODD VOLUMES
  On the ART OF OLD JAPAN![45]

The poem, whose dactylic trimeter and clubbable irony recall the Savoy operas, delights in an eccentricity that is nonetheless emphatically ethnic; this is an *English* oddness, and part of the Englishness here lightly lampooned is a presumption of expertise on a subject so apparently "odd" as Japanese art. The following verse, however, mobilizes Toryish good humor in the service of a decidedly exceptionalist narrative of Japanese modernity:

His *Oddship* asked Captain Kawara
  (I've named him as near as I can),
To respond for the civilization
  And culture of newest Japan.
He spoke with aplomb and conviction,
  His speech very much seemed to please;
But pray don't ask me to report it,

For I don't understand Japanese.
O, the Culture of newest Japan!
Civilization of newest Japan!
The Japs are out-Europing Europe,
I fear, in their newest Japan!

What had been cheerful English ignorance recurs as a species of historical irrelevance. The "Captain Kawara" lecturing these oddballs on Japanese modernity would find himself at a major figurehead of Japanese imperial power, as the captain of the cruiser *Yoshino* (built in Newcastle docks). The *Yoshino* was one of three Japanese warships involved in the ambush on the Chinese navy known as the "Battle of Pungdo," (July 25, 1894), the first engagement of the First Sino-Japanese War that concluded with the Japanese occupation of Korea, Taiwan, and the Liaodong Peninsula. Japanese victory in the war pleased the London literati greatly.[46]

The period's paradigmatic Japanese eccentric was the aforementioned Sadakichi Hartmann himself. According to his magisterially improbable autobiography, he left the mechanical island of Dejima for Hamburg, Germany, in "18?? (date of arrival in Germany unknown)," his mother having died in childbirth. He read "Goethe and Schiller" by the age of nine, and exported his considerable cultural capital to Paris in 1882 (where he became friends with Stéphane Mallarmé), Philadelphia later that year (where he occasionally crossed the Delaware to take notes for Walt Whitman after 1884), Boston in 1887, New York in 1889 (where he was crowned "the King of Greenwich Village"), and eventually Los Angeles in 1923 (in which year he appeared in the early action flick *The Thief of Baghdad*, against a young and pulsing Douglas Fairbanks). Hartmann revels in the privileges afforded to the "white chrysanthemum" (another of his many memorable self-soubriquets), leaving it to others to record that, for example, his relationship with Whitman was brought to an end after other Whitmanian acolytes expressed anxiety about his proximity to the master, who eventually cut off all relations with "that damn Japanee."[47]

Styling himself as "the first Eurasian," Sadakichi (rarely to himself or others "Hartmann," though whether through simple enthusiasm, or miscomprehension of Japanese patronymy, remains unclear) details the enthusiasm with which his literary magniloquence and personal elegance were received, as a modern major-general to whom "all doors opened!" The irony of the remark feels much stronger in retrospect: after the bombing of Pearl Harbor, Sadakichi lost the extraordinary privilege accrued over his literary career, and spent his last years under investigation by American authorities, narrowly avoiding the internment that other Japanese people in America suffered, until his death in 1944. Despite his having been occasionally resuscitated as a witty and unusual literary eccentric, his reputation hardly recovered, and he is still remembered, when he is, mostly as one of the "lost generation" of America's *belle époque*, as Ezra Pound puts it in his note on Hartmann in *Canto LXXX*.[48] After the dramatic escalation of racial violence that followed the outbreak of war between Japan and the United States, the exceptional quality that had so frequently been attributed to Hartmann (Pound: "Sadakichi has lived. Has so lived that if one hadn't been oneself it wd. have been worth while to have been Sadakichi") evaporated.[49]

Hartmann has proven difficult to place into history precisely on account of his eccentricity. He was excluded by name from the *Aiiieeeee!!* anthology that inaugurated the tradition of Asian American literary criticism on the historical grounds that that category could only make sense in the age of an American midcentury imperialism that reconfigured the nineteenth century's ferociously patrolled distinctions between Japanese and Chinese migrants.[50] Along with Yone Noguchi, the *Aiiieeeee!!* authors argue, Hartmann "momentarily influenced American writing with the quaintness of the Orient but said nothing about Asian America, because, in fact, these writers weren't Asian-Americans but Americanized Asians."[51] If we cannot speak here of a "queer temporality," as our contemporary lexicon frequently does, we can perhaps designate the history of the eccentric as conditioned by a *quaint temporality*: an aesthetic and elliptical feeling of historicalness that nonetheless seeks to exempt itself from the more muscular historical explanations that have, in recent debates within Victorian studies for example, sometimes been seen as exhaustive of historicism *per se*.[52]

The *Aiiieeeee!* editors ascribed to Hartmann two distinct kinds of conspicuous minorness: first, he did not have much of an impact because he neither came from, nor wrote from within, the major ethnic category of "Asian America." Devoid of ethnic identity, Hartmann's impact could be, at best, *anomalous*; not even a "native informant," in the sense that he was neither native (to Asian America) nor informing on it. Second, the effect that Hartmann *did* have, on the white Americans who interacted with his work, was muted and defunct, concerned merely with "the quaintness of the Orient," rather than with the more major affects—love, hate, recognition, enchantment, terror—associated with cultural work. Thus "quaintness" as a critical formulation performs, in Chin et al.'s reading of Hartmann, both historiographical and aesthetic work, operating both as a kind of exceptional but shallow alternative to the dominant, nonquaint literatures (in this case, the white avant-gardes of Boston and New York), squib literatures that, alas, prove only that the dominant literature is better after all; and as an emptied out remnant of what once might have been "charm"—quaintness as a low-intensity aesthetic fondness, enabled and finally marred by its reassuring historical irrelevance.

Chin et al. did not stipulate the relation between these two senses of quaint, and their position on the merits of Hartmann's writing (relative, that is, to the avant-garde work of the Asian American poets the collection promotes) is not one I'm going to dispute, exactly. The problem is that Hartmann's purported quaintness was merely an extreme example of the general case of how *Japan* was treated by Western thinkers at a far larger scale, no longer of a local avant-garde literary scene in an East Coast metropole, but of the global community of nations. Nineteenth-century Japanese writers and artists were keenly aware that their fetishization by Western aesthetes was something of a poisoned chalice: while, doubtless, it helped to facilitate East/West trade and travel, it deprived Japanese people of a sense of historical efficacy. In the introduction to *Things Japanese*, an encyclopedia of vignettes concerning Japanese culture, the Orientalist Basil Hall Chamberlain recalls a visit by Sir Edwin Arnold to Japan. Arnold, who had been known as an enthusiastic Japanophile, as well as a comparative religious scholar and Oriental linguist, gave a speech extolling Japanese culture: "so fairy-like, said he, is its scenery, so exquisite its art, so many more lovely still that almost divine sweetness of disposition, that charm of demeanour."[53] Lest any reader mistake the condescending and babying tone of Arnold's address, Chamberlain recalls an article in the Tokyo press published the next day, in which the editor takes Arnold's call as an implicit challenge to Japanese industrial and military power. "Art forsooth, scenery, sweetness of disposition! cries this editor. Why did not Sir Edwin praise us for huge industrial enterprises, for commercial talent, for wealth, political sagacity, powerful armaments? Of course it is because he could not honestly do so. He has gauged us at our true value, and tells us in effect that we are only pretty weaklings."[54] To be the most beautiful thing in the world is still, it would seem, to be merely a thing.

The editor's implication that aesthetic appreciation compensates for a lack of political will (figured as military or industrial power) is a narrative familiar to scholars of late nineteenth-century European culture as an assessment of the period's "decadence," its putative squandering of social energies in aesthetic projects that betray the century's earlier reforming spirit, and which needed in turn to be renovated by modernism's radicalization of the aesthetic project a little later. It is a narrative to which Chamberlain (whose account of the exchange between Arnold and the editor is all that remains, and whose motivations will be discussed in this book's second chapter) may very well have subscribed.[55] The figure of the "pretty weakling" would serve such a narrative not merely as a descriptor for the feminized Japanese man, but also for the effeminate Western aesthete. Such an assessment appears in the American abolitionist Thomas Wentworth Higginson's well-known denunciation of Oscar Wilde as having abandoned the just cause of Irish independence for a certain kind of art: "Is it manhood for [Ireland's] gifted sons to stay at home and help work out the problem; or to cross the Atlantic and pose in ladies' boudoirs or write prurient poems which their hostesses must discreetly ignore?"[56] In Higginson's account, as in that of Chamberlain's editor, the cosmopolitan mobility of aesthetic culture transgressed not merely the boundaries of nation, but the narratives of national growth and power that sustained them.

In other words, the aestheticization of Japanese contemporary history *racialized* a narrative about aestheticized eccentricity that was deployed domestically against both Japanese migrant writers in Britain and the United States, and the pretty weaklings, effeminates, and homosexuals of (particularly) the British aesthetic movement. The analogy was not merely formal: these two worlds were institutionally imbricated, too. The Japanese Anglophone writers shared, often, such institutional spaces with British Orientalists: in Arthur Diosy's London-based Japan Society, for example, where Yone Noguchi lectured a handful of times, or in the publisher John Murray's "Wisdom of the East" series, which printed Noguchi's *Spirit of Japanese Poetry* alongside Laurence Binyon's survey of Chinese and Japanese art, *The Flight of the Dragon*.[57] Indeed, it is striking the degree to which Orientalist and anti-Orientalist positions—or perhaps we should say "allo-Orientalizing" and "auto-Orientalizing" positions—were staked within the same cultural and institutional settings, with destabilizing effects both domestically and transnationally. Aesthetic investments in Japan metastasized into libidinal ones, and vice versa; "Japanese young man" became a euphemism for an effeminate aesthete; Japan was imaginatively transformed into a space of sexually dissident utopian longing. Despite the appeal of Japan to British aesthetes occurring partly on the basis of Japan's minorness, the aesthetic idea of Japan drew together, in the margins of British public culture, two of the most self-consciously major historical narratives of which Victorians were aware: (1) the sexualization of subjectivity (of which the Wilde trials were among the most spectacular demonstrations), and (2) the terminal project of globalization, whose major flashpoints—the Berlin conference of 1884–85; the growing global consensus around GMT as the epicenter of universal time—occurred during the period of high aestheticism.[58] In that sense, the late-Victorian idea of Japan as eccentric, producing exquisite art, and subject only to quaint styles of memorialization laid the groundwork for the influential post-structuralist historiographies of the twentieth century.

V. Victorian Postmodernity

A quaint temporality continually conditions accounts of Japanese culture within the broad Continental philosophical tradition we now designate as "theory," through Japan's apparently elliptical relation to the historical phenomenon that, whether singular or plural, gets called "modernity."[59] Roland Barthes writes that the "very specialty" of Japan is "its modernity."[60] As we have seen, many nineteenth-century observers would have agreed. But what kind of modernity is it, after all, that is defined through this distantiation that, while charged with affective and aesthetic content, is not located on any kind of timeline? Japan did not appear—and Barthes did not think it did—"modern" in the sense in which we discriminate the moderns from the ancients, or from the primitives. If the modernity of Japan distinguished itself from anything, indeed, it was precisely from *modernity*, as usually construed by Western writers. Japanese modernity functioned primarily as a criticism of a narcissistic Western modernity gone wrong. Nearer to the end of the century, this version of modernity was exhibited (almost literally) by Rudyard Kipling, in one of the two most widely cited passages about Japan that the fin de siècle produced. During a trip to Japan, Kipling meets a (fictional) Western professor, and the two begin a conversation about the superiority of Japanese over British "curios," and grieving that Japanese culture is under threat from Westernization.

> We stayed long in the half-light of that quaint place, and when we went away we grieved afresh that such a people should have a "constitution" or should dress every tenth young man in European clothes, put a white iron-clad in Kobé harbor, and send a dozen myopic lieutenants in baggy uniforms about the streets.
>
> "It would pay us," said the Professor, his head in a clog-shop, "it would pay us to establish an international suzerainty over Japan to take away any fear of invasion or annexation, and pay the country as much as ever it chose, on condition that it simply sat still and went on making beautiful things while our men learned. It would pay us to put the whole Empire in a glass case and mark it, 'Hors concours,' Exhibit A."
>
> "H'mm," said I. "Who's us?"
>
> "Oh, we generally—the Sahib log all the world over. Our workmen—a few of them—can do as good work in certain lines, but you don't find whole towns full of clean, capable, dainty, designful people in Europe." (334–35)

The Professor's allegory draws on a slew of occasionally contradictory suppositions about Japanese aesthetics. Here we have the trope of miniaturization, for example, vividly reconstructed: "the whole Empire" can be placed under a bell jar and taken in, presumably, by the singular gaze of the "Sahib log."[61] Less remarked, however, has been the strange placement of Japan in time: distanced from "our men" by virtue of their advanced skill (which the Sahib can nonetheless be presumed to pick up, given the opportunity), Japan must be told to "stand still" so that we can catch up. Underneath the glass case, Japan is protected from the Western version of modernity, here figured in both military terms ("invasion") and as cultural influence (the "European clothes"), but its temporal eccentricity remains fully intact. Like the bottle-city of Kandor, Japan sits among its own curios (which are, anyway, more metaphor than metonym) as a microcosmic ensign from the future.

The aestheticized form of modernity—perhaps, to adapt the title of a recent collection of essays on Japanese modernization, a "mirror of modernity"—has been frequently aligned with a now altogether less fashionable periodic designation: postmodernity.[62] In their introduction to a 1989 collection entitled *Japan and Postmodernism*, Masao Miyoshi and H. D. Harootunian offer a pair of explanations for the appeal of Japanese culture to Western theorists of the postmodern. They explain that the heyday of "postmodernism" coincided with the so-called "Japanese economic miracle" of the 1980s, which in turn prompted an Orientalist panic on the part of Western commentators about the possibility that economic growth threatened to make Japan "the hegemon of the twenty-first century" (ix). While Miyoshi and Harootunian are critical of the Orientalist tone of the op-eds they cite, and while they historicize this postmodernization of Japan within the longer history of "Yellow Peril" discourses, they offer the following important discrimination: "it looks far more legitimate this time around, simply because the threat of Japan's economic power is perceived to be real" (ix). Their second argument for the postmodernity of Japan concerns the persistence of a Japanese colonial historiography in Japan itself—a grand narrative in which Japan and the West are cast as the two great protagonists of global modernity—which has been (in "serious error," they think) adapted to suit postmodernist claims about the "end of history." It is this latter that Miyoshi and Harootunian take to be a repetition of a nineteenth-century plot: "Japan's identification of itself with the first world might be a repeat performance of the archetypal colonial gesture, lusting after the coveted membership in the utopian sanctuary. Japan has lived through this process before in the mid-nineteenth century. Does it need to repeat it?" (xi).

The ascription of a postmodern dimension to the premodernist historiography of the nineteenth century was, to be sure, a staple of poststructuralist theory. As, indeed, was the kind of Orientalist rhapsodizing on Japanese capitalism that Miyoshi and Harootunian align with Japanese colonial historiography. The first published of Jean-François Lyotard's *Postmodern Fables*, indeed, is entitled "Marie Goes to Japan," and depicts the eponymous Marie, a (Western) professor of postmodern theory, reflecting on the elegant fakery of her profession while moving through Tokyo airport on her way to give a talk:

> The *stream of cultural capital* [in English in original]. But that's me, Marie tells herself, while watching the baggage return rotate at Narita airport. A little stream, but still a stream. Cultural, that's for sure, they buy culture from me. Capital too. I'm not the owner, thank God, nor the manager. Just a little cultural labor force they can exploit. But correctly, under contract, let me add, with my signature. No great discovery here. (3)

Lightly dragged up as Marie, Lyotard reflects on his commodification as a stream of cultural revenue, with the same routinized reflexivity of the baggage carousel. Jean Baudrillard, who visited Japan a number of times, offered an imago less carousel and more mirror: "a strong culture [that] reflects back to us the image of our degraded one."[63] A similar ambush befalls Michel Foucault, in an awkward interview by a Buddhist priest, conducted in a temple in Uenohara. Foucault offers the following, blushing summary of his thoughts about Japan:

> PRIEST: Your interest in Japan is it deep or superficial?
>
> FOUCAULT: Honestly, I am not constantly interested in Japan. What interests me is the Western history of rationality and its limit. On this point, Japan poses a problem that we can't avoid, and it's an illustration of this problem. Because Japan is an enigma, very difficult to decode. That doesn't mean to say that it is that which opposes itself to Western reality. In reality, that rationality constructs colonies everywhere else, whereas Japan is far from building one, it is, on the contrary, colonized by Japan.
>
> PRIEST: I have been told you are interested in mysticism. In your opinion, do mysticism and esotericism mean the same thing?
>
> FOUCAULT: No.[64]

The rhetorical difficulty by which Foucault is beset—a series of yes/no questions with little room to maneuver—produces an elliptical and costive response. Japan both is and is not the limit case for this "Western history of rationality" in which Foucault declares his interest: knowing the game of Orientalist discourse, but unable to free himself from its double bind, his answers drift towards sulky negativity.

That Orientalism was one of poststructuralist theory's constitutive blind spots has been a mainstay of critical studies for a generation, and though I am fascinated by the *sociological* conformity of these various moments (French academics confronted with both the portability of their expertise and its hard limits), I've not cited these Lyotard, Baudrillard, and Foucault passages merely to discredit them—and certainly not to assimilate either their Orientalisms or their broader theoretical projects. My point is rather that the distinction of Japan in these accounts is that it both belongs and does not belong to the history of Western rationality; it can neither be simply included nor excluded from the colonial historiography that each of these theorists has set out to debunk. It cannot, because of the uniquely quaint position that Japan occupies for these theorists, as for the Victorians I have been discussing: *modern*, but not *in the way that everybody else is*.

Such is the condition of a Japan not merely as postmodern, but actually as post-historical—and such is the ideology that is at the root of the poststructuralists' accounts, as Miyoshi and Harootunian imply. This dimension of poststructuralist thought has generally been ascribed to the important influence of Alexandre Kojève, whose foundational reading of Hegel's *Phenomenology* was subject to "a radical change of opinion" after his 1959 trip to Japan, and whose thoughts on the subject were cited explicitly by Baudrillard and Félix Guattari.[65] A "one of a kind" society, Japan alone affords Kojève with an example of a society living at "the end of history," and had indeed dwelled there for "three centuries."[66] This condition had been brought about by, precisely, the aestheticization of modernity: the replacement, in Japan, of "Religion, Morals, or Politics" by "*Snobbery* in its pure form," whose primary forms of expression are Noh theater, the tea ceremony, and *ikebana* (162). The consequences for his reading of Hegel were definitive. Kojève had initially thought that the dialectic would pull humanity through language and towards a new kind of animality—that therefore the "post-historical" moment that would conclude the historical dialectic would lead to the abolition of the "human." But since Japan's post-historical quality was characterized by "Snobbery," or, as he calls it shortly after, "a position to live according to totally *formalized* values," and since, further, "no animal can be a snob," Japan opens up the possibility of a post-historical future in which humanness is preserved, but as *form*, rather than content. That is to say, the example of Japan allows Kojève to conceive of the (Hegelian) subject as such in terms of a kind of aesthetic patterning.

Kojève's diagnosis of Japan as the "end of history" catalyzed the development of American neoconservative ideology through the work of Francis Fukuyama, whose reading of Kojève motivates *The End of History and the Last Man* (New York: Free Press, 1992). On one level, Fukuyama's treatment of Japan conforms to the standard exceptionalist line: "Japan, the first East Asian state to modernize, was the first to achieve a stable liberal democracy. (Japan's democratization was accomplished at the point of a gun, so to speak, but the result proved durable long past the point where democracy could be said to have been imposed coercively)" (110). Yet his reading of Kojève's ("Japanese") aesthetics proves difficult to adopt into the version of liberalism he extends under the banner of *pax Americana*, since while "the Japanese demonstrated that it is possible to continue to be human through the invention of a series of perfectly contentless formal arts, . . . in the United States, our utilitarian traditions make it difficult for even the fine arts to become purely formal." Accordingly, in America, art will eventually cease to mean *either* what it meant for Kojève's Japanese, or contemporary Americans: "Artists like to convince themselves that they are being socially responsible in addition to being committed to aesthetic values. But the end of history will mean the end, among other things, of all art that could be considered socially useful, and hence the descent of artistic activity into the empty formalism of the traditional Japanese arts."

Yet for all the idiosyncrasies of Kojève's reading of *Phenomenology*, his understanding of Japan as a portent of an aesthetic future to come conforms in large part to that of a nineteenth-century American Hegelian, Ernest Fenollosa.[67] Mostly now read through Ezra Pound, who edited and published his essay on the possibility of importing the Chinese ideogram into Anglophone poetry, Fenollosa taught philosophy at Tokyo Imperial University off and on from 1878 until the end of the century—and is particularly credited with helping to establish the first national art institutions in Japan.[68] His essays of the 1890s treating what he called "the theater of the East" (153) described Japanese modernity in almost apocalyptic terms, as the fulfillment of the Hegelian historical dialectic—the movement of history from the East to the West. Fenollosa writes:

> We cannot shirk the responsibility if we would. Whether we like it or not, our lot is thrown with it, for good or ill, from now on, *and to all time*. The test is mutual. It is not merely that the West shall from its own point of view tolerate the East, nor the East the West; not even that the West shall try to understand the East from the Eastern point of view–but that both, planting their faith in the divine destinies of man, shall with co-operation aim at a new world-type, rich in those million possibilities of thought and achievement that exclusion blindly stifles.
>
> For this fusion is to be not only worldwide, but final. The future historian will look back upon our crisis as unique, the most breathless in human annals. Heretofore race unions have existed for limited areas only–composite cultures whose defects and abuses outlying types might eventually rectify. Rome was regenerated by Teutonic character, and Hun tyranny by Tartar freedom. But today each of the pledged factors absorbs the power

> and hope of a hemisphere. The Western type of culture is marked, scarred, cast into a hard mould for all Aryan people; the Eastern is full, over-ripe, despairing of new expression in its worn-out words. Each has exhausted the separate fruitage of its seeds. If the union fail now, the defect must be consanguineous to the end; for there is no new blood, no outlying culture-germ for subsequent infusion. Such as we make it now, it must remain till the end. This is man's final experiment.

Fenollosa's apocalyptic tone derives from his sense of the historical exceptionality of his moment: the 1898 Spanish-American War (a culmination of another sort: the first war to be fought westwards across the Pacific) had both necessitated and enabled a "coming fusion of East and West," in which the two hemispheres would finally stand "soul to soul, as if in the sudden meeting of two brothers parted since childhood" (155). And although Fenollosa did not go as far as Kojève, who argues that Japan had *already been* post-historical since the commencement of the Tokugawa Shogunate, as my second epigraph demonstrates, he did think that the coming fusion is both singular and final—that it will produce the end of history, or at least of history as it can be conceptualized through the Hegelian dialectic.[69] Notwithstanding the partisan delight with which Fenollosa considers the American imperial expansion into the Pacific, one might conclude that Fenollosa's Japan is apprehended with the same mixture of apocalyptic excitement and existential dread as Kojève's.

Japan: a precondition for the exquisite aesthetic structure implicit in Kant's description of aesthetic judgment; an Other Empire radically threatening the cultural chauvinism of late-Victorian Britain; an eccentric modernity populated by eccentric men, and a model, therefore, for the subcultural socialities of British aestheticism; a material source of influential writers and artists shaping the emerging aesthetic discourses, usually *away* from the interests of the white avant-gardes whose achievements are all-too-frequently centered in cultural histories of the period; an influence, direct *and* indirect, on the post-structuralist historiographies of theory, and therefore embedded, invisibly, in many of our most cherished categories of cultural analysis. *That* is the Japan this book is about.

The chapters are organized more or less chronologically, with a couple of wrinkles: from (1) *The Mikado* [1885]; (2) British aestheticism [ca. 1880–ca. 1900]; (3) Noguchi's "My love's lengthened hair" [1902]; (4) Mikimoto's Ruskin collection [1921–40]; (5) a chronological study of the theme of the Japanese sword, from the *Madame Chrysanthème/Madame Butterfly* books, through the work of Winifred Eaton published under the name "Onoto Watanna," to the contemporary movies *Audition* (1999) and *Kill Bill* (2003–4). Each of these time frames, however, is broken to enable discussion of later texts that elucidate some of the formal or theoretical issues raised in the chapter: with *The Mikado*, I examine a speech by a Conservative Home Secretary and a Stephen Sondheim musical; with aestheticism, a different kind of afterlife—the posthumous circulation of luxury editions of Wilde's works; with haiku, the later experiments in haiku-like forms by W. B. Yeats and Richard Wright; with *Madame Butterfly*, the durability of the plot itself (on Broadway) and the spectacle of Asian femininity's exquisite revenge in *Audition* (1999); in Mikimoto, more implicitly, with queer theory's own return to archival affects in the work of Ann Cvetkovich. Throughout, I explore the convergence of beauty and pain that I take to be the consequence of the encounter with Other Empires that I have described, and the ramifications of that for particular aesthetic and literary forms.

In addition to that chapter breakdown, it has been suggested to me by some of my generous readers that a quick description of the relations between this book's major categories might be useful at this point. So:

—***exquisite***: the book's main aesthetic category, which describes the idea of Japan when it is figured aesthetically (i.e., as the resolution to the melancholy condition of the subjective universal judgment of taste);

—***quaint***: the name the book gives both to the manner in which exquisite objects become (or fail to become) historical evidence, and for the book's own method, which seeks to activate quaint attachments in order to develop a richer engagement with obsolete aesthetic categories than traditional historicism generally accesses;

—***eccentric***: the character-type of the quaint temporal mode, which in my book describes both individuals detached from historical metanarratives (e.g., Sadakichi Hartmann and Yone Noguchi), and the idea of Japan as a uniquely—but somehow therefore inconsequentially—modern empire;

—***minor***: I mean this term, quite conventionally, to describe literary and cultural texts, individuals, and movements of less importance—causing fewer secondary phenomena; affecting fewer people or historical events; being generally less influential or just less good—than major texts, individuals, and movements;

—***historical abandonment***: the book's term to describe the affective condition of an eccentric individual realizing they are eccentric, that their own participation in history is conspicuously quaint. Many of the figures here—chiefly but by no means solely Mikimoto Ryuzo—

> wrote extensively about the feeling of having been left behind (often by somebody long dead, or something very remote), a feeling of loneliness that I take to be the concluding movement of the aesthetic judgment that the book, as a whole, describes.

Lastly, as this book presses on, it also moves incrementally further away from its center of gravity: the literary culture of Britain (more specifically: London) at the end of the nineteenth century and the beginning of the twentieth. The first chapter aims to redirect an opera that is *too often* dislocated from that scene back within its boundaries; the second makes an argument about the meaning of Japanese art to the major figures within that environment. The third discusses one particular intervention into late-Victorian literary culture by a writer, Yone Noguchi, who is generally understood, and understood himself, as an outsider to it. In the fourth, we will visit the United Kingdom with a Japanese literary tourist in the 1920s, searching alongside him for vestiges of Ruskinian utopian sentiment in an interwar period from which such ideas have been wholly absented—Ruskin's complex ideas, spoken out of context and somewhat garbled, amounting to little more than passionately articulated commonplaces. By the book's final chapter, on the distinctive aesthetic features of the katana sword, from the *Madame Chrysanthème* story through to *Kill Bill,* the argument's Victorian prehistory will have been submerged by many other determining aesthetic choices and influences—film noir, the revenge tragedy, psychoanalytic film theory—that interact with but do not fundamentally condition the central formal categories of the book. My book, then, begins at an epicenter of one collapsing, but still hegemonic, empire (London, 1885), and ends at another (Los Angeles, 2004). Since part of my argument (indeed, a premise of cultural studies since its inception) is that the discourse of aesthetics reflects geopolitical power relations, it has made sense for me to range outside the boundaries of the British Empire at the moment when the idea of Japan I am describing—itself an idea with connections to French and German Orientalisms—did so.

Each chapter, then, will not only ask the reader to take one more step away from the Victorians, but also to maintain some kind of contact with the aesthetic self-formation in the metropolitan center of a global empire in terminal crisis. This is not to endow that period or that place with any particular kind of cultural authority; rather, it is to explore the diffusion of Victorian ideas and feelings throughout a post-Victorian world in which that authority is all-too-frequently asserted. That "Victorian values" does not mean what, for example, the neoconservative political commentator Michael Barone would have it mean will surprise nobody who has engaged the field since it was reconfigured by Steven Marcus's *The Other Victorians* (1966).[70] Yet the event of modernism sometimes causes the British nineteenth century to appear as a mere prologue—the cusp of something, whether that be cultural modernism; the militant success of anticolonial nationalist movements; the First World War. *Quaint, Exquisite* is about, among other things, forms of historical attachment that fail or refuse that logic—the logic of the historically *major*. As Japan to the Victorians, in some senses, so the Victorians to us.

1

Not About Japan

It is a commonplace among Savoyards that *The Mikado* is about England, not Japan: the joke was that what seemed utterly remote from the audience was in fact all about themselves. But if you actually change the location of the opera to England, as Dr. Miller did, then you not only make the joke too obvious: you actually destroy it. *The Mikado* becomes an opera about England which is actually—surprise, surprise—about England. Where's the fun in that?

—ANDREW CROWTHER, LETTER TO THE *MUSICAL TIMES*, JULY 1992.

Pooh Bah, it will be remembered, traced his ancestry back to a "protoplasmal primordial atomic globule"; consequently no Japanese gentleman of rank, however sensitive, could imagine himself or his progenitors to have been made the subject of the English author's satire.

—FRANÇOIS CELLIER, *GILBERT AND SULLIVAN AND THEIR OPERAS*, 1914.

I. Aboutness

It might seem absurd to claim that something as trivial as Gilbert and Sullivan's *The Mikado* could be "about" anything much at all. Yet critics have had no difficulty formulating the case in the negative: it's *not* about Japan.[1] That assessment, almost ubiquitous in both scholarly and popular writing on Gilbert and Sullivan's 1885 opera, performs several useful functions: it reassures enthusiasts of the popular work that nobody is calling them racist; it demonstrates an intellectual savoir faire, by overcoming sullen literal-mindedness; and it locates a problem play in the relatively safe hermeneutic space of domestic satire. This chapter, too, will stop short of exhibiting Japan as the secret referent of *The Mikado*; but will, rather, explore the interpretive practices that have installed this certainty within critical approaches to such a semiotically complex work. Early productions proudly exhibited its Japanese qualities: the putatively authentic sword and costumes onstage; the Japanese women recruited to teach the British actors how to dance; the "Miya Sama" theme, incorporated almost without amendment from a Japanese source.[2] It was not until the aftermath of the Russo-Japanese War of 1904–5, when the Japanese Empire confronted British audiences and critics with a newly threatening aspect, that critics collectively decided, never to recant, that the opera did not contain "a single joke against Japan," as G. K. Chesterton put it, but was rather wholly designed to satirize and caricature British political culture.[3] As such the affinities between *The Mikado* and a particular aspect of late-Victorian Orientalism have been obscured, and the semiotic problem Japanese culture posed to Victorians has been oversimplified.

Orientalist writing dealing with Japan has long been characterized by a desire to fictionalize or formalize its object, to assure that readers realize the knowledge on offer is not to be taken too literally, or too seriously. Roland Barthes famously writes, at the beginning of *Empire of Signs* (1970), that his Japan is nothing more than a "system" formed from the assessment of features of a "faraway" place, "in no way claiming to represent or to analyze reality itself."[4] Rather than a belated critique of high Orientalism, Barthes's gesture conforms strikingly with many similar moves by turn-of-the-century writers on Japan. One of the foremost Western authorities on Japanese culture, Lafcadio Hearn, begins his haltingly titled *Japan: An Attempt at Interpretation* (1904) with the disclaimer that "no work fully interpreting [Japanese] life . . . can be written for at least another fifty years"; and goes on, "after having discovered that I cannot understand the Japanese at all,—I feel better qualified to attempt this essay."[5] Hearn's qualifications derive not from knowledge or expertise, but from the frank admission of their absence; his knowledge advances in the space of avowed ignorance, and the authority of his claims depends on the paradoxical weakening of the claimant. In the course of this essay, we will see comparable moves in a wider range of Orientalist writing, as well as inchoately in *The Mikado* itself, which appears less idiosyncratic than it is sometimes thought to be: a text in which the loud antipositivism of Hearn and Barthes appears in a more muted tone.

An Orientalist caught between fantasy and knowledge might be diagnosed with a classical paranoia: he both projects authority and wishes not to be taken seriously; he loudly asserts the value of this or that truth-claim and then promptly withdraws it when confronted. His is a position quite different to that of the Orientalist elaborated by Edward Said, who describes the "apogee of Orientalist confidence" as an affective disposition within which "no merely asserted generality is denied the dignity of truth; no theoretical list of Oriental attributes is without application to Orientals in the real world."[6] Though Orientalist writing might seem committed to an aesthetic of realism, we might gloss Said as saying, it is neither, in the end, true nor realistic. By contrast, Barthes and Hearn derive their critical dignity from something quite other than truth: the "real world" is precisely, and in such terms, what they foreclose any access to, even when their abstractions are thoroughly researched, rather than "merely asserted." Such genial and convenient disavowal has made it has difficult to determine how these writers, and the Orientalist ideology that informs both them and *The Mikado*, located themselves in the real world: a world that had to adapt to the emergence of a non-Western, but modern, empire that contradicted the unipolar stereotype on which Orientalism had hitherto relied.

The task of reading *The Mikado*, then, is that of finding a middle ground between truth-claim ("it's about Japan/England") and disclaimer ("it's not about Japan"); to describe the movement *between* a fantasy of knowledge and the fantasy of its dissolution. Questions of this kind have motivated a number of recent returns to the theory of realism, as scholars such as Catherine Gallagher and Fredric Jameson have challenged the dogmatically ethical or naively mimetic stereotypes of the nineteenth-century novel by emphasizing its internal dynamism, its dialectical traffic between the familiar and the strange.[7] In Gallagher's terms, George Eliot's realism inheres not in her capacity to categorize particularities into types or classes, but to mutate such particulars into new, eroticized configurations. "George Eliot is the greatest English realist," Gallagher writes, "because she not only makes us curious about the quotidian, not only convinces us that knowing its particularity is our ultimate ethical duty, but also, and supremely, makes us want it."[8] From such a perspective, realism is a mode triply attuned to its own absence: predicated on a curiosity about the world around us, on an ethical duty to an other, and on an erotic *lack* of that other, Gallagher's realism proceeds by grappling with the not (yet) categorized, the not (quite) known. Referentiality matters less to such a system than does the subjective posture out of which references are made, an ecstatic tendency that refuses the schematic authority of the fable (in Jameson's vocabulary, the "*récit*") in favor of the mutual transformation of universal and particular. For these purposes, then, realism will not be located in the verisimilitude or even referentiality of a line about Japan, of which *The Mikado* contains many: it will rather be sought in those of the opera's generic and formal patterns that cannot *but* ground themselves in the world outside the Savoy Theater; those moments, that is, when the opera touches its own membrane.

The reality effect enacted by the Orientalists mentioned above takes the rhetorical form of *praeteritio*: "I don't really know anything about Japan, but—". The Orientalist argument worlds itself by insisting on the otherworldliness of its object. Likewise, *The Mikado*'s jovial ambiguity about its location makes claims about the real world (that which we might call the *epistemological* ambition of realism) while refusing to represent that world realistically (realism's *aesthetic* strategy). I have come to refer to this position—affirming realism's epistemology while negating its aesthetic—as *queer realism*. While the queerness of such does not depend on any repressed homosexual desire that one might find within the text, the strategic evasions both practiced and thematized by *The Mikado*—an opera whose plot revolves entirely around a desire punishable by death—helped to install "Japan" as a placeholder object for queer men negotiating queer identities at the fin de siècle. In this sense, "queer realism" operates as the precise antipode of the "epistemology of the closet."[9] Whereas the late nineteenth century, according to Sedgwick's formulation, engendered a discourse in which homosexuality was everywhere known but nowhere spoken; the queerness of Japan was everywhere spoken, and nowhere known. In this sense, *The Mikado* might be seen as both a transitional text in the history of British Orientalism *and* as an attempt to retrain realism's worlding strategies on the queerer world of the late nineteenth century.

A queer realism concerning Japan also motivates D. A. Miller's remarkable rehabilitation of Barthes's Japanophilia in *Bringing Out Roland Barthes*, a text in which not merely an erotic but also an ethical value is placed on the act of exoticization that accompanies specifically homosexual forms of socialized desire. Miller offers an extraordinary defense of Barthes's exoticizing descriptions of Japanese bodies as antibodies to virulent racializations to which liberalism responds only with euphemism and obfuscation:

> Barthes's writing practice is never more directly provocative of our thinking about the inscription of the body than when in *Empire of Signs* he dares to look the Japanese *in the eye*, the eye that has been the favored referent of racist insult to the bodies of Japanese and other Asian people. Now the white Western liberal characteristically refrains from taking any notice whatever of the racially other's body, under the assumption that no such notice *can* be taken without repeating or in some way reinforcing the abusive mythologization of this body. With this paradoxical result: the white Western liberal respect for the racially other takes the form of *denying* his body, whose specificities are surrendered without a struggle to the racism that is, for its part, more than willing to describe this body concretely, but only, in deriding it, to justify the often institutionalized cultural aggression against it. . . . In its willingness to write on the very site of racist stereotype, then, Barthes's text on "the Japanese eye" also breaks with the liberal reticence whose embarrassment unwittingly assents to that stereotype. Any attempt to make the operation of Barthes's sexuality peripheral to this

> initiative would be simply to let another version of such reticence fall on the difference of the other. Entirely devoid of that liberal advocacy which in defending "them" is even more concerned to establish the advocate's own humanity, Barthes writes out of his patent pleasure in Japanese bodies, faces, eyes, on which he bestows his own look of love. This inevitably means that the Japanese eye gets configured in terms of *writing*—that is, as an instance of a cherished signifying process that no meaning can ever annul or arrest.

In this account, the most "real" dimension of the Japanese body is the "patent pleasure" it produces in its observer, a pleasure that circumvents the various ideological postures of both Orientalism and the critique of Orientalism. Inveighing against the invisibilization of the racialized body by a euphemizing "white Western liberal" whose priorities are to "establish the advocate's own humanity" and, relatedly, to repress his desires, Miller reinflects a theme from Edward Said. *Orientalism* embarks from a critique of "the textual attitude," an aspect of Orientalist consciousness that contrasts "the schematic authority of a text" with "the disorientations of direct encounters with the human" (93), and finds in favor of textual authority over the body, every time. Said chooses the noun "disorientations" carefully: the "direct encounter" (which Said variously figures via bodies, via desire, via the face-to-face, and, as here, via "the human") disorients and, thereby, disorientalizes. If, as Sara Ahmed argues, *Orientalism* is a phenomenological manual about the conscious experience of space, then "direct encounters with the human" are those that replace the confusions of orientation with presence and plenitude.[10] *The Mikado*'s queer realism, if it does not allow itself the same delight of Miller on Barthes, nonetheless discloses through its form the imprint of a felt history that, for real reasons, it cannot represent realistically.

It need hardly be remarked that realism is not a genre to which *The Mikado* could be said unproblematically to belong. The more obvious, and better-trodden, generic pathways by which it has been explored explain more of its distinctive features—parody, extravaganza, and light opera, especially. Although none of the characters represented (prince in disguise, a ludicrously oleaginous bureaucrat, a lascivious older woman straight out of a Restoration comedy) could be described as a realist protagonist, and although none of the plotlines (a tortuous jurisprudential fiction, a swashbuckling romantic tale) could be assimilated comfortably into realist narrative, Gilbert's libretto consistently displays a *metatheatrical* awareness of how the opera's very performance locates its performers and audiences. It is at this meta-level, then, that we might be able to discern a grounding realism, of which the protagonist is not the character but the actor, its plot not the presented narrative but the fate of the opera itself. The protagonist of this realism is a public theatrical performance, striving to assert its own identity against the ministrations of worldly powers such as censors, diplomats, and audiences.

The libretto engages such figures on a small scale when, for example, the world of the Town of Titipu is incorporated into the familiar world of 1880s London, as when the Lord High Executioner informs the Mikado that the Prince has gone abroad to "Knightsbridge!" (*Complete Annotated,* 631). (Knightsbridge, in South West London, was from 1885–87 the location of a "Japanese Village," where the seamstresses and dancers who trained the Savoyards were exhibiting their craftwork.)[11] Koko's metatheatrical joke both assimilates the world of *The Mikado* and the real world, and disaggregates the two: the audience laughs, in part, because it has been folded into the fictional space, but in part at the improbability at their having been so; that is, at the sheer scale of the distance transgressed between Titipu and Knightsbridge. As hinted in this essay's first epigraph, *The Mikado*'s wit derives from the incongruity of that distance with the fact that, indeed, there are at present Japanese people in London. Scholars have occasionally further suggested that the name "Titipu" itself is a slightly bawdy reworking of the town of Chichibu, the site of a peasant revolt in 1884, and the source of some of the fabrics on display at the Japanese village.[12] Whether or not such material is incorporated into the libretto knowingly, the Chichibu connection has been an important element of the play's mythology for Japanese performers seeking to *reworld* the opera as both an archive of Japanese cultural tropes in the West, and a record of Orientalist fascination with those tropes.

More importantly, however, *The Mikado*'s problematic geolocation is a conspicuous feature of Gilbert's method of introducing and representing *characters.* The first scene opens on a "Chorus of Nobles" who are "discovered," according to the libretto's stage directions, "standing and sitting in attitudes suggested by native drawings" (*Complete Annotated,* 559). Whether or not that suggestion has been imprinted on the opera's stage designer, or on its audience, is a question that the libretto leaves unresolved, and only amplifies in the Chorus' opening number:

If you want to know who we are,
We are gentlemen of Japan:
On many a vase and jar—
On many a screen and fan,
We figure in lively paint:
Our attitude's queer and quaint—
You're wrong if you think it ain't, oh!

If you think we are worked by strings,
Like a Japanese marionette,
You don't understand these things:
It is simply Court etiquette.
Perhaps you suppose this throng
Can't keep it up all day long?
If that's your idea, you're wrong, oh! (559)

The lyric's syntax constructs meaning wittily and prettily; identifying the characters at first hypothetically ("*if* you want to know who we are") and then defensively ("you're wrong if you think it ain't"), as though the very identity of the characters could only be established indirectly, —queerly and quaintly. Yet what is most striking is the song's analogizing of the Chorus' presentation of character to the depiction of Japanese figures on a series of visual media—vase, jar, screen, fan—presumably familiar to the audience. The portability of these objects, and their broad circulation within the material culture of 1880s London, familiarizes the characters even as it defamiliarizes them. Yet there is a further twist. The finite verb of the second clause, "figure," condenses these movements brilliantly, since to an audience listening rather than reading, it shifts the meaning of the foregoing lines. Until that "figure," the preceding "on"-phrases seemed as though they modified the noun phrase "gentlemen of Japan": as though the Chorus were representing not "gentlemen" themselves, but *representations* of gentlemen on the vase and jar; representations of representations. Once the finite clause arrives, we learn that these are indeed characters more conventionally understood, but ones become metatheatrically aware of their figurativeness, and indeed of the queer-and-quaintness of that figuration.

The song sustains, I suggest, a realism without referent, which combines the listing of familiar objects (a classical realist strategy) with the estrangement of the subject from his identity. If Lukácsian realism depends on the possibility of commuting an individual's narrative into a historical situation—as in the idea of a "typical" character—*The Mikado*'s "If you want to know who we are" performs that action in the vivid sense that it grants historical consciousness to an *object*. The historical situation in which such characters are planted, a situation engendered by the unprecedented event of Japanese modernity, is not one the opera can fully grasp, but neither is it a reality from which Gilbert's libretto absents itself entirely. As with Barthes and Hearn, the "real world" cannot but exert a pressure on the Orientalist ego, and the text reverberates with its disorienting effects. I will proceed by examining the opera's situation of itself in that world: first, by comparing its representation of legal authority with its own legal fortunes; second, by drawing connections between its comic Orientalism and broadly contemporary works "about Japan"; and lastly by returning to the British 1880s to reconsider the opera's queerness in the light of the Labouchere Amendment, passed in the same year as *The Mikado*'s opening performance. For some attendees of the Savoy in 1885, the worlding realism of an opera in which flirtation was punishable by death would have been all-too-disturbingly apparent.

II. A Japanese Gentleman of Rank

On April 30, 1887, a crowd of men and women gathered outside Yokohama Gaiety Theater, waiting to hear whether they would be seated for the Salinger Opera Bouffe Company's performance of *The Mikado*. The chances did not look good. Two days previously, a scheduled production had been canceled by the British consul in Yokohama, whose extraterritorial legal authority over British subjects had been established by the first of the "unequal treaties" between the British and Japanese governments, the 1858 Anglo-Japanese Treaty of Amity and Commerce. Sir Francis Plunkett, the British minister at Tokyo, had refused to allow Salinger to present his *Mikado* until certain elements of the play, a farcical treatment of the legal culture of a Japanese town, had been changed to erase, or at least mitigate, any offense to Japanese viewers. The characters' names ("Nanki-Poo," "Pooh-Bah," etc.) were allowed to stand, presumably since no Japanese spectator would think them to suggest Japanese words, but all references to "Japan" would have to be replaced by the word "country" and all references to the "Mikado" would be replaced by simply "king." Accordingly, the title of the opera needed to be changed and, shortly after a messenger from Plunkett arrived conveying the emperor's personal approval of the censored script, the curtain went up on *Sotyugo Shita Sannin no Otome*, "Three Graduated Debutantes," or, more loosely, "Three Little Maids from School."[13]

Accounts differ on the composition of the audience, and although the *Taranaki Herald*'s claim that it was "entirely Japanese" lacks credibility given the Gaiety Theater's location in "The Bluff," a cosmopolitan residential area of Japan's major port populated primarily by European and American merchants. That there were *some* Japanese spectators is, nonetheless, established; so too that Plunkett's edits had failed to disguise the play's original setting: Fukuchi Gen'ichiro, the reviewer for the *Nichi Nichi Shimbun*, wrote that the opera "showed a good understanding of traditional Japanese society." For a British spectator who described his experience in the *Times*, however, such good humor could not be taken for granted on the part of the Japanese audience members: "There were many Japanese among the audience, who laughed heartily at the performance, but whether their mirth was due to a genuine appreciation of the fun of the play or was provided by ludicrous inaccuracies in the representation of themselves and their ways it would be impossible to say" (Leiter, 128). The correspondent recalls, then, watching two performances, one by the actors in Salinger's company, and the other by the Japanese spectators, whose Orientalized inscrutability was apparently amplified, rather than mitigated, by their apparent good humor. Indeed, the Japanese audience's laughter provoked on the part of the correspondent a desire to preempt, and ultimately to manage, its unruly affective consequences.

Such a desire clearly motivated G. K. Chesterton's impatient assessment, in 1907, that *The Mikado* had nothing whatever to do with Japan: it is from his note in *Littell's Living Age* that most critics have directly or indirectly derived authority for that position. His language draws on military metaphors and projects something closer to Saidian confidence than anything one finds in *The Mikado* itself:

> The cannon ball simply rebounded. And we were earnestly concerned about whether the camion would cannon and hit our Gallant Allies. I doubt there is a single joke in the whole play that fits the Japanese. But all the jokes in the play fit the English, if they would put on the cap. The great creation of the play is Pooh-Bah. I have never heard, I do not believe, that the combination of inconsistent functions is specially a vice of the extreme East. I should guess the contrary: I should guess that the East tends to split into steady and inherited trades or castes; so that the torturer is a torturer and the priest a priest. But about England Pooh-Bah is something more than a satire: he is the truth. ("Pooh-Bah," 248)

Like those of Hearn and Barthes, Chesterton's assertions about Japan derive rhetorical authority from his admissions of ignorance: "I doubt"; "I have never heard"; "I do not believe"; "I should guess." But the rhetorical force is still stronger, working successfully to exclude the Japanese referent *entirely* from the opera on the basis of the critic's own ignorance. Chesterton's call for the individualization of the British bureaucrat echoes the influential Fabian theory that British society was bogged down by an "inefficiency" engendered by capitalism, and soluble only by state intervention.[14] Yet he does not elaborate the specific Englishness of Pooh-Bah in as much detail as he speculates about the peculiarities of the "extreme East." There is no need for him to do to, since, for the purposes of the argument, England is the part of the opera that remains once Japan has been deleted.[15]

Chesterton's article in *Littell's* was written for a specific purpose: protesting the censorship of *The Mikado* for the duration of a state visit to London by Prince Fushimi Sadanaru in May 1907, the first since the conclusion of hostilities between Japan and Russia in 1905. The Lord Chamberlain's decision to refuse the Savoyards a license to revive the show was never explicitly explained, but was widely interpreted as a move designed to avoid offending London's Japanese visitors. As such it was condemned as spineless pandering in a variety of editorials like Chesterton's in the *Daily News*, the *Era*, and elsewhere; public letters of support for the ban were fewer.[16] Also unclear was whether the ban was the Lord Chamberlain's own idea, or whether he was responding to representations made by Japanese diplomats, as Gilbert believed.[17] In any case, the potentially querulous Prince furnished the Savoyards with a "real world" example of the capricious Oriental authority whose presence suffuses every aspect of *The Mikado*.

Although the titular character's appearance onstage is delayed until the second act, he is fearfully anticipated for much of the first. He has decreed, we learn in an early number, that "All who flirted, leered, or winked / (Unless connubially linked), / Should forthwith be beheaded" (*Complete Annotated*, 563)—a law that, while apparently popular, has necessitated the first of the plot's many legal fixes, since the sentence, if rigorously applied, would lead to the extirpation of the towns people. So, the person who was supposed to be executed next is appointed as the Lord High Executioner (since "Who's next to be decapited / Cannot cut off another's head / Until he's cut his own off" [565]). The elegance of both the law and its evasion are glossed in the same way by a chorus satisfied by the playing out of good form: "And we are right, I think you'll say / To argue in this kind of way / And I am right / And you are right / And all is right—too-looral-lay!" (565). From the start, then, the opera sets an unimpeachable law against its cunning circumvention, and stages that plot repeatedly as the avoidance of accountability to the despotic emperor. Consequentially its characters dwell in perpetual dread of the "short sharp shock" (591) that will follow from the Mikado's eventual appearance, presaged in a letter received towards the end of the first act in which the emperor "decrees that unless somebody is beheaded within one month the post of Lord High Executioner shall be abolished, and the city reduced to the rank of a village!" (587).

That the death sentence *is* successfully avoided in the denouement is, to be sure, a generic necessity: unlike realist novels, or indeed grand opera, Gilbert and Sullivan's opera cannot end love plots by killing off half of the characters. In *The Mikado*, however, that outcome is not brokered through legal reform, or through the Mikado's being persuaded to change his mind, but rather through the hyperbolization of his legal authority. It is Koko, the executioner himself, who eventually hits on the solution:

KOKO: It's like this: When your Majesty says, "Let a thing be done," it's as good as done—practically, it *is* done—because your Majesty's will is

> law. Your Majesty says, "Kill a gentleman," and a gentleman is told off to be killed. Consequently, that gentleman is as good as dead—practically, he *is* dead—and if he is dead, why not say so?
>
> MIKADO: I see. Nothing could possibly be more satisfactory! (649)

Many of Gilbert's plots revolve around legal fixes. The famous "paradox" of *The Pirates of Penzance,* for instance, is that the pirate apprentice Frederic is denied the freedom promised to him on his twenty-first birthday because, having been born on February 29, "if we go by birthdays, you're only five and a little bit over" (*Complete Annotated,* 239). Yet where the pirates are eventually chastened, and their grip on Frederic loosened, by their loyalty to a greater sovereign ("because, with all our faults, we love our Queen" [261]), the authority of the Mikado is strengthened, rather than abandoned, in the plot's conclusion.

These legal fictions demarcate one border at which the imaginary meets the real, and begin to connect *The Mikado*'s (extradiegetic) fear of a Japanese audience in Yokohama or in the Greenwich docks, with its (intradiegetic) fear of the Oriental despot that motivates much of its plot. Yet we might reasonably ask: can affects such as paranoia, anxiety, fear, anticipation, and excitement—all of which postulate their own condition as one of unknowing—sustain a realism of whatever kind? What conditions of *unknowing* might construct the reality principle of a queer world? In order to understand, then, what kinds of knowledge "Japan" could produce for Victorians, I turn to a handful of other texts that offer comical accounts of Japanese culture: Tobias Smollett's *The Adventures of an Atom* (1769); Basil Hall Chamberlain's *Things Japanese* (1891); Donald Sladen's *Queer Things about Japan* (1901), and its sequel *More Queer Things about Japan* (1904).

III. Queer Things about Japan

Smollett's *The History and Adventures of an Atom* offers both an early example of comic writing about Japan and an example of what *The Mikado* might look like if it *were* unambiguously a satire of English political culture. A picaresque it-narrative told by a roguish atom to an amanuensis named Nathaniel Peacock, the novel describes a trip around Japan, comprising a number of eccentric "political anecdotes."[18] Like those in *The Mikado,* the Japanese politicians described are variously ruthless, stupid, and pedantic, and given to pointless arguments—though, written at the high watermark of English *picaresque,* the jokes are much bawdier than Gilbert's, and the narrative involves a punishingly detailed series of ass-kissing scenes, both literal and figurative. Characters' names, too, share with Nanki-Poo and Pooh-Bah a queasily euphemistic anality: Nin-kom-poo-po, Fika-kaka, Sti-phi-rum-poo. Yet the most striking difference from *The Mikado* is that *Adventures of an Atom* rests on a tight allegorical correspondence between its characters and the British political figures it has set out to describe in the service of a critique of the Seven Years' War of 1754–63. Taycho, known for his "fluency of abuse" (104), is a mockery of William Pitt, and Lords Chatham and Bute also appear under pseudonyms.[19] Walter Scott understood *Adventures of an Atom* not as a set of claims about Japan, but as a patriotic work, designed "to inspire a national horror of continental connexions" (159). Smollett's novel, apparently, was not about Japan. But it did, certainly, use Japan as a setting that was *particularly* suitable for the purpose of not being thematized, and one which could lead to spectacular scenes of eroticized violence; a setting that then shaped the generic conventions of explicitly nonfictional writing about Japan a century later.

A scholar and diplomat of repute both within and without Japan, Basil Hall Chamberlain might be expected to write the antithesis of Smollett's prurient gag-book. Yet even in his attempt to establish an entirely serious, modern, and respectful tone in which English writing about Japan might proceed, one detects vestiges of the comic queer-and-quaintness of the picaresque. His career as a Japanologist is detailed at length in Yuzo Ota's sympathetic biography,[20] but might be exemplified by his having been appointed as the first Western scholar to have taught Japanese at Tokyo Imperial University, which he did from 1873 until his retirement, aged forty-one, in 1891. (Hearn taught English literature at the same school, around the same time.) Along with E. M. Satow and W. G. Aston, Chamberlain was one of the three most distinguished British scholars of Japan, scholars whose writing helped to shift the perceptions of Japan in the minds of British readers from the folkloric depictions of Edwin Arnold and A. E. Mitford to appreciation of Japanese military and industrial power. Chamberlain's position on Japanese military strength fluctuated over his career—he notoriously called the Sino-Japanese War of 1894 "our war," but became critical of militarist deployments of folk myths in the later Taisho and Showa periods. Consistently, however, he maintained a commitment to representing Japanese modernity, rather than tradition. The most widely read of his Anglophone books on Japan, *Things Japanese*, opens with an implicit rebuke of the tone of Edwin Arnold's writing on Japan, noting the distaste with which an audience of Japanese diplomats, academics, and journalists received a speech of Arnold's praising Japanese folk traditions. Adopting the first-person voice of an editor of a Japanese newspaper, Chamberlain writes: "Art forsooth, scenery, sweetness of disposition! cries this editor. Why did not Sir Edwin praise us for huge industrial enterprises, for commercial talent, for wealth, political sagacity, powerful armaments? Of course it is because he could not honestly do so. He has gauged us at our true value, and tells us in effect that we are only pretty weaklings."[21] The editor, in Chamberlain's account, resolves to ensure that the enfeeblement of Japan in Orientalist representations is made more difficult, and Chamberlain responds by seeking a new genre for Japan-writing, and a new tone in which to conduct it.

Chamberlain responded to the political exigencies of a modernizing Japan not merely argumentatively, but in the hybrid form of his text: an alphabetized anthology of brief essays on Japanese culture that he calls "a dictionary, not of words but of things." Part travel guide, part encyclopedia, Chamberlain addresses at the outset the generic hybridity of his collection:

> We are perpetually being asked questions about Japan. Here then are the answers, put into the shape of a dictionary, not of words but of things,—or shall we rather say a guide-book, less to places than to subjects?—not an encyclopedia, mind you, not the vain attempt by one man to treat exhaustively of all things, but only sketches of many things. The old and the new will be found cheek by jowl. What will not be found is padding: for padding is unpardonable in any book on Japan, where the material is so plentiful that the chief difficulty is to know what to omit. (2)

At another moment, Chamberlain describes the collection as a memorial to the "Old Japan" whose passing marks the present historical moment: "This unpretentious book is intended to be, the epitaph recording the many and extraordinary virtues of the deceased—his virtues, but also his frailties" (6–7). Defined by a series of hesitant designations followed by their negations, *Things Japanese* is presented to its reader as an impressionistic and subjectivist collation of "sketches," a text whose argument is a series of moving parts, rather than a unified whole. Chamberlain's ambition is analytic, rather than synthetic, his critical insights always entailing the splitting of apparently unified identities into a series of shifting, incommensurate entities. Romantic and fragmented perhaps even against Chamberlain's explicit aims for the collection, then, *Things Japanese* is founded on an ideology of discrimination and difference, which the author politicizes in relation to both modernity and Orientalist assumptions concerning Asia. The introductory peroration proposes a schematic counterexample to the text's own method, in which Chamberlain enumerates the various assumptions that comprise "Europe's illusions about the Far East" (9). The foundational mistake is the unification of discrete Asian "peoples" by the singular designation "Orientals" or "Asiatics" (9). The fragmentary form of *Things Japanese* responds primarily to Japanese modernity, but also proposes an Orientalism of parts as a corrective to the simplistically synthesized Orientalisms of Chamberlain's contemporaries.

If Chamberlain's newly particularized scholarly content needed to be mobilized as a series of almost epigrammatic entries, more populist writing on

Japan took a comic tone as a prerequisite for the modernity that Chamberlain had striven to manage, and turned to the picaresque as a model for knowledge production. Douglas Sladen, for example, opens his book *Queer Things about Japan* (1901) with the Horatian motto "Ridentem dicere verum quid vetat?" (what is to stop a joker from telling the truth?),[22] positioning himself as a jester whose gnomic jokes about Japan might prove a firmer ground for knowing Japanese culture than a more serious tone. "I am so fond of Japan that I should not have cared to criticise the Japanese directly" (vii). His Japan is full of playful analogies and witty exuberance: the resort town of Miyanoshita, for example, appears as "the Brighton of Japan" (317), where "Nice young people with European lovers go sentimental walks into the glen [*sic*]" (325). Like Chamberlain's "things Japanese," each of Sladen's "queer things" is a vignette, a series of gently descriptive passages held together by a lightly grasped narrative, in which the narrator appears as a character, though rarely a central one. When the tone or subject matter appears to require an elevated register, Sladen punctures it as quickly as possible: the chapter named "The Sacred City of Nikko, and its Golden Shrines" begins "A sacred city in Japan need not be taken *au grand sérieux*, as it must in some countries" (341).

Sladen's sequel, *More Queer Things about Japan*, provides a rich source of information concerning the rapid change in British representations of Japan in the wake of the Russo-Japanese War.[23] The book initially comprised four heterogeneous, but each fairly lighthearted, sections: "Japan from a Woman's Point of View" (written by Sladen's partner, Norma Lorimer); "The Letters of Will Adams from Japan, 1611–1617"; "A Life of Napoleon, Written and Illustrated by Japanese in the First Half of the Nineteenth Century"; and "Japan from a Man's Point of View." But, after the conclusion of the Russo-Japanese War, Lorimer and Sladen put out a "Peace Edition," which inserted an utterly flat-affect timeline of the war, charting in bullet points the major events of almost every day from February 5, 1904, until September 5, 1905. The reprinted "Peace Edition" starkly displays the dramatic and rapid changes in the kinds of literary form that writing about Japan could take.

Yet *The Mikado* is not merely another instance of this loose genre of comic writing about Japan. Rather, it registers, both metatheatrically and at the level of plot, the fractious internal dynamics that would eventually produce the emphatically antipositivist Orientalisms of Hearn and Barthes, working through the epistemological problems Japanology had posed at the level of theatrical form. It is an opera in which the capacity of themes to be adequately encapsulated by language (of something to be "about" something) is subjected to a relentless examination—especially through its inquiries into the force and nature of legal authority. The Mikado's edict that motivates the plot's beginnings—that flirtation shall be made punishable by execution—links speech with death, and the articulation of one's thinking with a profound risk. The universe of the play, in other words, is one in which all speech is by nature a circumlocution, as is made dramatically clear when the "Lord High Everything Else" Pooh-Bah is forced to give entirely conflicting advice as he cycles through his personae—"Of course, as First Lord of the Treasury, I could propose a special vote that would cover all expenses, if it were not that, as leader of the Opposition, it would be my duty to resist it tooth and nail" (575). Williams rightly notes that these parodic performances of identity unsettle the play's gender performances, and indeed a broader array of constructions of gender that Victorian theater enacted. But, amplifying Williams's sense of the opera's queerness, I will end by arguing that the weakness of *The Mikado*'s performative act—the text's ambivalence, that is, concerning the thematic presence of "Japan"—enables a new kind of nonsovereign *critical* practice, an interpretive practice that leaves itself open to revision and reconstruction. There is at the heart of the opera itself an incipient theory of speech contrived to avoid the executioner's axe, that might disclose itself briefly, but then be able to smile, gauge an audience's reaction, and hurriedly add "just kidding" should it be necessary to do so: a paranoid claim to subjective authority.

IV. Dull Dark Dock

To *flirt*, to *leer*, to *wink*: the Mikado has established as capital crimes not sex itself, but its solicitation. Rather than criminalize consummation, he has banned pursuit; or, perhaps, rather than the act, the identity. If this substitution might initially seem to be possible because sex is so far from the horizon as to be unthinkable, *The Mikado* repeatedly sets the matter straight: sexual words are everywhere, from the characters' names to the sweet nothings mumbled by the dumb creatures close by. Like "The Raven," Koko's (bad faith) plaint of love to Katisha pulls hard on a single word tweeted by an unwitting (but potentially all-knowing) bird; like Poe's narrator, Koko grows increasingly and morbidly fascinated by the repetition; unlike "nevermore," "titwillow" (*Complete Annotated*, 641) seems to have been chosen as much for its vulgarity as for its euphony. Deprived of a sexual object, language is treated by the Mikado's law as an object in itself, and so it becomes a worldly and conspicuous object. The most illustrative example of such speech is, moreover, the first appearance in the libretto of the Japanese language, from a chorus shouting "o ni! bikkuri shakkuri to!" (601) in order to drown out the spurned lover Katisha, who is on the cusp of informing them that Nanki-Poo is the Mikado's son, and not a minstrel at all. The exclamatory fragment of words suggests (though few of the Savoyards could have been expected to know) hiccupping in shock, and so emerges onstage as both a confabulation of nonsense *and* as a corporate body resisting knowledge through a homeostatic response. Here, as with the opening "gentlemen of Japan" number, there is a blurring of the line between the textual world of the libretto and the metatexual world of performance: queer realism places the performer in the world without her knowledge.

If, under pressure of law, language appears in *The Mikado* as a privileged object of erotic desire, the form that fantasy takes is accordingly judicial. The moment when the voices of Koko, Pooh-Bah, and Pish-Tush (the messenger who has brought the Mikado's letter) converge to express their desire not

> To sit in solemn silence in a dull dark dock,
> In a pestilential prison, with a life-long lock,
> Awaiting the sensation of a short, sharp shock,
> From a cheap and chippy chopper on a big black block! (591)

is not eroticized solely by its thrilling trisyllabic line endings, alliterative molossi that depart dramatically from the two tetrasyllabic feet that precede them. The moment captures three voices coming together in a shared, and intimate, exposure of their abject humanity. For the foregoing couple of minutes, each character has been rapidly pattering over the others, muttering a different excuse for not volunteering to die, and all now sing the same words, united in hypocrisy and anxiety. The moment is not merely intimate but implicitly sexual, since the punishment in question, decapitation, has been established from the start as the opera's code word for sex, the consummation that has taken its place in the Mikado's regime. Fantasies about legal power also motivate not one but two of *The Mikado*'s showstoppers, moreover, which take the form of gleeful indulgences of legal violence. In "As Some Day It May Happen," it is Koko who playfully lists the social undesirables his position as executioner may allow him to kill (571); later the Mikado proudly and happily announces his "object all sublime" to be "to make each prisoner pent / Unwillingly represent / A source of innocent merriment, of innocent merriment!" (623).

I have been arguing that the "queer realism" of *The Mikado*, its stretching out into a world it can only struggle to inhabit, was enabled by the particularities of its Japanese setting. On the one hand, I have argued, Japan produced a number of literary subgenres in which knowledge about an Orient was advanced tentatively and comically, and that the hybrid genres of texts about Japan resolve some of the hermeneutic problems that *The Mikado* has posed for audiences and critics. On the other, I have suggested that the historical emergence of Japan as a modern and military power in the late nineteenth century necessarily conditioned both those genres and the version of "the real world" that they were able to represent; these texts, after all, are Orientalisms neither propelled by colonial desire nor nourished by Saidian "confidence." By way of concluding, however, I will turn to one of *The Mikado*'s domestic contexts in order to understand one other aspect of these orientations.[24] I do not do so in order to join the consensus that this opera is about Britain after all, but rather to suggest that the Orientalist genres I have been adumbrating form one historical basis for a critical engagement with the legal status of homosexuality in the late nineteenth century.

Bluntly: a world in which the phrase "sex crime" described not sex itself, but the eroticization of language and of the eye, was indeed the world in which *The Mikado* was first performed. Or, almost: the play opened on March 14, 1885, but it was not until August 7, towards the end of a long summer of sex panic, that the Liberal MP Henri Labouchere successfully appended the following amendment to the Criminal Law Amendment Act:

> Any male person who, in public or private, commits, or is a party to the commission of, or procures, or attempts to procure the commission by any male person of, any act of gross indecency with another male person, shall be guilty of a misdemeanour, and being convicted thereof, shall be liable at the discretion of the Court to be imprisoned for any term not exceeding two years, with or without hard labour.[25]

There is a patter-song quality to Labouchere's legalese as it conducts its subordinated clauses and antimetabolic caesurae towards their murderous peroration. Foregrounding the capacity of language to induce an indecency that neither will nor can be further defined, Labouchere's own words rely on connotation and rumor, legislating neither this act nor that, but Sedgwick's open secret itself. Legal language as such is not, in general, written to be spoken out loud except under specific circumstances, but the "blackmailer's charter," as it came to be known, was a different kind of tongue-twister, one that stifled the flirtatious speech of men and treated imprecise language as positive evidence. Symptomatically, if not consequentially, the most famous case it produced comprised a protracted and agonizing attempt to force silence into speech, from the properly impossible question "what is 'the love that dare not speak its name?' " through to the judge's attempt to "prevent one's self from describing, in language that I would rather not use, the sentiments which must rise to the breast of every man of honour who has heard the details of these two terrible trials." The usually loquacious defendant's response was a minimally constructed question to which silence was the ambiguous answer: "May I say nothing, my Lord?"[26]

In the libretto of Gilbert and Sullivan's satire of the aesthetic movement, *Patience*, a word that appears twice as a shorthand for queerness is "Japanese": the first time when the "fleshly poet" Bunthorne (*Complete Annotated*, 266) confesses in an aside to the audience that he isn't a fop after all ("I do *not* long for all one sees / that's Japanese" [291]); the second when he playfully reassumes the role ("Conceive me if you can / A Japanese young man" [345–47]). It is surely the second of these that the anthropologist Sheila K. Johnson is recalling, however unconsciously, when, in the context of a slightly phobic argument about Americans in Japan, she claims: "The existence, in Japan, of 'pretty young men' is no doubt another reason why American homosexuals are attracted to the country. . . . [Some] prefer the slim, beardless, high-cheekboned, aesthetic-looking youths often found in Japan."[27] (Despite being published in 1988, this passage exhibits an exquisitely fin-de-siècle usage of "aesthetic.") The phrase "pretty young men" is not, as far as I can tell, a quotation *from* anywhere; it is only a semi-citation, much as it is at the beginning of Oscar Wilde's essay "Art and the Handicraftsman," where Wilde imagines his own Japaneseness as an ugly rumor: "You have heard of me . . . as, if not a 'Japanese young man,' at least a young man to whom the rush and clamour of the modern world were distasteful."[28]

Gilbert and Sullivan did not invent the queerness of Japan for British audiences: as I have suggested, there is a longer generic history to the association. Yet *The Mikado* stands as the fullest articulation of the particular affinity between the two themes that the period produced. By constructing a realism defined by its incapacity to inhabit the world "confidently," *The Mikado* expresses both the eroticism and the distinctive social posture of an emergent queer identity. Accordingly, it is not merely the history of British anti-Japanese sentiment that is obscured by the assessment that it is "not about Japan": one also risks misconstruing the opera's distinctive response to British culture itself. No doubt because of the grotesque violence represented in "As Some Day It May Happen," contemporary performances tend to amend the lyrics to reflect whichever repository of the abject seems most within the production's reach: in Jonathan Miller's 1987 production for the English National Opera, for example, Eric Idle's Koko cited "people who host chat shows and the guests what's on 'em too."[29] But the song's enduring capacity to name and degrade the economic, racial, gendered, and sexual outcasts from within a British conservative ideology was made stunningly clear at the Conservative Party's 1992 conference, at which Peter Lilley, the secretary of state for social security who was regarded as one of the most right-wing members of John Major's government, came to give his speech:

> I'm closing down the "something for nothing" society. This summer I announced new rules affecting so-called "New-Age Travelers." Most people were as sickened as I was by the sight of these spongers descending like locusts demanding benefits with menaces. . . . But there are scores of other

> frauds to tackle. So, Mr. Chairman, just like in *The Mikado*, I've got a little list. Of benefit offenders who I'll soon be rooting out, and who never would be missed. They never would be missed. There's those who make up bogus claims in half a dozen names, and counselors who draw the dole to run left-wing campaigns. They never would be missed. They never would be missed. There's young ladies who get pregnant just to jump the housing queue, and Dads who won't support the kids of the ladies they have . . . kissed. And I haven't even mentioned all those sponging socialists. I've got *them* on my list, and there's none of *them*'d be missed, there's none of them'd be missed.[30]

The ellipsis I have placed in Lilley's quite accomplished prosody (particularly accomplished before the parody starts, in fact: the tetrametric crescendo that weighs "spongers," "locusts," "benefits," and "menaces" produces forceful rhythms and chilling feminine rhymes) marks a moment of euphemism in which "screwed"—which would not, exactly, have rhymed with "queue"—is overwritten in a manner that could certainly be called "quaint," although hardly queer. And Lilley's deployment of "sponging" as a name for the exuberant expenditure of communal values on fripperies hardly maps onto Gilbert's own horror at the threats of amateurism and effeminization.

"I've Got a Little List" presents, then, a kind of comic elaboration of the problem of the Ship of Theseus: is it still the same list, if all the items have been replaced? The same formal problem is dramatized to a different political end in Stephen Sondheim's 1976 Broadway musical *Pacific Overtures*, in its eight-minute act 1 showstopper, "Please Hello." Staged in a Kabuki style, and featuring (in its original performance) Japanese and Japanese American actors, "Please Hello" depicts Matthew Perry's arrival in Japan and its aftermath as a series of short songs sung by a sequence of Western diplomats, the style of each of which is marked as ethnic pastiche. The American diplomat's appearance is announced by Yankee brass; the French ambassador's campy number recalls Offenbach; the Dutchman's in a manner Sondheim's libretto describes as "Weber-and-Fields style, complete with Hans Brinker pockets and heavy clogs." The British admiral delivers a patter song in the unmistakable *primus paeon* of the Major-General's song from *The Pirates of Penzance*:

> Hello, I come with letters from Her Majesty Victoria
> Who, learning how you're trading now, sang "Hallelujah, Gloria!"
> And sent me to convey to you her positive euphoria
> As well as little gifts from Britain's various emporia.
> . . . .
>
> Her letters do contain a few proposals to your Emperor
> Which if, of course, he won't endorse, will put her in a temper, or

More happily, should he agree, will serve to keep her placid, or
At least till I am followed by a permanent ambassador.

. . . .

Her Majesty considers the arrangements to be tentative
Until we ship a proper diplomatic representative.
We don't foresee that you will be the least bit argumentative,
So please ignore the man-of-war we brought as a preventative.

"Please Hello" wittily explores the difficulty of formalizing partial knowledge: the problem, too, of *The Mikado*. Though the five ambassadors all *sound* different, they *perform* in the same Kabuki style. But more pressingly, the lyrics expose a connection between aesthetic form and historical violence that Perry's bravado had sought to conceal: the deeply unequal power relations between the admiral and the Japanese diplomatic to whom his euphemistic address is made. The formal parity that, in his own published account, Perry imagined as the coming together of two smooth membranes, in other words, protects him against the realization that, in this negotiation, he is far from the underdog he repeatedly presents.[31] Forms govern the mode of discussion between Perry and his Japanese counterparts: they are, in that sense, metadiegetic. But "form" also serves him as the representation of ideology *within* ideology: a euphemism whose very extravagance debunks it.

These objects—the Savoy Opera, the Lilley speech, the Sondheim number—share certain formal features: they combine a librettist's virtuosic control of rhyme and meter with a performer's virtuosic control of breath; their satirical energies are directed against a kind of speech they typify as bureaucratically overdetermined; their euphemisms serve ostentatiously to disguise, and therefore surreptitiously to foreground their violent themes. What I have been describing as the Gilbertian queer realism—a realism built up around a *real* aporia—might also be understood as an exquisite revision of the older genre of Menippean satire—the witty invective against the totalizing epistemologies of the *philosophus gloriosus* whose closest antecedent would be Thomas Carlyle's *Sartor Resartus* (1836) and Samuel Butler's *Erewhon* (1872), but whose best known examples in English are eighteenth-century fictions: *Gulliver's Travels* and *Tristram Shandy*. Such satires are formal, rather than thematic: they do not assail the abuses of this or that (political or intellectual) system, but the very impulse to system building itself, given the association (since Plato) between system building and the exclusion of the poets. Accordingly, argued Northrop Frye in his elaboration of the Menippean genre, "Satire on systems of reasoning, especially on the social effects of such systems, is art's first line of defense against all such invasions."[32] Yet, the patter song redirects the genre's exhaustive cataloguing energies—that conventional Menippean satire channels into the erection of monstrous paragraphs and tomes—into *prosody*. The conversion of a satirical prose genre into verse effects an aestheticization of the fact, which in *The Mikado* amounts to an epistemology of the exquisite. One cannot know the opera's object *entirely*; but nor can one avoid, prompted by the virtuosic prosodic stimuli, transmitting back to the opera a *desire* to know. Thus, though Gilbert and Sullivan were peripheral to the British aesthetic movement I discuss in the following chapter, their work too bears the mark of having been called towards, and then recoiled from, the irreducibly aesthetic idea of Japan.

2

All Margin

There was more margin; margin in every sense was in demand, and I remember, looking at the poems of John Gray (then considered the incomparable poet of the age), when I saw the tiniest rivulet of text meandering through the very largest meadow of margin, I suggested to Oscar Wilde that he should go a step further than these minor poets; that he should publish a book *all* margin; full of beautiful unwritten thoughts, and have this blank volume bound in some Nile-green skin powdered with gilt nenuphars and smoothed with hard ivory, decorated with gold by Ricketts (if not Shannon) and printed on Japanese paper; each volume must be a collector's piece, a numbered one of a limited "first" (and last) edition: "very rare."

He approved.

"It shall be dedicated to you, and the unwritten text illustrated by Aubrey Beardsley. There must be five hundred signed copies for particular friends, six for the general public, and one for America."

—ADA LEVERSON, *REMINISCENCES*[1]

I. Too Near and Too Far Away

"You will blow your brains out, of course": J.A.M. Whistler's characteristically cool, but uncharacteristically hot, telegram was delivered first to Mortimer Menpes, and then to *Truth* magazine, where it was published on March 28, 1889.[2] Like Whistler's ever-changing signature, a mutant butterfly with a sting in its tail, the note is both violently punctual and too-too light, the trace of an intimacy maintained even in its closure, a wounding kind of softness. The apparent cause of Whistler's ire had been an interview Menpes had given the *Philadelphia Daily News*, but the latter's memoirs tell a different story. The two men had met in the early 1880s, and discovered a shared admiration for

the *Philadelphia Daily News*. Mr. Whistler sent on his own copy to the pretender, with the following note :—

" You will blow your brains out, of course. Pigott has shown you what to do under the circumstances, and you know your way to Spain. Good-bye ! "

FIGURE 2.1. J. A. M. Whistler, "A Suggestion", *The Gentle Art of Making Enemies* (Chelsea: Heinemann, 1929).

ukiyo-e printing, and in different ways attempted to adopt some of its formal features.[3] Menpes, twenty-one years younger than one of the most divisive and visible painter in London, apprenticed himself to the man he would call "Master," and enjoyed his patronage and institutional support until, in 1887, he decided to travel to Yokohama to train with local printers, and sketch a handful of still-life images. This, Whistler could not abide: "Japan should have been saved for the Master. I must admit that I really did slip off like a naughty boy sneaking out of school. I felt that he would resent my leaving him."[4] It was not a decision Menpes took lightly; indeed, the account of the trip offered in *Whistler as I Knew Him* suggests (as the book's title itself attests) that the project was in part calculated to stage a departure from the Master's tutelage, a betrayal to be remembered as fond agony: "I blamed myself bitterly for leaving him," Menpes goes on, "I yearned for the old days when I lived in the intimacy of his studio and we worked together and almost thought together."[5] An intimate space had been violated by the real Japanese craftsman, suddenly real enough to be a rival. And there's another poignant element to this convergence of erotic and aesthetic antagonisms: underneath the publication of the telegram in *Truth* was signed the name of the periodical's publisher, the Liberal MP Henry Labouchere, author of the "blackmailer's charter" under which Oscar Wilde was imprisoned. Wilde himself had attempted to corral various friends into trips to Japan: first Whistler, then Walter Sickert, and eventually a young man he met in Lincoln, Nebraska. Like Whistler, he never made the trip.

The British aesthetic movement, if it was a movement, was a movement without momentum: it is difficult to say what it wanted, or where it thought it was heading. "To burn always with this hard, gem-like flame, to maintain this ecstasy," was Walter Pater's famous formulation of "success in life," a presentist formulation whose antireformist energies characterized, too, the explicit political statements of many of the movement's luminaries.[6] Scholars generally, and understandably, write about aestheticism more as a cultural formation than either a body of theoretically viable writing (the way, for instance, that the aesthetics of the Frankfurt School are still widely discussed) or as a social movement.[7] So the aesthetic movement—or "aestheticism"—needs to be grasped sociologically, as the codes and protocols of certain historical individuals and groups, especially since I have so far been describing the exquisite aesthetics of the encounter between Britain and Japan in relatively abstract terms. At the same time, defining aestheticism in the highly restrictive sense in which it is sometimes construed—highly educated men and women, publishing essays and books on the meaning and power of art, between roughly 1870 and 1900: among whom, Wilde, Whistler, Pater, and Vernon Lee are the central Anglophone figures, and Joris-Karl Huysmans's stream-of-consciousness novel *À Rebours* the essential formal type—creates a stronger sense that aestheticism was an Oxbridge *coterie* than is justifiable. So, following Foucault's distinction between a "history of ideas" and a "history of thought," I propose to treat the aestheticism of the late nineteenth century as representing the social form of aesthetics itself: that it was through the embodied and socially embedded practices of cultivating beauty that the exquisite limits of aesthetic thinking were formulated as a historical problematic.[8] By this I mean: while British aestheticism's engagement with Japan plugged into the hole of Kantian subjective universal, by supplying a set of objects immediately, absolutely, and universally legible as beautiful, it also brought painfully close to home the narcissistic threat of the Other Empire.

This is not to say that the artists and writers of the British aesthetic movement would accept this formulation of their condition. Kant's influence on, especially, Wilde, has been overestimated. Wilde's Oxford notebooks reveal the early intellectual life of a thinker fascinated by Greek tragedy, and then the Hegelian account of aesthetics as grounded in historical and cultural assemblages that dominated the intellectual culture of Oxford in the 1870s. The young Wilde's references to Kant are relatively cool: "object of philosophy according to Kant is what can I know? what ought I to do? what can I hope for? the last two resolve themselves into the first: and this philosophy must rest on science and *psychology*. While psychology rests on the physiology of the nervous system the popular notion of mind is that it is a metaphysical entity seated in the head like a telegraph operator—modern science contends it is a function of the brain."[9] Oxford Hegelianism, on the other hand, may afford a surprisingly fruitful resource for thinking about the erotics of Victorian aestheticism. Pater, a fateful figure of influence and inspiration for Wilde, wrote the *Studies in the History of the Renaissance* partly to test the viability of Hegelian historical materialism as a theory of aesthetic judgment.[10] In his essay on Winckelmann, Pater cited Hegel directly: "The arts may thus be ranged in a series which corresponds to a series of developments in the human mind itself" (182). Nonetheless, while in his famous "Conclusion" to the *Studies,* Pater argued that aestheticism amounted to "never acquiescing in a facile orthodoxy of Comte or of Hegel," Wilde would conclude one of his most important essays "it is only in art-criticism, and through it, that we can realize Hegel's system of contraries. The truths of metaphysics are the truths of masks."[11] Wilde's dialectical relation to Pater—incorporating, negating, upholding—is only one aspect of his thinking that bears the trace of Hegelian method; his famous "inversions" of familiar adages into subversive epigrams, as in the "Phrases and Philosophies for the Use of the Young" themselves model, on that account, a dialectical procedure in miniature.[12]

Pater's career as a Brasenose classicist was, as is well known, marred by a homosexual romance with an undergraduate named William Money Hardinge; the other major homosexual scandal that played out in Oxford during Wilde's time there concerned J. A. Symonds, the author of *A Problem in Greek Ethics*—an early scholarly text dealing with homosexual aspects of Greek culture. Symonds's book was composed in 1873, but not published immediately, partly due to the censure of Benjamin Jowett; in 1883, ten copies were printed privately, and then, in 1908, an unexpurgated version was printed again—still privately, but for a broader readership—under the title *A Problem in Greek Ethics.*[13] As early as 1867, however, Hegelian aesthetics interested Symonds, and he considered writing an expanded translation and commentary on the *Lectures on the Fine Arts.* He *did* publish an essay on "Theocritean landscape" that was attended by a kind of aestheticized embarrassment for which Hegel was partly responsible. Writing to a friend:

> There is a certain cripple of mine which, having got itself into print, will presumedly appear in native and artificial deformity in the next *North British.* Look at it. It is an article on Theocritean landscape. Verily, I shall end with being what the French call a *polygraphe fécond*—a jack of all trades, aesthetical, and a humbug who has gorged and disgorged Hegel.[14]

As with the thematics of suffering touched on above, however, the direct representation of homosexuality was, for many of these authors, less central to an aesthetic project than was a more general obliquity of form, an indirectness that governed aestheticism's modes of representation. Recognizing that counterintuitive, but historically observable, phenomenon, queer theoretical dealing with the late nineteenth and early twentieth century distinguished itself from the earlier gay and lesbian studies, by positioning itself as a theory of form. Queer theory has maintained more of an interest in the habits, structures, tones, and cultural codes that govern relations of sexual and gendered difference, and often refrained from speculating about the precise content of those relations. From this perspective, one need not hazard guesses about what exactly transpired between Dorian Gray and Adrian Singleton (part of the point, Eve Sedgwick might say, is that everybody *knows* anyway) in order to designate the relationship as paradigmatically conditioned by queerness. David Kurnick describes the novel of interiority in queer terms as a project of "dethematizing" subjectivity; "Japan," likewise, was incapable of sustaining the strong form of referential thematics that, since Edward Said, we have habitually associated with Orientalist writing.[15] Powerfully *thematizing the dethematization* in *The Picture of Dorian Gray*, indeed, is the book Dorian considers in the aftermath of the murder of Basil Hallward—"Gautier's *Émaux et Camées*, Charpentier's Japanese-paper edition, with the Jacquemart edging"—where "Japanese" refers to one of a number of mediating forms governing relations between the two men.[16] It is not that we can use this "Japanese-paper edition" as evidence for or against Dorian, but that the exquisite detail triangulates and mediates an intimate relation through a set of thematic conditions (chiefly, here: luxury) that might appear, on first glance, to operate as distancing or alienating effects. One essential element of the idea of Japan for Victorians was that, by the paradoxical virtue of being extremely far away, it could flesh out and formalize relations that were ruinously close.

II. A Blue and White Young Man

For many Victorian aesthetes, such relations took the metaphorical form of the Japanese craftsman: a fantastical emblem uniting tradition with industry, a masculine body with an aesthetic conception of spirit, and the knowable with the desirable. That association confronted the aesthetic movement with two related paradoxes: (1) that some realist or materialist conception of labor was not incompatible with a celebration of abstraction, and in some senses was even a precondition of it; (2) that the Japanese craft of the book, with its elegantly textured pages and harmonically organized book designs, subverted in salutary but also threatening ways the distinction between visual and textual media. Wilde explores the first of these problems directly in "The Decay of Lying," in which Japanese cultural practices aroused not merely aesthetic enthusiasm, but an allergic response to the all-too-real presence of Japanese artists and art objects in Menpes's work:

> In fact, the whole of Japan is a pure invention. There is no such country, there are no such people. One of our most charming painters went recently

> to the Land of the Chrysanthemum in the foolish hope of seeing the Japanese. All he saw, all he had the chance of painting, were a few lanterns and some fans. He was quite unable to discover the inhabitants, as his delightful exhibition at Messrs Dowdeswell's Gallery showed only too well. He did not know that the Japanese people are, as I have said, simply a mode of style, an exquisite fancy of art.[17]

Wilde himself might have had grounds for sympathy with Menpes, not only because he too had seen the sharp side of Whistler's pen, but also because the younger artist was godfather (third choice) to Vyvyan.[18] But instead he is cast as an unfortunate stooge who has mistaken the *formal* potential of Japanese art for its mere *thematic* content. Japan as abstraction: dethematized, aerosolized, diffuse.

Yet this is only one half of the paradox: although "there is no such country, there are no such people," the *style* of Japaneseness has been, Wilde suggests, only grasped by artists who happen to have been Japanese. He goes on: "The Japanese people are the deliberate, self-conscious creation of certain individual artists. If you set a picture by Hokusai or Hokkei, or any of the great native painters, beside a real Japanese gentleman or lady, you will see that there is not the slightest resemblance between them" (1088). The "individual artists" on whose *real* labor Wilde premises his defense of the *irreality* of the "Japanese effect" occupied in that sense an interstitial space within the Victorian aesthetic imagination, de-particularized as instantiations of an ethnic generality, but individuated as singularly "great native painters." The Japanese artist then occupies a place in the scheme of Japanese art at once highly privileged and profoundly threatening: he originates the system, but through the fact of objective existence threatens to desublimate the airy beauty of Japanese art into one more material product.

Wilde does not say this, of course: his epigrammatic argumentative mode formalizes a tendency to sustain paradoxes, rather than prolong them. Yet the figure of the Japanese artist—at once the originator and murderer of aesthetic abstraction—played a somewhat surprising role in Wilde's own growth as an epigrammatist and dandy. One name that Victorians gave to such a person as Wilde was, indeed, "Japanese young man": In *Patience*, the Savoy Opera that he was sent to America to promote, the "fleshly poet" Bunthorne describes himself as, "A Japanese young man, / A blue-and-white young man / Francesca da Rimini, miminy, priminy, / *Je ne sais quoi* young man!"[19] In Gilbert's dashing lyric, the word "Japanese" projects an indexical force quite in excess of its demonymic usage. The young man is Japanese because he has admired too many Japanese craftworks—he has become one of them, object and subject blurred into each other, as they are in Wilde's early epigram: "I find it harder and harder to live up to my blue china."[20] The man himself is at risk of becoming "blue and white," his surface recolored and reoriented. And Wilde, too. He opens his essay on craftwork with an anxious disclaimer: "You have heard of me, I fear, through the medium of your somewhat imaginative newspapers as, if not a 'Japanese young man,' at least a young man to whom the rush and clamour of the modern world were distasteful."[21]

The second paradox of Japanese art was its mobilization of both textual and visual effects, and not just in the popular ukiyo-e prints (such as the Hokusai and Hokkei) that deployed both text and image, and which were, in that sense at least, apprehensible within the generic conventions of cartoons that suffused much of the Victorian popular press. Victorians attempted to model literary texts after Japanese art—often quite literally, as in Whistler's self-designed book *The Gentle Art of Making Enemies*, with its black lines dividing columns of white space, or his butterfly signature—somehow a text, an image, and an art object in itself. Often less than literally, too. In his review of W. E. Henley's poem "Ballade of a Toyokuni Colour-Print," Wilde drew the connection directly: "The Toyokuni colour-print that suggested it could not be more delightful. It seems to have kept all the willful fantastic charm of the original."[22] The theory of mimesis underpinning this assessment is less orthodox than it might appear—or, at least, the fact that the original is a *print* requires the introjection of another layer of mediation. Any individual print is by definition one of a series, infinitely extensible provided that the woodblocks still exist. This is another paradoxical dimension of the Japanese craftwork: it is both unique ("original") and imbued with an ethnic, generalizing style, such that it is not the product of an individual, but of a portable, abstracted figure.

As Wilde attests, Henley's poetry revels in the capacity of Japaneseness to undo categorical distinctions. From his collection "Bric-à-Brac":

Back-View

To D. F.

I WATCHED you saunter down the sand:
Serene and large, the golden weather
Flowed radiant around your peacock feather
And glistened from your jeweled hand.
Your tawny hair, turned strand on strand
And bound with blue ribands together,
Streaked like the rough tartan, green like heather,

That round your lissome shoulder spanned.
Your grace was quick my sense to seize:
The quaint looped hat, the twisted tresses,

The close-drawn scarf, and under these
The flowing, flapping draperies--
My thought an outline still caresses,
Enchanting, comic, Japanese![23]

There is nothing in this poem that has equipped us to read that last word, whose exclamation mark underscores, rather than mitigates, the semantic impoverishment at this last, bathetic gasp. The boundedness and containment of the first stanza present a body harmonized with a natural environment, albeit rather precariously—the "golden weather" itself encircling, sexualizing the body's extremities, Zeus to Danae. But that solidity is slowly unwoven by a second stanza that recites, only to strip off, a set of clothes, until what is left is as close as possible to nothing, an "outline" held close by the poem's speaker. That closeness feels queasy, partly because of the chintziness of the late-Victorian style, with its cheap alliteration and too much flapping about. But partly too because Henley's diminuating, precious adjectives recreate *us* (the "you") as an abject, fragile shard, unfit for the caresses of the voyeur stalking us, whose anal eroticism ("peacock feather") can hardly be anything else but an embarrassment. Interlocking masculine and feminine rhymes, and indeed the gender-free initials of the poem's dedicatee, tell us what we already know: that the body being watched is sexless, that the fetishistic economy of the poet's gaze *requires* that it be unsexed. "Japanese" here is not a demonym,—this figure must be Scottish?—but the poem functions to reduce that word to a pure edge, a minimal Orientalism that by virtue of remaining merely *outline* also remains all-*encompassing*.

Towards the end of this chapter, we will return to the visual/textual distinction in order to consider the particular importance of the printed page as a site in which the problematic visual dimension of textual form was explored. But turning to the materials, let me leave Japan for a moment to bind this Henley, an originating author (according to Wilde) of the Japanese style in English literature, more tightly to the social setting in which my own narrative is embedded—indeed, to show that setting to be constituted through a risk of estrangement, exile, and loss of which Japan furnishes an exemplar. Wilde met Henley around 1887—at just the time that, as far as we know, he began a romance with Robbie Ross, and began working on "The Portrait of Mr. W. H.," the first of his texts to thematize homosexual desire directly. For a couple of years, Wilde and Ross attended dinner parties at Henley's house together. All three were intimate, if one can judge by Wilde's nickname for Henley: "my last pet lunatic."[24] Henley moved to Edinburgh in 1889 to edit the *Scots Observer*, which printed on July 6 that year an unsigned and critical review of Wilde's newly published "Portrait": "With the exception of one article which is out of place in *Maga*—or indeed, in any popular magazine—the July number of *Blackwood* is particularly good."[25] The moralizing tone of that notice was enough to prompt an angry epistle from Wilde: "The Philistines in their vilest forms have seized on you. I am so disappointed."[26] The friendship drifted; Henley published a number of similarly critical reviews of Wilde's work. Shortly after Wilde's release in 1897, however, Henley was clearly on his mind: other than "The Ballad of Reading Gaol," his only piece of new writing that year was a "character" of Henley, to be published by Max Beerbohm alongside a caricature by Will Rothenstein, but eventually rejected because it was considered too hostile. The "character" is among the most semantically opaque passages anywhere in Wilde's oeuvre:

> He founded a school, and has survived all his disciples. He has always thought too much about himself, which is wise; and written too much about others, which is foolish. His prose is the beautiful prose of a poet, and his poetry the beautiful poetry of a prose-writer. His personality is insistent. To converse with him is a physical no less than an intellectual recreation. He is never forgotten by his enemies, and often forgiven by his friends. He has added several new words to the language, and his style is an open secret. He has fought a good fight, and has had to face every difficulty except popularity.
>
> !!! !!![27]

An "open secret": is it too much to read between these lines the same thwarted intimacy one finds in Menpes—routed not now through Japan, but through style itself? Is it mere pedantry or prurience to wonder whether this letter, and the wound through which one must reach to find it, offer us, in the person of William Henley, a portrait of Mr. W. H.?

III. Finish, Gloss

Friedrich von Wenckstern's *Bibliography of the Japanese Empire* lists books and articles published in Europe, North America, and East Asia on the subject of Japanese culture, arranging texts first by subject matter, then by author. In part 15, "Fine Arts and Fine Art Industries," Wenckstern lists seven subcategories of Japanese art practice: Drama, Enamels and Carving, Lacquer, Metallurgy/Magic Mirror, Music, Pictorial Arts, and Pottery.[28] Of these, lacquered objects in particular engage a wide range of scholars and enthusiasts, producing works ranging from scientific textbooks, such as O. Korschelt and H. Yoshida's *The Chemistry of Japanese Lacquer* (1884), to arguments concerning military strategy, such as Lieutenant J. B. Murdock's fascinating call in "The Protection of the Hulls of Vessels by Lacquer" for the use of Japanese lacquering techniques in protecting the steel hulls of military vessels.[29] But aside from the technological and scientific questions posed by Japanese lacquer, the subject was frequently deployed as a metonym for a nonspecific Japanese ethnicity—the beautiful but inscrutable wood preserving as aesthetic form features of a beautiful but inscrutable *racialized aesthetic* form.[30] The American astronomer and Orientalist Percival Lowell, for example, develops such an analogy in *The Soul of the Far East* (1888):

> For it is as true of the Japanese as of the proverbial Russian, though in a more scientific sense, that if you scratch him you will find the ancestral Tartar. But it is no less true that the descendants of this rude forefather have now taken on a polish of which their own exquisite lacquer gives but a faint reflection. The surface was perfected after the substance was formed. Our word finish, with its double meaning, expresses both the process and the result.[31]

Extending the popular adage frequently attributed to Napoleon—*grattez le Russe, vous trouverez le Cosaque*—Lowell generates a complex explanation of Japanese acculturation. Perhaps counterintuitively, the act of "finishing" renders invisible the inner processes that construct the Japanese subject. The kind of lacquer so valued for its elegance is merely a "faint reflection" of that different, more perfect, surface.

Lowell's "double meaning" of the English word "finish" perceives a tension in lacquering between the perfect completion of an object and the revelation of the process of that completion—a difference perhaps analogous to that between preterite and imperfect verb tenses in English. This tension is visible, though less theorized, in a number of contemporary essays on lacquered wood. An article in *The Architect and Contract Reporter*, for example, notes that "Lacquer work is prized, in the first place, in proportion to its delicate and accurate finish, representing artistic and manipulative skill; and, in the second, in proportion to the degree of relief given to its ornamentation, representing time, care, and labour."[32] The perfect completion of an object is then taken to "represent," in some sense, the accretive processes that produced it. Christopher Bush takes lacquered wood to be archetypal of a category he calls "anticommodities"—beautiful products of unalienated labor, which remains somehow visible in the completed work.[33] But this is only half the story: paradoxically, the capacity of lacquered wood to signify such unalienated work depends on the *occlusion* of marks of labor as part of a process of finishing, leading to a formula such as: the full expression of the artisan is the erasure of all of the marks of labor. The laboring body remains most proximate when his presence is least felt.

Whistler's admiration for Japanese art was derived from a sense that that work, with its subdued and invisible menace, was "finished" in precisely the right way. He famously took a strong position on the question of when a work of art is finished in the second of his "propositions": "A picture is finished when all trace of the means used to bring about the end has disappeared."[34] Over the course of a career spent publishing critical dispatches in London newspapers and journals, Whistler developed this axiom into an argumentative, as well as a visual, style: his notes are brief, punctual, and witty—form and content working together to depict an aesthetic consciousness unconfined by literary convention. Whistler's literary style accorded fully with his critique of the institutions of art criticism, which he typified as unnecessary verbiage around an unnarratable, indeed nonlinguistic, experience.[35] In the development of his sparse literary style, as in much else, Whistler turned to aesthetic practices he takes to be Japanese, taking as his signature an ever-changing butterfly that, his biographers Elizabeth and Joseph Pennell speculated, he derived from his study of Japanese prints.[36] When he finally collated his various epistles into a collected volume, *The Gentle Art of Making Enemies* (1891), critics attributed the minimalist design of the text—expansive white space of pages divided by elegant, forceful black lines, text centered both vertically and horizontally—to a Japanese sensibility.[37]

For Whistler as much as for his critics, Japaneseness indicated open white space and strong black lines; a painting without visible labor and a text without excess of language. Above all, Japanese art had no need for any kind of linguistic supplement or exegesis: as he writes at the end of his lecture "Ten O'Clock," "the story of the beautiful is already complete—hewn in the marbles of the Parthenon—and broidered, with the birds, upon the fan of Hokusai—at the foot of Fusiyama."[38] (29) The timelessness of Fusiyama would not, for Whistler, brook any narration, freezing the diegetic progress of Western art much as Wilde uses Orientalist imagery to arrest time in *The Picture of Dorian Gray*.[39] But whereas Wilde used descriptive language to impede the drive to narrative progress, Whistler's aesthetics implicitly took description and narration to be indissociably linked, and took the example of Japan to point to nonlinguistic representations, even at the level of the page's surface. The harmonic arrangements and blank space of *The Gentle Art of Making Enemies* is an extension of Whistler's stylistic insistence on brevity, and distaste for excess of language.

In another article for the *Pall Mall Gazette* in 1885, the author of "The Critic as Artist" naturally disagreed with Whistler about the value of critical commentary on art, noting: "Nor do I accept the dictum that only a painter is a judge of painting. I say that only an artist is a judge of art; there is a wide difference."[40] Algernon Swinburne, however, took a far stronger line—indeed, pursued an outright attack on Whistler's lecture in the *Fortnightly Review*. The difference between Wilde and Whistler concerned the value of criticism, but they took essentially compatible positions on the value of admiring Japanese art. For Swinburne, such an admiration (which in any case occurred only briefly in the "Ten O'Clock") is precisely Whistler's fault: "Japanese art is not merely the incomparable achievement of certain harmonies in colour; *it is the negation, the immolation, the annihilation of everything else*."[41] Swinburne explosively frames his disagreement with Whistler as the difference between an Orientalist abolition of meaning, feeling, and intellect in the name of "harmony," and an art in which theme and subject can exist with, and even outlast, composition and form. His argument counterposes the harmonic and the literary, continuing: "It is true, again, that Mr. Whistler's own merest 'arrangements' in colour are lovely and effective; but his portraits, to speak of these alone, are liable to the damning and intolerable imputation of possessing not merely other qualities than these, but qualities which actually appeal—I blush to remember and I shudder to record it—to the intelligence and the emotions, to the mind and heart of the spectator."[42] Of these portraits, it is Whistler's depiction of Thomas Carlyle that most invites Swinburne's admiration since it involves "study of character and revelation of intellect"—that is, that the effects of the painting are revelatory and intellectually satisfying, rather than simply harmonic. It is no accident that Swinburne picks the portrait of Carlyle— his aim is to demonstrate that Whistler's painting is already circumscribed by literature and language. Japanese art, for Swinburne, is "finished" in the sense that it is beautiful but unreadable, and he introduces to Lowell's pair a third meaning of "finish"—this time as a transitive verb: "it is the negation, the immolation, the annihilation of everything else." The Japanese aesthetic, all surface and no depth, presents an existential threat to Swinburne's self-conception as a subject capable of signifying with language, of possessing a communicable interiority.

As the title under which it is printed—"An Apostasy"—attests, Swinburne's disagreement with Whistler interrupted a collaborative friendship that had, indeed, been cemented through engagement with Japanese themes. The two met early in the 1860s, and in 1864 Whistler began work on "The Little White Girl"—eventually retitled "Symphony in White, No. 2"—a portrait of Jo Heffernan holding a fan, with a blue-and-white vase placed on the mantelpiece on which the model leans. In addition to those two representations of Asian objects, and the pink flowers in the painting's foreground, there is a curious Orientalized thematics to the painting's backdrop, in which a mirror, bisected with a thick black seam, reflects both Heffernan's face and a pair of impressionistic paintings hung on the green wall opposite. The effect is to render the mirror as a kind of screen, whose representation amounts to a third Orientalized object, alongside the fan and the vase—both of which, in addition to being objects, are works of visual design in their own right. The strange effect of the backdrop (among with much else) aligns "The Little White Girl" with another of Whistler's 1864 compositions, "Caprice in Purple and Gold: The Golden Screen," the background of which is corrugated by a Japanese screen—whose black seam is in a similar spot on the canvas—and which similarly locates its model, all the more conspicuously, in front of a visual field whose richness and plenitude seems to hem her in. Background serves another disorienting function in "The Little White Girl," moreover: while our model's gaze is clearly directed towards the vase, her reflection's eyes seem decidedly to point *to that same vase*, rather than to its virtual representation in the mirror, which is only glimpsed in the far right hand side of the canvas. Indeed, given the skew of the painting's gaze upon its subjects, composed (presumably) to allow the painter to depict Heffernan in profile and in three-quarters profile, it is all the more striking that the vase appears as the focal point for two sightlines, as an impossible point in which real and virtual objects converge.[43]

These features and others led Whistler's critics to point at once to his use of not merely Japanese objects, but Japanese decorative forms that informed his own painterly practice. The critic and anthologist Francis Turner Palgrave wrote that "[s]truck with the eminent beauty in color and the *naïf* inventiveness in design displayed by the Japanese, Mr. Whistler has not only studied their decorative painting till he has made its secrets his own, but seems now impelled to endeavor to reproduce it in England."[44] Palgrave had published an essay in 1863 arguing, along lines opened by the designer John Leighton, that the primary quality of both Japanese design and Japanese high art was its "passion for *irregularity*" and distaste for symmetry: in these two paintings, even one of the most basic conceits of symmetry, that between background and foreground, is ruthlessly disrupted by tricks of perspective and the stark divisions of the back field.[45] Other critics found Whistler's attempt to form a practice out of Japanese art less persuasive, not merely on the grounds that Japanese art was distasteful, but on the grounds that the ethnic humor of Japanese design, like the "*naïf* quality" with which Palgrave associated it, was impossible to fake. "Genuine Japanese art," wrote a reviewer for the *Spectator* in 1865, "reveals a humour which is more difficult to imitate, and of which there is no trace in the European counterfeit."[46]

"The Little White Girl" was exhibited at the Royal Academy in 1865, three years after the Academy had rejected an earlier painting, "The White Girl," with a similar theme. That work has been widely interpreted as an inflection point in Whistler's turn away from narrative painting, and an early practical

FIGURE 2.2 J. A. M. Whistler, *Symphony in White No. 2: The Little White Girl* (1864).

example of the kind of antitextual theories that governed Whistler's aesthetic theory from the mid-1860s onwards. The retitling of the later painting performs precisely such a maneuver: substituting the painting's thematic content for an intermedial description of its form, Whistler deprives "The Little White Girl," likewise, of linguistic referent, and endows it with a nonlinguistic basis. All the more striking, then, that "The Little White Girl" was exhibited with a poem by Swinburne, commissioned for the occasion. "Before the Mirror (Verses Written under a Picture)" also appeared in Swinburne's *Poems and*

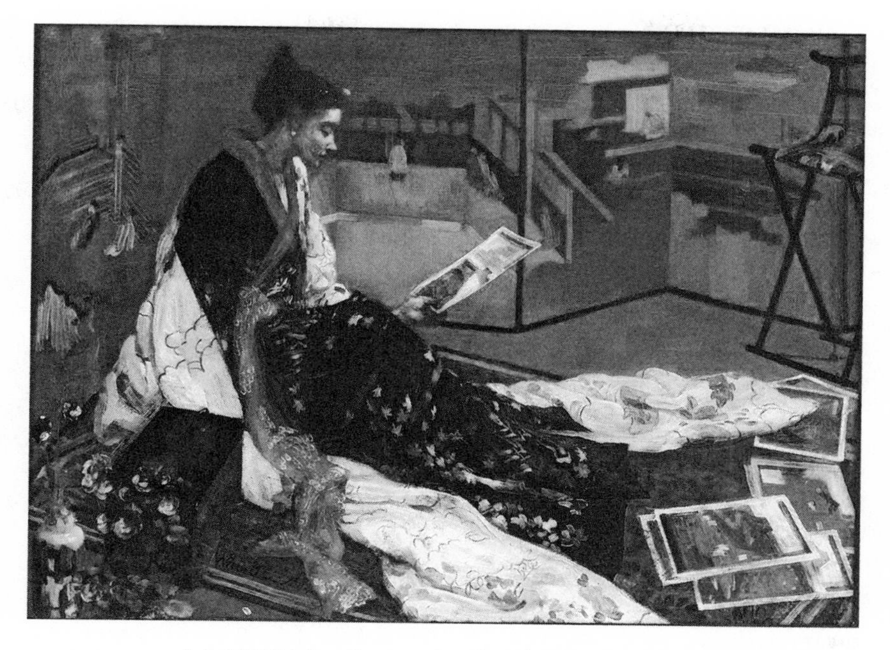

FIGURE 2.3. J. A. M. Whistler, *Caprice in Purple and Gold: The Golden Screen* (1864).

Ballads (1866), where it was then marked as "Inscribed to J. A. Whistler." Notwithstanding J. Hillis Miller's observation that "The Little White Girl" and "Before the Mirror" comprise a "double work of art," the coexistence on the painting and the poem would seem to resist Whistler's attempt to establish for visual art a relative autonomy from text.[47] T. S. Eliot, implying from the other side the incompatibility of the objective and the literary in this field, used "Before the Mirror" as the basis for his claim that, in Swinburne, "you will find always that the object was not there—only the word."[48]

Swinburne's poem does not reference the Orientalist form or theme of Whistler's composition, unless a reader feels the need to stretch a brief reference to the wind—"the hard East blows"—to such an end.[49] It does, however, pick up on the play with perspective in the painting, beginning with the careful, contradictory prepositions of its tripartite title: before, under, to. "Before the Mirror" comprises nine stanzas grouped into threes, each offering a distinct perspective on the scene of a woman's contemplation: the first, in allegorical mode, speculates on her thinking, apostrophizing her as a third party ("Behind the veil, forbidden, / Shut up from sight / Love, is there sorrow hidden, / Is there delight?"); the second allows the subject to articulate her own thoughts within quotation marks ("I cannot see what pleasures / Or what pains were; / What pale new loves and treasures / New years will bear");

and the third glosses and extols her thoughts from without ("Glad, but not flushed with gladness, / Since joys go by; / Sad, but not bent with sadness, / Since sorrows die;"). Looking at the poem's subject from these three perspectives, Swinburne's gaze settles on the little white girl in much the way that three points of view settle on the vase in Whistler's painting: the viewer, the subject, and the reflection.

The matter gets still more complicated when the poem's compositional history is taken into account. Submitting the lines to Whistler on April 2, 1865, Swinburne declares that they were "written the first thing after breakfast and brought off at once," adding "I think myself the idea is pretty: I know it was entirely and only suggested to me by the picture, where I found at once the metaphor of the rose and the notion of sad and glad mystery in the face languidly contemplative of its own phantom and all things seen by their phantoms."[50] Rather than depicting a face contemplating "its own phantom," however, Whistler has been careful to direct the viewer's gaze towards the vase: it is the viewer who, thanks to the oblique angle of the painting, is alone able to see both face and reflection.[51] Swinburne's slip reveals in advance a complication that, tactfully, he withholds from Whistler: that although the majority of the poem had indeed been composed after seeing "The Little White Girl," the final trio of stanzas had been written a few years previously, and have been located in an unpublished manuscript from the late 1850s entitled "The Dreamer." In addition to the three stanzas that complete "Before the Mirror," "The Dreamer" includes an extra one in the third position of four, which reads:

> A painted dream, beholden,
>   Of no man's eye,
> Framed in far memories, golden,
>   As hope when nigh
> Holds fast her soul that hears
> Faint waters flow like tears
> By shores no sunbeam cheers
>   From all the sky.

This omitted stanza mounts an assault on the autonomy of the visual object by explicitly thematizing, and indeed framing, the visual field in language. Vividly ekphrastic, Swinburne's suppressed verse treats consciousness as a verbal field in which visual imagery is processed and narrated: no more cognitively accessible than the face behind the mirror, but nonetheless amenable to literary treatment. If this is a "double work of art," in other words, its doubleness might be thought of in terms of contradiction, rather than collaboration: the germ, perhaps, of the outright hostilities over the place of meaning in visual representation that would end the friendship between its cocreators nearly a quarter-century later.

Swinburne's encapsulation of this threatening capacity of Japanese beauty might help to explain a part of this story that would otherwise be rather surprising: the relative coolness of British arts-and-crafts luminaries on Japanese aesthetics—for William Morris, Walter Crane, and others, the ukiyo-e craftsman was a mere craftsman. In Crane's faint and patronizing praise, Japanese craftsmanship is "in the condition of a European country in the Middle Ages," under the influence not of the "real constructive power of design" but "a free and informal naturalism."[52] Or as Wilde put it later, flipping Crane's opinion inside out, and drawing out its blind spot in his own paradoxical and perverse way, Japanese craftsmen display a "perfect knowledge of how to make a space decorative without decorating it."[53] Crane's sense of such design as a simulacrum, or a *mise-en-abîme*, was already clear in the generally enthusiastic responses to the "Japanese village" of artisans resident in Knightsbridge from 1885 to 1887, who, in the employ of a Dutch entrepreneur named Tannaker Buhicrosan, were displayed making various handicrafts while Londoners paid for the privilege of watching. Buhicrosan had developed an interest in Japanese craftworks at the Great London Exhibition in 1862, and decided not to exhibit the works, but the workers: as a review in the *Furniture Gazette* had it, "the surpassing superiority of the work was . . . principally due to the painstaking character of the workmen."[54] What most struck the *Gazette's* reviewer, as others, was the fastidious attention paid to even the most degraded commodities, chief among which was the "toy": "the main characteristic of all Japanese work was its conscientious perfection of detail in every particular, in that which was hidden as well as in that which was exposed to the eye; and this might be seen in the cheapest and most trifling toys almost as well as in the costly lacquered cabinet or the enameled cloisonné."[55] The hyperbole emerges so unassumingly that it is quite possible to avoid noticing this reviewer's claim that the main "characteristic" of the particular form of labor ascribed here to the Japanese artisan is "the perfection of detail in every particular"; that is, of absolute perfection in the execution of even the most trivial tasks. Another review uses similar language with a slightly different emphasis: "[the workman's] very ignorance of machinery serves him in good stead, making his dexterity as perfect as his eye for form, color and arrangement. . . . It is impossible to note all the subtle ways in which the Japanese artisan and artist differ in technique from our own."[56]

If the popularity of the village rendered the Japanese artisan a human embodiment of exquisite *technique*, it thereby risked returning the figure of the artist to the very stereotype that the Victorian aesthetic ideology had striven, at great cost, to escape: the idea of the human body as nothing more than a kind of machine. In that sense, Morris's treatment of the Japanese artisan racialized the antipathy to the modern worker famously developed by John Ruskin in *The Stones of Venice* (1851–53). In a famous passage dealing with the advantages of Gothic architecture over modern craft, Ruskin dwells on the shallow perfection of modern glasswork. "Our modern glass is exquisitely clear in its substance," he writes, "true in its form, accurate in its cutting. We are proud of this. We ought to be ashamed of it." The uniformity of craftwork was evidence, for Ruskin, that the individuality of the worker had been subtracted from his work—and for Ruskin, too, the enemy of the lush aesthetic signification of interiority was called "finish." "Choose whether you will pay for the lovely form or the perfect finish," he explains, "and choose at the same moment whether you will make the worker a man or a grindstone."[57] In a lecture entitled "Textile Fabrics," Morris forcefully made the case against imitating the Japanese architectural style in terms explicitly indebted to Ruskin:

> It may be well here to warn those occupied in embroidery against the feeble imitations of Japanese art which are so disastrously common amongst us. The Japanese are admirable naturalists, wonderfully skilled draughtsmen, deft beyond all others in mere execution of whatever they take in hand; and also great masters of style within certain limitations. But with all this a Japanese design is absolutely worthless unless it is executed with Japanese skill. In truth, with all their brilliant qualities as handicraftsmen, which have so dazzled us, the Japanese have no architectural, and therefore no decorative, instinct. Their works of art are isolated and blankly individualistic, and in consequence, unless where they rise, as they sometimes do, to the dignity of a suggestion for a picture (always devoid of human interest) they remain mere wonderful toys, things quite outside the pale of the evolution of art, which, I repeat, cannot be carried on without the architectural sense that connects it with the history of mankind.[58]

His biographer Aymer Vallance glosses Morris's claim that Japanese art is ahistorical because nonarchitectural by explaining that all buildings in Japan "are liable to be overthrown at any moment by earthquakes," and therefore not sources of cultural pride.[59] According to another biographer, Morris was an enthusiastic reader of Mitford's *Tales of Old Japan*—and, to look at the problem from another direction, there is abundant evidence that Japanese artists and critics began to respond to Morris from 1891.[60] But nonetheless, these short notices reveal Morris to be quite unambiguously resistant to the import of Japanese forms into the British scene of labor, harboring the fantasy of provincial laboring bodies mutated into "mere wonderful toys."

Why such hostility to an aesthetics of craftsmanship that, at the time of his writing, would appear to offer a mass-cultural platform for many of Morris's own commitments? Representations of Japan began to amplify differences within the internal politics of aestheticism from the 1880s onwards, schismatically dividing the effeminacy of Wilde's branch of the aesthetic movement from the straight manliness promoted by William Morris. The Japanese artisan was too pleasurable, too cute: that sentence in "Textile Fabrics" that begins "their works of art" turns on the finite clause "they remain mere wonderful toys," where the "they" could pertain either to the works or to the "they" which generated them. Again, it is the figure of the plaything, enjoyable but infantile, that allows for worker and object to become interchangeable. The association with toys was irresistible, and Morris returns to the theme in his utopian novel *News From Nowhere* (1891), in an early scene designed to affirm a causal relationship between free labor and beautiful craftwork. A young girl has carved a pipe, which she presents to the novel's narrator, William Guest, to whom it appears "as pretty and as gay a toy as I had ever seen,—something like the best kind of Japanese work, but better."[61] Although the reference to Japan is hesitant and ultimately disclaimed, the Orientalist fragrance secreted by the pipe can not be entirely expurgated, as Guest goes on to turn down the girl's gift on the grounds that it "is altogether too grand for me, or for anybody but the Emperor of the World."[62] This moment, in which a pseudo-Orientalist object occasions a bashfulness in the baffled time-traveler, might seem to confirm John Plotz's insight that Morris "recoils against the notion that an investment in poignant particulars is the best avenue toward the universal."[63] Plotz reads Morris's romances as adaptations of the allegorical and "antiparticularizing" socialist narratives published in Chartist newspapers, and develops his argument by discussing moments where affectively charged objects appear in Morris's work as focal points, nodes around which diverse individuals might forge political collectivities, only for the narrative to have them spectacularly fail to achieve that task. Yet Guest's rejection of the pipe is more than a failed attempt to forge such a collectivity. The rejection, however subtle, marks the exclusion of a Japanese object from a world system that may enable the formation of bonds between colonizer and colonized, but could never incorporate the idea of Japan. The remark's delicate irony notwithstanding, toy registers Morris's trepidation over the narcissistic threat of Japanese culture: the threat of a universalism whose locus is not Britain, nor even Europe, but somewhere beyond even the long reach of the empire.

IV. Your Wretched, Degraded, Humiliated Brother

The position Vivian takes in "The Decay of Lying"—that in order to see a "Japanese effect" one should not "behave like a tourist" and visit Japan—was not Wilde's own.[64] At least, it was not that of the young Wilde who, writing to Helena Sickert from Fremont, Nebraska, in April 1882, described the effect of a trip to "the great prison" in Lincoln: "every day I see something curious and new, and now think of going to Japan and wish Walter would come or could come with me."[65] That wish to go to Japan *with a painter*, born (as far as the archive will tell us) in a Nebraska prison, did not disappear quickly: it seems to have preoccupied Wilde for a few months—most letters sent from that leg of his American tour offer some version of "I must go to Japan and live there with sweet little Japanese girls," and, as late as July, Wilde writes to C. E. Norton that he has only "a three-weeks holiday before Japan."[66] After no response from Walter Sickert, Wilde tapped up Whistler: "Also when will you come to Japan? Fancy the book, I to write it, you to illustrate it. We would be rich."[67] He didn't get a response. An Iowan painter named Spencer Blake was approached next, and he accepted the offer, but the trip never happened.[68] But what was left was the book Wilde never wrote in Japan, a conceptual object that exerts a pull over not just Wilde's work but aestheticism as such—the collective enterprise described by Ada Leverson in this chapter's epigraph.

In a novel that overwhelms its characters and readers with the power of the material text, a luxurious edition of Théophile Gautier's poetic collection *Émaux et Camées* bears a unique and strange kind of meaning. A gift from Adrian Singleton to Dorian Gray, the Gautier does not quite resemble the famous "yellow book" that Lord Henry gave him, of which he buys five more, binding them in rainbow colors—"so that they might suit his various moods" (65).[69] Singleton's gift expresses no part of Dorian's internal life, and offers no lesson about the world at large. Our attention is redirected quickly from a description of the material text to a incantation of the immaterial—but not before the book has been lovingly, alliteratively accounted for: it bears the marks of its exotic provenance, and narrates a history at once personal and geopolitical: "It was Gautier's *Émaux et Camées*, Charpentier's Japanese-paper edition, with the Jacquemart etching. The binding was of citron-green leather, with a design of gilt trellis-work and dotted pomegranates" (87).[70] "Japanese paper," usually manufactured in Japan largely for the export market, and a familiar choice for expensive editions of aesthetic movement literature, is one of a number of features that suggest both absolute distance and odd proximity—the latter even slightly nauseating, when the narrator's deictic "the" assumes readerly familiarity with *this* rather than *that* luxury edition of *Émaux et Camées*. Stuck between the very far and the too near, the book furnishes Wilde's novel with a trace of the unspeakable, remote intimacy of Singleton and Dorian, a strange proximity like that of the East to the West, whose nature is never stipulated, and which could feel at once like presence and absence.

Advertisements for luxury editions, sometimes signed, populate the back matter of late-Victorian magazines, journals, collected volumes, pamphlets, books of poetry, and catalogues. More constant than any idea, word, or proper noun, these advertisements co-construct the *format* not of a particular poetic form, but of aestheticism as such; these advertisements mark the half-acknowledged limit of a text's capacity to transcend its own materiality.[71] That limit was defined by a need for commercial forms of circulation, and by the outsourced production of artisanal goods that sustained the ideology of the book as an aestheticized object, an ideology vital to both the plot of *The Picture of Dorian Gray* and, more widely, to literary aestheticism's self-representation.

Given Wilde's appreciation, in 1891, of the luxury and richness of the Japanese paper, and given moreover the close connections the novel draws between the luxury books it describes and its own material form, why could readers not pay the surcharge to pick up such a copy of *The Picture of Dorian Gray* itself? The answer has more to do with his publishers than the author himself: John Lane, the most important publisher of aesthetic movement texts and Wilde's own, generally preferred Indian paper for his luxury editions. But Wilde could certainly have pushed harder than he did to see his work in such materials—as indeed he did for the first edition of his poem "The Sphinx," which he had printed on Dutch paper for collectors.[72] Japanese paper betokened luxury of a different order of magnitude. It was the most expensive, and required the least florid advertising copy: contrast, for example, "Limited edition of Five Hundred Copies on superior English vellum paper, and printed in Grasset characters in red and black,"[73]—and the more austere advertisement for the more expensive—"Fifty copies on Japanese paper."[74] The priciest and most valuable edition of a text, though, was that printed on "Japanese vellum,"—a thicker, rougher pulp. Japanese vellum editions were usually numbered, and occasionally signed by the author, and generally retailed at two guineas. Like other expensive editions printed on "India paper" and "handmade English paper," but usually more expensive, the Japanese vellum copy furnished its purchaser with the pleasure of considering the hemispheric distance traveled by the paper, bringing the Orient into the domestic scene of reading. Smooth, but unevenly cut, its bumps and contours intrude upon the flatness of the page, rematerializing prose that appears to pull away from the material, imbuing airy arguments with an earthly sensuousness. The pleasure of the book is derived from contemplating matter exquisitely but imperfectly yoked to form, while also conferring social distinction on the buyer through an elevated price and restricted circulation. The luxury edition retains the material traces of its production, as surely as lacquering wood erased them. Such luxury volumes provide aestheticism with a material basis for its investigation of art's epiphanic power, its capacity to forge connections between people, though they be separated by time, space, or legal injunction.

This is why, I suggest, luxury editions of Wilde's work—including and especially editions on Japanese vellum and paper—began to circulate in the years of his financial, moral, and somatic ruin. Dropped by Lane, Wilde found a publisher willing to risk scandal in Leonard Smithers, a pornographer notable for both his cheap "smut" and his high-quality "erotika."[75] Smithers understood that although the number of Wilde readers had shrunk dramatically since his trials, the remaining constituency had only grown more ardent in their affection. Wilde's reputation had narrowed and deepened: his brutal treatment had become a focal point for homosexual activists and penal reformers, even as his name had become synonymous with sexual dissolution in more public registers.[76] And although it wasn't Wilde's idea to put out such editions, his letters to friends and supporters demonstrate a growing sensitivity to the aesthetic and affective possibilities of the luxury edition. Along with a letter from Paris in 1899 to congratulate his friend Frances Forbes-Robertson on her recent marriage, Wilde included a bound copy of *The Importance of Being Earnest* in Japanese vellum along with the following description: "The dress is pretty, it wears Japanese vellum and belongs to a limited family of nine and is not on speaking terms with the popular edition: it refuses to recognize the poor relations whose only value is seven and sixpence. Such is the pride of birth. Such is the pride of birth. It is a lesson."[77] At first Wilde describes the high-quality paper as clothing for the text to wear, but then the metaphor switches, such that the Japanese edition is a wealthy family member excised from the common social life of poor relatives—what had been mere adornment now signifies the social and intimate relations between texts and readers. Yet it is not just the social isolation of the Japanese object—its exilic condition—which linked Japanese vellum to Wilde's own self-conception in the years of his exile. The exceptional status that had once caused the vellum to appear especially beautiful now appears disfigured, evoking not only "pride," but also the fall, and shame, which follows from it. Wilde's tone is playful, but the passage is nonetheless poignant: the aesthetic object itself has come to take on the form of a rarefied but scorned aristocratic relative, a branch snapped off from the family tree. Like its author, the book has been feminized, deracinated, and abandoned to its whimsical melancholia.

Eight hundred impressions on Dutch paper, and thirty on Japanese vellum, were published on the first press of "The Ballad of Reading Gaol," which Wilde published under the pseudonym C.3.3.—his cell number at Reading Gaol. (The first text to be published on luxury edition in its entirety: illustrations and boards had been printed on the vellum for *The Happy Prince and Other Stories* (1888), and the Beardsley-illustrated *Salomé*.) The pseudonymity of publication, however, did not deter Wilde from personally signing a number of the luxury editions—as though it were clear that anybody who cared to spend two shillings and sixpence on the book deserved to know, and could be trusted to keep faith with, the identity of its author. On January 24, 1898, Smithers published four hundred standard editions of the "Ballad" and thirty vellum editions, retailing at twenty-one shillings. Even the standard edition was to be printed only on high-quality handmade paper, "thick, good paper, not tissue," Wilde demanded, since "I cannot correct tissue, and one should not waste tissue."[78] "The Ballad of Reading Gaol" was the last original work he wrote—his translation of Barbey D'Aurevilly's romance *Love Never Dies* is usually not counted, and in any case no longer makes it into the Collins *Complete Works*—but the last three years of his life would see him instructing his publishers to include a very limited run of these Japanese codices alongside standard editions of the first publications of *An Ideal Husband* and *The Importance of Being Earnest*, which had been hitherto unavailable in print. Each of these limited runs sold out very quickly, with Wilde himself getting a lot of them from Smithers himself, intending to give these luxury editions as gifts to loyal friends such as Forbes-Robertson.[79]

Of the twelve (not nine) numbered vellum editions of *Earnest*, a minority were traded freely: one was donated to the British Museum, where it remains, another to Robert Ross; others were donated to friends and ended up in private collections. Posthumous publications—first of *De Profundis* and then of Wilde's other works—also carried limited-run editions on Japanese paper or vellum, usually with prices inflated even beyond those of the three texts whose publication Wilde oversaw. By the time of his death, the association of Wilde with the luxury Japanese material text became so strong that any monograph still being published about Wilde carried a Japanese paper edition at an inflated price. Robert Ross's collection of Wilde's letters written in exile to him, published under the title *After Reading*, was published on a limited run of 475 copies, of which the first seventy-five were on Japanese vellum. (Editing work had been finished by More Adey after Ross's death in 1918.) They sold so quickly that Beaumont quickly put out a sequel called *After Bernaval*, for which Adey edited Ross's remaining papers, which was published in the same way the same year. Even more striking, perhaps, is a privately printed edition of the transcripts of Wilde's three trials, edited anonymously and published as *The Trial of Oscar Wilde: From the Shorthand Reports*. Though no name appears on the edition, it is generally agreed that the publisher was Charles Carrington, another pornographer who was at the time preparing to publish a new edition of *The Picture of Dorian Gray* along with a defense of Wilde.[80] Most of these express fury and contempt for the hypocrisy of Wilde's accusers. Against the opening statement of the first trial, for instance, is inscribed: " 'In all men's hearts a slumbering swine lies low,' says the French poet; so come ye, whose porcine instincts have never yet been awakened, or if rampant successfully hidden, and hurl the biggest, sharpest stones you can lay your hands on at your wretched, degraded, humiliated brother, *who has been found out.*"[81] The limited print-runs that produced these luxury editions advertised forthcoming publications that might be relevant to those people still prepared to read Wilde enthusiastically in 1905: new translations of his work in French, "One Hundred Merrie and Delightsome Stories," and forthcoming sexological manuals.

An edition of *The Trial of Oscar Wilde* I inspected at the National Library of Ireland bore the "ex libris" card of Dennis Wheatley—presumably the bacchanalian occult novelist of the same name—with an ornate image of a forest of trees, representing the Garden of Eden. The Tree of Knowledge stood in the center, with an open book in its branches and a parchment nailed to the trunk, while in the background Eve floated in a large vulvular cloud emerging from the Tree of Knowledge, on the trunk of which Adam is hanging from manacles. In the foreground, a satyr sat on a rocky mound, recounting a story to a nude younger man sitting among the daisies. Next to the mound nestled an open bottle of sparkling wine and an alto saxophone. The caption read:

> One admires EVE for having tasted of the FORBIDEN [*sic*] TREE OF KNOWLEDGE:—But what a WONDERFUL EXPERIENCE she missed when she overlooked the TREE OF LIFE. I should have eaten of not ONE but ALL the trees in the garden—and THAT; dear boy—is what I hope for YOU.

The design is signed by the artist, Frank C. Papé, and depicts Wheatly instructing his protégé, a handsome young man identified as Eric Gordon-Tombe. The "ex libris" card depicts an intimate relationship between the reader and the author, as if to underline the intimacy among strangers brought into being by the Japanese vellum edition, and the community of secret readers that the text's private circulation comprised. Papé's imagery amplifies the citational power of the paper itself, its capacity to conjure up Dorian's relationship with Singleton, Wilde's relationship with his readers, and the community of loyal readers convened in Wilde's name in the years after his exile and death.

Japanese vellum tells its own story of this intimacy, of the too-close modulated by the too-remote, of the isolation of the aesthetic subject—to dip, again, into Bersani's terminology.[82] Yet, in a sense, what might appear to be a story of vitalism—the motive signifying force, what Jane Bennett might call the "thing-power" of the object—reveals itself rather as a series of humiliating mistakes, failures, and concessions. In this, the social relations of aestheticism conform to Bersani's description of intimacy as the inverse of agency, as a relational structure in which each participant must accede to all the others. Like Menpes, Whistler, Wilde, Morris, Swinburne, and Henley, the vellum copy

FIGURE 2.4. Ex libris card, bearing the name Dennis Wheatley, found in *The Trial of Oscar Wilde*, (1906), National Library of Ireland, July 2011.

"refuses to recognize"—on the face of it, a cognitively improbable task—not just its "relations" but, ultimately, itself. It fails to locate itself correctly either in the small world of gift exchange or the large one of the global trade in commodities. The poetics of lacquer are different: its refusal to signify labor is a sign of the becoming inanimate of the laborer, either for erotic good (as for Whistler) or political ill (as for Morris). But, in both cases, an erotic finish is the sign for a political unfinishedness. A final example of this failure: for all the conversations I have had with book specialists, all the fingers I have run up and down the uncut Japanese vellum editions in libraries and antiquarian bookstores, all the gifts of lacquered boxes that are now every birthday present from my closest kin, all the gasps of joy as I encounter another beautifully oxymoronic signed/anonymous edition of "The Ballad of Reading Gaol" on sale for €25,000—after all these, I confess I cannot tell the difference between the Japanese type of vellum and any other. Or, rather, I rely on a paratextual auxiliary in order to do so: the words "printed on Japanese vellum"—a performative text-act that, placed on the luxurious page, self-immolates. The high value of the material text is asserted, but only through a gesture that assumes that value to be undetectable except through the power of an immaterial fragment of language. I must conclude either that the institutional structures that would enable me to make such a distinction without such guide have eroded. Perhaps it's just that I, particularly, have no gift for making them. Or perhaps the distinctions asserted by these Victorian bibliophiles never existed in the first place, except as a phantasmatic negotiation between language and object, the impossible wish for material confirmation that one's delight was not, after all, a mistake. But even if it was nothing more than aesthetic ideology disguised as real intimacy, these circuits I have been tracing afforded aestheticism with a resource in which queer sociality could be configured out of the exquisite isolation of aesthetic contemplation—an isolation in which the scholar can find herself, too.

3

The Pre-Raphaelite Haiku

From these three random and virtually impromptu remarks, I should merely like to draw a working hypothesis: that we consider stylistic features as *transformations*, derived either from collective formulas (of unrecoverable origin, literary or preliterary) or, by metaphoric interplay, from idiolectal forms; in both cases, which should govern the stylistic task is the search for models, for patterns: sentential structures, syntagmatic clichés, divisions and clausulae of sentences; and what should animate the task is the conviction that style is essentially a citational procedure, a body of formulas, a memory (almost in the cybernetic sense of the word), an inheritance based on culture and not on expressivity.

—ROLAND BARTHES, "STYLE AND ITS IMAGE," (1969)[1]

I count syllables not out of any allegiance to tradition but because I want the indifference and inflexibility of a seventeen-syllable limit to balance my self-expressive yearnings. With the form in place, the act of composition becomes a negotiation between one's subjective urges and the rules of order, which in this case could not be simpler or firmer. My hope is that such fixity will keep the pulsations of the ego in check by encouraging a degree of humility in the face of the form.

—BILLY COLLINS, "INTRODUCTION" TO *HAIKU IN ENGLISH* (2013)[2]

His unnaturalness was most natural, his formalism a living fire in itself.

—YONE NOGUCHI, OF D. G. ROSSETTI, "MY LONDON EXPERIENCE," (1911)

I. Inverted Historicism

So far, I have argued that the cultural forms of Japanese modernity confronted the Euro-American powers of the late nineteenth century as aesthetic signs of a unique Other Empire; that, therefore, not only did many conspicuously aesthetic themes and forms reflect an engagement with Japan that sometimes called itself "influence," but also that the geopolitical fact of Japanese power interfered with that narcissistic ego-appropriation in a variety of ways. So, what I have called *The Mikado*'s "queer realism"—an effort realistically to represent an object that resists representation for real historical reasons—bursts its banks not, as might have been expected, when absorbed back into the dominant imperialist ideology of the late-Victorian moment, but on account of a *reaction formation*, penned by London's conservative theater critics but authored, in a more primary sense, by the emerging power that had defeated the Russian navy in a sea war, and now maintained ships in Greenwich docks. In the second chapter, the idea of Japan enabled Whistler and Wilde to explore the material limits of abstraction, the affective and objective grounds from which the aesthetic movement's speculations drew power. Yet despite the causative force that I have ascribed to the idea of Japan, that idea has so far remained phantasmatic and indirect—its causative force is triangulated *through* the Western agents in whom the idea of Japan has stirred a reaction formation. I have yet to describe a decisive intervention, articulated in the *name* of that idea, into the history of aesthetic form. This chapter narrates precisely such an intervention: the establishment of Japanese-style haiku poetry as the definitive genre of exquisite aestheticism within English-language verse, a position that (I submit) haiku has occupied since the outset of the twentieth century until the present time. That assessment may seem rash, given the lack of canonical Anglophone poets known primarily for haiku writing, and the relatively cool, and scarce, attention that haiku verse receives from scholars. Yet, in a domain beyond the university—but certainly encompassing the kindergarten, the doctor's waiting room, and the online message board, haiku has only consolidated its position as the apogee of a kind of formally contrived poetry that, howsoever contrived, *works*, as the exquisite always does. It has done so, we shall see, not by repeating the modernist impulsive sometimes ascribed to it, but by bypassing modernist poetics entirely and activating the quaint Victorian versification strategies that, at its origin, haiku was designed to preserve.

So, my unusual origin story of the Anglophone haiku begins in a newly post-Victorian London. It begins early in 1903, with a Japanese poet named Yone Noguchi. Noguchi composed at least four original Anglophone haiku in English that year, of which the first was composed in Hyde Park, London, a decade before Ezra Pound's "In the Station of the Metro" was first published in *Poetry*. The four poems appear underneath a note entitled "A Proposal to American Poets" in the February 1904 number of the *Reader*, in which Noguchi exhorts his American readership to "try Japanese Hokku." The following year, slightly different versions of the poems (detailed below) appeared in a bilingual book entitled *Japan of Sword and Love,* coauthored with the Oakland poet Joaquin Miller. Dedicated "to the Meiji spirit which declared war against Russia," *Japan of Sword and Love* juxtaposes Noguchi's militaristic odes ("Let Us March on Towards Manchuria!") with Miller's homoerotic ballads ("The Wee Brown Men").[3] Two essays are interposed, a prose ode of Miller's in which he rhapsodizes "The Little Brown Men of Nippon" (littleness and brownness are recurring themes in the titles of his contributions), and an essay of Noguchi's entitled "The Outcome of the War for Japan" in which he defends the Japanese conduct of the Russo-Japanese War, and predicts a Pacific alliance as its outcome: "America will be the chief gainer from the Russia-Japan war."[4] Although the American version was published before the Japanese, one might deduce from Noguchi's 1918 essay "On Japanese Hokku" that it was the version in *Japan of Sword and Love* that more closely resembled the poem as it was originally conceived. The poem's composition is presented as an epiphany whose decathetic energies initially recall Pound's own "impasse," in which the futile labors of translation are overcome, and an original composition—an entirely new thing in the English language—sprang into being:

> by the skyscrapers of New York, again in the London 'bus, I often tried to translate the *Hokku* of our old masters, but I gave up hope when I had written the following in English:
>
> My Love's lengthened hair
> Swings o'er me from Heaven's gate:
> Lo, Evening's shadow!
>
> It was in London, to say more particularly, Hyde Park, that I wrote the above *Hokku* in English, where I walked slowly, my mind being filled with the thought of the long hair of Rossetti's women as I perhaps had visited Tate's Gallery that afternoon; pray, believe me when I say the dusk that descended from the sky swung like that lengthened hair. I exclaimed then: "What use to try the impossibility in translation, when I have a moment to feel a *Hokku* feeling and write about it in English!" . . . Let me wait patiently for a moment to come when I become a *Hokku* poet in my beloved English.[5]

Yet there are several impediments to the historical project of recovery that promises to establish Noguchi's as anything the *original haiku*; in fact, it is precisely originality that is at stake in both the form and history of Noguchi's poem. So, three important caveats. First, this is an early *original* composition, but Victorian readers had been familiar with translations of Japanese poetry (including haiku) since Basil Hall Chamberlain's *The Classical Poetry of the Japanese* (1880) offered both a set of translations of Japanese verse and a theory of their ethnic expressiveness. That account laid much of the ground for Noguchi's understanding of the priority of form over content in the haiku—although he critically engages Chamberlain in the 1918 essay. The expressiveness of Japanese poetry could not easily be taken for granted, since the one indispensable characteristic that Chamberlain attributed to "Old Japan" was imitativeness, a contentless characteristic that for that reason foregrounds the mediatic quality of Japanese cultural forms.[6] That vacancy was expressed by the "lilliputian" Japanese prosody, which, Chamberlain held, "regards neither rhyme, tone, accent, quantity, nor alliteration, nor does its rather frequent parallelism follow any regular method. Its only essential rule is that every poem must consist of alternate lines of five and seven syllables, with, generally, an extra line of seven syllables to mark the close. It is, indeed, prosody reduced to its simplest expression."[7] In his encyclopedia *Things Japanese* (1890) and in an essay on Basho, Chamberlain refers to short Japanese verse forms as "epigrams"—augmenting the *internal* vacuity of the haiku with a serial modularity, and presenting haiku as a set of disarticulated parts that "in the hands of our poets, are evolved as parts or members of an organic whole, but would in Japanese literature each stand alone as an independent composition."[8] In "Japanese Hokku Poems" Noguchi himself took issue with the term "epigram," which he understood to name something that "is or at least looks to have one object, [whose] beauty, if it has any, is like that of a *netsuke* or *okimono* carved in ivory or wood, decorative at its best."[9] The value of a good haiku, Noguchi felt, "is not in its physical directness but in its psychological indirectness."[10]

Likewise, this was an early original haiku in English: it was not the first published poetic composition by a Japanese Anglophone author. Circa 1890, a bilingual poetic collection entitled *New of Pom and Song the English and Japanese* circulated in Tokyo.[11] The date of the collection is unclear, but 1890 provides us with a *terminus ante quem*, since Chamberlain cites two poems from it ("The Midnight Winds" and "Her Glee") in *Things Japanese*, under the heading "English as She Is Japped," in which he pokes fun at the misconstructions and infelicities of Japanese Anglophony. The entry compiles examples of the style with minimal glossing, and culminates with an apology for its own obvious offensiveness in language whose bad faith is revealed as a curiously stiff and formal—that is, in context, *Orientalist*—tone: "rise not in your wrath to indict us of treachery and unkindness. We mean nothing against the honour of Japan" (144). As if through a kind of autoimmunity, Chamberlain's own English was Orientalized by his own theme.

A. M. Thompson's 1911 travel memoir, *Japan for a Week (Britain for Ever!)*, which was written in the same comic style as Douglas Sladen's books described in the first chapter, drew on *New of Pom and Song* to develop a more synoptic theory of "Japaneso-English," examples of which are described as "better in intention than effect," and analogous to "the pregnant prose of Mr. Henry James."[12] Responding to an anonymous poem entitled "The Waterfall at Yoro, near Lake Biwa," published in the *Japanese Mail*, Thompson gives voice to the poignant sadism of the melancholy critic, addressing the (merely *presumptively* young, *presumptively* male, *presumptively* unhappy, etc.) poet: "It is a beautiful poem, though it leaves one wondering, wondering as to the gentle, gentle very poor boy, why, in the noble words of another Japanese poet, 'why his gleamy grew gloomy?' " (133). The cloying, gakky tone here, in which a critic produces and rehearses an image of the Japanese poet as sad, had, by 1911, already come to typify critical notices of Noguchi's work—and, indeed, the accounts of his own creative process he frequently wrote himself.[13] The ascription of loneliness: an observation of the Other's melancholic attachment to an aesthetic object, and also a performative severance that enacts the isolation it seeks to obtain.

Finally, the originality of the poem itself cannot be taken for granted, since, rather than merely thinking about the long hair in Dante Gabriel Rossetti's paintings after a visit to the Tate, Noguchi seems to have been cribbing directly from Rossetti's *poetry*, specifically from "The Blessed Damozel." This is not to discredit the origin story as he narrates it—not least because, in his autobiography, *The Story of Yone Noguchi, Told by Himself* (1914), Noguchi goes out of his way to assimilate Rossetti's visual and verbal aesthetics.[14] The point rather is to specify the peculiar form of originality that Noguchi explored in the haiku form, an idea of originality to which he understood less as the generation of wholly new material, and more as a new way of inhabiting an existing literary tradition. In the case of the haiku, counterintuitively, that was the tradition of Victorian verse, but that was not his first attempt at approaching originality through an indirect means. His early poetic career in the United States had been impeded by an early claim of plagiarism: in the December 1896 number of the *Literary Digest*, he was publicly accused of having plagiarized Poe's *Eulalie* for a poem published in *The Philistine* entitled "Lines."[15] In one sense, it was more or less a fair cop. Poe's lines: "I dwelt alone / In a world of moan, / And my soul was a stagnant tide."[16] Noguchi's: "I dwell alone, / Like one-eyed star, / In frightened, darksome willow threads, / In a world of moan."[17] In his autobiography, Noguchi admitted the resonance, but refused to see his adaptation of *Eulalie* as any kind of slight upon Poe's original. Rather, he feels that the innocent repetition of Poe's writing brought him close to an admired forebear. "I was glad for having the moment when I felt the same thing with Poe, and I could not understand why I could not say the same thing if I wanted to say it; and I declared I should like to understand poetry from the point that it would be a journal of one's feeling or the footmark of one's soul's experience."[18]

FIGURE 3.1. The Purple Cow. *The Book Buyer* Vol. 12, p. 286.

The *Literary Digest* article that criticized Noguchi took the familiar trope that Japanese poetry was merely imitative—in this case, plagiarized—and extended the analogy to cover the not merely the author's poem, but his very racial identity itself. The poet *himself* is not original, as the *Digest* article satirically recites from Noguchi's "Lines," "Alas—I'm not all of me!"[19] But this is only one aspect of the broader drive to discredit Noguchi's poetic practices—to write him out of literary history altogether. That story began with his first book, *Seen and Unseen: Monologues of a Homeless Snail* (1897), published in San Francisco. At once readers began to suspect that its very fidelity to a preconceived notion of Japanese style—what another, approving, reviewer called his "radical and audacious use of Japanese words and phrases"[20]—marked it out as a *hoax* being perpetrated on the public by Gelett Burgess, the comic verse writer and author of, among other anthologized pieces, "The Purple Cow."[21] The originator of that theory, according to an 1897 editorial in *Book Notes* magazine, was the critic Vance Thompson, who eventually confirmed "from Mr. Burgess's own lips, that *he* was Yone Noguchi, and that the whole was one of the former's clever jokes, ingeniously invented and systematically carried out."[22] By 1933, when Noguchi was living in Japan but publishing Anglophone critical prose in Britain, critics could make the claim more baldly: a reviewer of *The Ukiyo-e Primitives* (1934) wondered openly whether "the author's use of Japanese-English" was not, itself, "a purposefully affected quaintness."[23] Less predictable, perhaps, has been the continued appeal of the trope for modern and contemporary critics of Noguchi's writing. For Earl Miner, Noguchi "seemed like the real thing to a generation who knew no Japanese," and "seemed not to question anything Japanese."[24] Even the eminent scholar of the Anglophone haiku and of Noguchi in particular, Yoshinobu Hakutani, treats the haiku of 1904 as forerunners to the genre, rather than inaugural examples, because they apparently don't contain a *kigo*. In the same text, Hakutani places Ezra Pound's short poem "In a Station of the Metro" at the head of the genre, arguing that if only it were relineated, each line would have the correct number of syllables.[25]

The critical contortions necessitated by that standard genealogy might be explained on the one hand by a drive to preserve the whiteness of the haiku genre. But as much energy is expended proving the *modernism* and *Americanness* of a form that, in Noguchi's work, drew more directly on nineteenth-century British poetry. The version of the poem published in the *Reader* for an American audience is written with a Cali twang, sharpened in poems like "Noguchi's Song unto Brother Americans" that he had been writing under Miller's influence at the Hights. In the *Reader*:

My girl's lengthy hair
Swung o'er me from Heaven's gate:
Lo, Evening's shadow!

The version published the following year, however, hews more closely (though not exactly) to the version cited above from the 1918 essay. In *Japan of Sword and Love*:

My Love's lengthened hair
Swings 'ver me from Heaven's gate:
Lo, Evening's shadow!

Juxtaposing the two versions, one encounters first a bathos in the 1904 version, "girl" for "Love," that seems to fit with the nominal addresses of the article—a slightly snooty edit made in condescension to American plain-spokenness. The Americanness of the *Reader* version, in other words, is a contrived effect of Noguchi's diction.

How might these paintings in the Tate help explain the haiku? Both of the Rossettis hanging at the Tate at the time of Noguchi's visit offer suggestive possible identifications for the poem's subject: "Portrait of Mrs. William Morris" (1868) and "Beata Beatrix" (1870).[26] The earlier of these depicts Jane Morris with her hair tied up—lengthy, then, but not lengthened—and carries a Latin inscription in which Rossetti's painting of his friend's wife is glossed as both a seduction and as a liberation from her dependence on her more celebrated husband's reputation: "Conjuge clara poetâ, et preclarissima vultu, / Denique picturâ clara sit illa meâ"; "famous for her poet husband, and most famous for her beauty, may she next be famous on account of my painting."[27] The inscription stages as a social contest the aesthetic contest between visual and literary representation—a contest of which, as we have seen, Victorians took Japanese art and literature to be exemplary. The themes of "Beata Beatrix" resonate more clearly. A depiction of Dante's *Beatrix* at the moment of death, the painting also displays a sundial with a long shadow at the moment of dusk; the sundial (though not the shadow) gesturing towards the long, unbound hair of the central figure—Elizabeth Siddal, Rossetti's by-now-late wife, model, and collaborator.

For a poetic predecessor to this haiku, however, it is impossible to overlook Rossetti's most important and most anthologized poem, "The Blessed Damozel." That poem, like "Beata Beatrix," concerns a dead lover, who leans out of the heavens in order to watch her lover, who remains alive, and overhears her rhapsodizing on the joys they will share when he finally ascends. The damozel's hair has become astrological—"the stars in her hair were seven"—and, as it emanates outward, seems to make a ghostly contact with the poem's speaker, who annotates the damozel's monologue in a set of parentheses:

(To one, it is ten years of years.
   . . . Yet now, and in this place,
Surely she leaned o'er me—her hair
Fell all about my face. . . .
Nothing: the autumn-fall of leaves.
   The whole year sets apace.)

As with the Noguchi, the lover's hair seems to descend but is likewise revealed as a natural phenomenon; Noguchi substitutes the long shadows of dusk for Rossetti's falling autumn leaves. The scene is laid with a psychoanalyst's sense of stagecraft. Suzanne M. Waldman reads the poem as the manifestation of a drive towards inclusion in a symbolic order from which one has been barred—and the damozel does indeed peek out from beyond "the gold bar of heaven."[28] But what this odd moment dramatizes most directly is the relationship between the season and the year: the speaker experiences a moment of disenchantment as what had felt like the touch of a lover's hair reveals itself to be a natural function of the season, a poetic effect hooked to a natural phenomenon at the expense of its auratic power. The dispirited final line finally attributes what might have appeared to be a single part of the year to its whole; autumn functions both as a marker of temporal particularity and as a symbol for seasonality as such.

If, though, we allow ourselves to read Noguchi's haiku as a "journal of one's feeling, or the footmark of one's soul's experience," that is, as a remediation, of lines 3–5 of this fourth stanza of "The Blessed Damozel," we notice a number of significant alterations. Whereas the damozel's hair *fell*; the Love's either *swings* or *swung*—pendulous and even threatening, the hair in the haiku evokes a castration complex more than it does the unboundedly phallic extension Waldman sees in the Rossetti. Unlike in "The Blessed Damozel," the connection Noguchi draws between the poetic image and the natural phenomenon entails no disenchantment—if anything, the exclamation on the second side of the colon amplifies the more mystical description. And then, perhaps most importantly of all, Noguchi replaces the seasonal temporality of "The Blessed Damozel" with a diurnal temporality: it is not autumn that has arrived, but evening. By making this change, Noguchi signals decisively that he will not adopt in English one of the most important aspects of the Japanese haiku, the kigo, or season-word.[29] The kigo has indeed been less central to the Anglophone haiku than the notorious syllabic conformity, and it is worth noting that although "In a Station of the Metro" does indeed contain a seasonal reference, "petals," it is part of a psychic, rather than natural, image: like Wordsworth's daffodils, Pound's petals can be recalled to mind at any time of the year.[30] On the other hand, Noguchi's first poem conspicuously refuses to include an element of the model text that, albeit unwittingly, actually conformed to the rules of the genre he was attempting to adapt.[31]

On one level, the omission of the kigo fits the poem's setting—a public park in a busy urban setting, rather than the less bounded rural world of contemplation and agriculture in which a large (but finite) number of natural phenomena can be taken, denotatively, as signs of a season.[32] But it also reflects Noguchi's principle that the Anglophone haiku would not precisely *import* aesthetic effects from the Japanese, but rather amplify and extend the somber naturalist romanticism that was already present in Rossetti's Pre-Raphaelite poetics. In his note, "A Japanese on the Poet Rossetti," Noguchi stresses the strictness of economy in Rossetti's poetry and painting alike: "He was one of the most fastidious workers in poetry as he was in painting; it seems to me that he hated nothing more than profusion, and from that great hatred of profusion, made his loam of life asunder to create a simple thing."[33] This "loam of life" having been jettisoned, what remained to Rossetti was "form and colour," Noguchi goes on to say, and "he was, in that respect, quite Oriental." This Orientalness consists, then, in the capacity to isolate and formalize simplicity in an overcrowded world—and, as Noguchi makes clear in his more systematic treatment of *The Spirit of Japanese Poetry* (1914), it is not an Orientalness that is Rossetti's alone, but rather runs throughout the mainstream of nineteenth-century British verse culture: "I can point out sometimes a *Hokku* effect of poetry even from the works of Tennyson and Browning; it is not too much to say that many of Wordsworth's poems could be successfully turned as a series of *Hokku* poems."[34]

Noguchi's observation is apposite, and not just because, by conspicuously extracting it, he has highlighted the presence of a kigo in his model text. Both compositions include a *kireji*, a "cutting word" that bisects the poem, allowing the reader to contemplate the diremption of two connected phenomena. Anglophone critics of haiku have sometimes explained the kireji as a species of *volta*, a switch or turn that reorients a poem's affective, tonal, or conceptual drift. Yet there is an important difference: while the *volta* turns, the kireji cuts. On the one hand, a redirected but continuous semantic procession; on the other, a radical break between one moment and another, the relationship between which is never spelled out. Pound's concept of the kireji's "superposition" has been picked up by some later critics;[35] Paul Fussell summarizes the function of a Petrarchan *volta* as analogous to the homeostatic procedures of a body, "the actions of inhaling and exhaling, or of contraction and release in the muscular system."[36] In treating Rossetti to a remodeling, nonetheless, Noguchi draws on the earlier poet's own experiments with cutting, closer in spirit to asyndeton than to anacoluthon.[37] In the inaugural sonnet of *The House of Life*, Rossetti bisects the first and second parts; rather than "open up for solution the problem advanced by the octave,"[38] he reasserts that problem, in terms not merely distinct but starkly incompatible:

A Sonnet is a moment's monument,––
   Memorial from the Soul's eternity
   To one dead deathless hour. Look that it be,
Whether for lustral rite or dire portent,
Of its own arduous fulness reverent:
   Carve it in ivory or in ebony
   As Day or Night may rule; and let Time see
Its flowering crest impearled and orient.

A Sonnet is a coin: its face reveals
   The soul,––its converse, to what Power 'tis due:––
Whether for tribute to the august appeals
   Of Life, or dower in Love's high retinue,
It serve; or 'mid the dark wharf's cavernous breath,
In Charon's palm it pay the toll to Death.

Like the coin that is one of its emblems, the sonnet can not be seen from both sides at once—Rossetti's sonnet perversely resists the closure that the sonnet has generally been held to perform. Unable to cash in the charge accrued in the octet for a sententious moral, the sonnet must remain uncompensated—or, as Bersani might have put it, unredeemed.[39]

In Noguchi's haiku as well as in "The Blessed Damozel," the poet performs two contradictory actions, severing sense perception from cognition and suturing the two together. In the Noguchi that effect is accomplished with a single punctuation mark, the colon at the end of the second line that marks the moment of realization, the beat at which the demystification of ideal into material transpires. The Rossetti, on the other hand, presents a morass of punctuation. The parenthesis with which the stanza begins marks a change in voice, from a third person narrator whose personal investments are obscured, to a lyrical, first-person confessional. But not quite. That first line identifies the subject of the parenthesis as "one," and gnomically resituates the poem in a doubled temporality, "years of years," that is not only difficult to decipher on its own terms, but sits uncomfortably next to the present-tense verb "is"; which colloquially suggests "has been," but also suggests a heavenly perspective on time, a long duration collapsed into an endless present. The first person doesn't enter at all until after the long ellipsis, which then functions as a secondary parenthesis; when it does so, it is as a pronoun in the indirect object position in the sentence, the subject of which is "her hair." Another elongated ellipsis, and then another mystical statement with no first person at all; the ellipses, not the parentheses, encapsulate the first person. That the forthcoming parentheses will subtract the ellipses, and that a lyric subject will (apparently unproblematically) inhabit them, is no disproof that in the fourth stanza the parentheses form only one of a pair of mediating typographical structures. The second ellipsis, then, marks the action of the stanza, the transition from subjective to objective narration, a demystification whose subject is "nothing"; an unvoiced beat, as in Noguchi's composition, but rather than a simple semicolon, Rossetti enacts something like a kireji through a typographical oddity whose instantiation in a word, "Nothing," reinforces a poetic effect whose primary agent was punctuation.

To treat Rossetti's ellipsis as a precursor to the kireji is, admittedly, to read backwards. But "The Blessed Damozel" is a poem whose critics, and indeed whose author, cannot resist that which D.M.R. Bentley calls, suggestively if derisively, "inverted historicism."[40] First composed by a young and pious Rossetti in 1847, it was first published in *The Germ* in 1850, the same year that Rossetti met Elizabeth Siddal, and ten years before they married. It underwent substantial revisions and republications three times before its final publication in *Ballads and Sonnets* (1881).[41] By this time, Siddal was long dead of laudanum poisoning, and subsequent critics have both seen this poem about a dead lover as autobiographical, and claimed that in 1847 the poem *already* reflected the eroticism avowed openly in Rossetti's later work.[42] Others have argued, more modestly, that Rossetti activated affective currents in his edited versions that were dormant or underdeveloped in the version in *The Germ*.[43] Rossetti himself, though, seems to have outdone his critics. In his 1932 discussion of the poem's various revisions, Kenneth Knickerbocker describes a single sheet of paper among Rossetti's papers in the Pierpont Morgan Library that establishes 1847 as the date of the poem's composition, in which lines from the poem are gathered together under the title "The Blessed Damsel," and signed "D.G.R. 1847."[44] That the lines are written in Rossetti's hand is undisputed. But in a dashing 1938 essay, J. A. Sanford claims quite conclusively that the manuscript was fraudulently inserted into his papers by Rossetti himself, certainly after 1856, and possibly much later, as an attempt to "substantiate the legend of his own precocity."[45] "The Blessed Damozel" is not merely an invitation to inverted historicism but, as with much of this poet's notoriously reprocessed verse, a performance of it.

Noguchi's pleated historicism worked both ways. Years after having returned to Japan, he sent some free verse compositions to the poet, illustrator, and homosexual rights campaigner Laurence Housman, which Housman—appreciating the work's "atmosphere and graceful fancies" but missing the meter—recomposed into metrical arrangement. Housman did not return the poem to Noguchi but, fifteen years later, published "Cradle-Song" in his own collection *The Heart of Peace* (1919):

Cradle-Song

SLEEP, my baby, your road of dreams
  By the fire-flies shall be lighted:
See them link their tingling teams
  Round you, lest you go be-nighted!

Off to-night your father flies
  Honey from the stars to bring:
Star-town, ah, how far it lies!
  Thither he goes travelling.

But at daybreak, big with news,
  Backward riding he shall come,
Bright of hoof across the dews,
  Beating on a golden drum! (90)

The jovial, adventuring tone, as well as the themes of cosmic exile and return, chime with the tone and content of Noguchi's earlier work, but the ballad meter is indisputably late Victorian—that of Henley, of Kipling, and of Housman. Yet syncretic as "Cradle-Song" feels, Housman reports his conscience untroubled by the work's publication in *The Heart of Peace*, and it was not until reading a review of Noguchi's poetry in the *Sunday Times* years later, in which the reviewer singled out *Noguchi*'s "Cradle-Song" for praise, that (by his own account) Housman realized what had happened: "It was in free verse—the words, as I read them, seemed strangely familiar. I sat up with a snort of indignation—here, surely, I began saying to myself, was bare-faced plagiarism! And then, memory smote me, and I suddenly realized what I had done! . . . [I] here express my humble thanks to Mr. Yone Noguchi that he has not prosecuted me for the theft" (261).

II. Some Impertinent Poet

Noguchi's description of Rossetti as "quite Oriental" exhibited as a biographical claim the fruits of a close, if not especially original, reading of certain formal features of his poetry. But no less importantly, it was an act of territorialization, a performative act of interpretation that uncomfortably moved towards two potentially incompatible perlocutionary goals. First, to inscribe himself within a Victorian poetic tradition for which Rossetti (and others) were made to stand: in this limited sense, it might be possible to understand Noguchi's procedure as something like what Harold Bloom calls a "strong misreading," the phase in the development of a poetic consciousness in which symbolic murder is enacted on an earlier poet cast in the quasi-Oedipal role of father.[46] But, second, by citing one of the leading figures of the Victorian verse tradition as Japanese or Oriental, Noguchi attempted to *con*scribe part of that tradition within a transnational cultural formation, over which a cosmopolitan Japanese Anglophone reader could assume stewardship. Noguchi's very adherence to the Victorian model text caught him in the double bind of authority and submission, which sets the price of speech as the use of others' words. As much as the syllabic arrangement and kireji, then, the submissiveness facing the cultural authority of that back-projected Other marks "My love's lengthened hair" out as a haiku: his poem did not merely conform to an inflexible syllabic arrangement, but to an inflexible cultural heritage that required its own kind of genuflection.

Although Noguchi's haiku does not, obviously enough, offer anything like an explicit political commitment, elsewhere he explored the traffic between authority and submission more directly, particularly in the novel he published in the United States shortly before he left for Britain, *The American Diary of a Japanese Girl* (1901). While traveling East across the Pacific in an early chapter of that book, the narrator (Miss Morning Glory) first calls to mind, and then rewrites, a few lines of Tennyson:

> I recalled a few passages of "The Lotos Eaters" by Lord Tennyson—it sounds better than "the poet Tennyson." I love titles, but they are thought of as common as millionaires nowadays.
>
> A Jap poet has a different mode of speech.
> Shall I pose as poet?
> 'Tis no great crime to do so.
> I began my "Lotos Eaters" with the following mighty lines:
>
> "O dreamy land of stealing shadows!
> O peace-breathing land of calm afternoon!
> O languid land of smile and lullaby!
> O land of fragrant bliss and flower!
> O eternal land of whispering Lotos Eaters!"
>
> Then I feared that some impertinent poet might have said the same thing many a year before.
>
> Poem manufacture is a slow job.
>
> Modern people slight it, calling it an old fashion. Shall I give it up for some more brilliant up-to-date pose?[47]

The passage stages a provocative and, in at least one sense, improbable confrontation between verse styles cast in Japanese, British, and American voices. Despite her playful and precocious casting off of poetry, Miss Morning Glory writes in a line-broken prose that for the most part adequates, as does the indented poem, sentence to line—the "mode of speech" to which she alludes brooks no distinction between prose and verse. Noguchi himself was fond of very long lines, and had in the years prior to writing *The American Diary* largely writing his Whitmanian odes at the Hights in Oakland—no doubt, in these poems, he understood his long line as an American line.[48] An improbable dimension is that Miss Morning Glory's poetic merging of these three elements—British model text, Japanese "mode of speech," and American lineation—coincides almost exactly with another joke about Tennyson by an early Asian American prose writer, Sui Sin Far. In her short story "Mrs. Spring Fragrance," one of the earliest short stories written by an Anglophone Chinese author, and composed around the same time as Noguchi's novel, the eponymous heroine reveals either her ignorance or her perceptiveness when she reassures her lovelorn young neighbor, "Is there not a beautiful American poem written by a noble American named Tennyson,—which says: "Tis better to have loved and lost, / than never to have loved at all?"[49] Notwithstanding that striking, if probably coincidental, apercu, Miss Morning Glory's treatment of Tennyson while virtuosic, must push through several layers of obsolescence: of aristocratic titles ("as common as millionaires"); of this specific poem's redundancy ("some impertinent poet might have said the same thing"); and finally, of poetry itself ("modern people slight it"). The narrator's mode of speech is superadded to a verse culture become moribund through overstuffing; she sets herself the task of imagining a "more brilliant up-to-date pose" even than poetry.

Beneath the poem, the pose: Noguchi moves from textual apprenticeship to the consideration of embodied identity. Miss Morning Glory's treatment of Tennyson hews far less closely to the model than does Noguchi's own use of Rossetti; she condenses into iterated apostrophes ("O peace-breathing land of calm afternoon!") passages that, in the model, are narrated in the third person ("In the afternoon they came unto a land / In which it seemed always afternoon").[50] Indeed, the passage imagines a practice of freedom that follows from poetry, and cannot be performed within it—a practice whose mode is not merely Japanese, but gleefully, immoderately girly. There are two travesties at work: of Tennyson, whose incipient sentimentality is rendered as Orientalist mock-epic, and of a stereotypical version of Japanese femininity. Critics have generally posed the ethical problem of this gendered presentation in polarizing terms: he either "bought into" or "rebelled against" Orientalist stereotypes.[51] Very frequently, discussions of this question have drawn on the language of economics: Noguchi "began to capitalize on his ethnicity," as Amy Sueyoshi puts it, treating *The American Diary* as a *volta* in Noguchi's own career, a pivot at which a queer anti-Orientalist poet becomes a proto-fascist stooge of Japanese imperialism.[52] As Miss Morning Glory's winsome decision to "pose" suggests, however, Noguchi's hybrid novel cannot easily be slotted into the binary logic whereby true can be finally distinguished from false consciousness. It rather conforms to the nuanced account of parody that Mikhail Bakhtin offers in his essay "From the Prehistory of Novelistic Discourse," in which generic parody is theorized not as a *critique* of the literary forms to which it appears to be attached, but as a renegotiation of the relationship between a subject and a reality whose edges have already been contoured by genre. Parody not as a satirical treatment of a genre's apparent contradictions, but as an accommodation to the contradictions that comprise reality as such. Between the false consciousness of Orientalist stereotype and the embodied consciousness of the ethnic subject, *The American Diary* expresses a "parodic-travestying consciousness" that explores the rules governing this ethnicized Anglophone style.[53]

The *American* diary of a *Japanese* girl: this curiously doubled title feels almost impossible, and foregrounds the dispossession of one ethnic object—the embodied girl—by another, the textual diary. Although Bakhtin's account of such consciousness does not, especially, privilege ethnicity as such, it clearly presupposes some degree of cultural hybridity and, so, a mobility of the kind Noguchi performs: "A new mode developed for working creatively with language: the creating artist began to look at language from the outside, with another's eyes, from the point of view of a potentially different language or style. It is, after all, precisely in the light of another potential language or style that a given straightforward style is parodied, travestied, ridiculed."[54] On the other hand, the drag performance of *The American Diary* affirms Rita Felski's insight that fin-de-siècle male writers who adopted feminine personae were not generally "in sympathy with the aims of feminism"; their gender play was rather "predicated upon a radical disavowal of and dissociation from the 'natural' body of woman."[55] In his essays, Noguchi repeatedly describes Japanese women as disembodied ghosts, "an allegory," "a vision of beauty itself," "a butterfly with magic wing," etc.[56] His later expressions of antipathy towards Onoto Watanna emphasized not just the bogusness of her ethnic presentation but her having entered into a textual field from which women would be better excluded.[57] On the other hand, Noguchi's performance of Tennyson-in-drag allows him to achieve an authority relative to his model text that the haiku form will not: Miss Morning Glory, poser and poet, subtly avows the eroticism of poetic submission if only in order to sublimate it.

Noguchi's play with style thus presents as a performative act of *appropriation*: of rendering an external phenomenon (the poetry of Rossetti, Poe, or Tennyson) one's own property. It is a distinctive mode of appropriation precisely because it is performed partly on behalf of an ethnic collectivity, and partly on behalf of an individual subject: these poems are *both* the work of a Japanese cultural actor engaging an undifferentiated stratum of Western culture, *and* the work of an individuated authorial style particularizing and reauthorizing the stylistic features of other individual men. Part of the strangeness of style is its ahistoricity, or perhaps its capacity to persuade us that it simply *is* history, and that it therefore will brook no supplementary historicism. The haiku again affords a paradigmatic case, since not only does it foreclose the account of style as a singularity, but it also gestures to a historical moment it need not prove existed, the "footmark," to repurpose Noguchi's word, of an irrefutable (because not real) event in historical time. The political force of that apparently rather rarefied question would reach a high pitch in Noguchi's late correspondence with his former friend Rabindranath Tagore concerning escalating Japanese aggression in China, written in 1937 in the weeks following the full-scale invasion of China in July, a policy of which Noguchi was an unambiguous supporter. For Tagore, Noguchi's enthusiasm for war, reflecting as it did an alliance with the fascist powers of Italy and Germany, was a betrayal of the cosmopolitan soul of the artist: "What is not amusing is that artists should echo such remarkable sentiments [as those of the Japanese government] that translate military swagger into spiritual bravado."[58] On the one hand, Noguchi's descriptions of the war are full of the kind of modernist fascist rhetoric associated with Marinetti: the war is "the inevitable means, terrible though it is, for establishing a great new world in the Asiatic continent," and "Japan's militarism is a tremendous affair."[59] On another level, Noguchi's defense of Japanese militarism exhibits the particular epistemological panic occasioned by modern techniques of propaganda, familiar to readers of Mark Wollaeger and Susan Sontag:[60] "So awful pictures they are—awful enough to make ten thousand enemies of Japan in a foreign country. But the pictures are nothing but a Chinese invention, simple and plain, because the people in the scenes are all Chinese, slaughterers and all."[61] But most important of all, for these purposes, is Noguchi's effective reproof of Tagore's romanticization of "the land of Bushido, of great Art and traditions of noble heroism" by insisting on the grounded militarism on which such aesthetic exceptionalization in fact depended:

> Supposing that we accept your advice to become a vanguard of humanity according to your prescription, and supposing that we leave China to her own will, and save ourselves from being a "betrayal of the intellectuals," who will promise us with the safety of Japanese spirit that we cultivated with pairs of thousand years, under the threat of communism across a fence? We don't want to barter our home land for an empty name of intellectuals. No, you mustn't talk nonsense! God forbid![62]

If the rhetorical power of this argument seems to extinguish the lightness of tone in *American Diary* and *Seen and Unseen*, it also warns its reader(s) against assuming an easy binary in which the airy realm of aesthetic forms might be treated in isolation from the grubby world of imperial violence and nationalist fervor. Noguchi's point was that the value of intellectual activity derives only from its fulfillment of patriotic duty, not that it is inherently empty.

Noguchi's thinking moved from aestheticism to fascism: this, perhaps, conforms to a familiar story about modernism in general, and indeed it is usually through a discussion of modernism that haiku is historicized and formalized by scholars. Yet the association between haiku and the white avant-gardes detaches haiku not only from its origins in a Japanese writer's attachment to Victorian verse, but from its contemporary existence as a mass cultural form consistently *distinguished* from modernist poetics and their avant-garde inheritors. So, what other stories about the politics of Anglophone haiku become possible, once Pound has been dislodged from, and Noguchi/Rossetti installed at, the origin?

III. Convention, Mobility, Provincialism: Haiku Mass Cultures

One of the most prolific composers of haiku in English, the African American novelist and critic Richard Wright adopted the form late in life, and most of his work in it has yet to find its way into print. Of the four thousand or so he composed over the last two years of his life, only 817 have been published, in a collection entitled *This Other World*. For all the frenzy and violence that critics have seen mobilized in Wright's major works, his haiku are slow, poignant, and fragile, leaving his daughter and editor Julia Wright to contemplate "a biographical enigma: how the creator of the inarticulate, frightened, and enraged Bigger Thomas ended up leaving us some of the most tender, unassuming, and gentle lines in African American poetry."[63] There is another conundrum: how twelve thousand lines of poetry—roughly the same number as *The Odyssey*, substantially more than *Paradise Lost*—might be understood by Julia Wright, and by other critics, as short-form literature? How does the haiku sequence, that is, pose the brevity of the individual poem with the potentially exorbitant extension of the series? Julia Wright herself offers a powerful somatic theory:

> worried as we all were by his drastic weight-loss (the haiku must have been easy to carry) and the strange slowness of his recovery, we did not immediately establish a link between his poetic practices and his ailing health. Today I know better. I believe his haiku were self-developed antidotes against illness, and that breaking down words into syllables matched the shortness of his breath, especially on the bad days when his inability to sit up at the typewriter restricted the very breadth of writing. (viii)

Her memory fastens the haiku to the body in three ways. The poems being short, each individual object did not require much paper, and was therefore light enough for the dying poet to carry—though here one hears the ambiguity of that term, as though the haiku were being taken with him, on that apparently inexorable journey towards death. The syllabic decomposition of semantic units matched, apparently, the short and irregular breathing: a body failing to fully be itself does not require that words have sense, or even sound, but only a unitary, syntagmatic quality. The haiku themselves thematize a dispossession that follows from the loss of name: "I am nobody," begins the first of the collection, "A red sinking autumn sun / Took my name away."[64] Linking the invalid's breath to the composition of the syllable, Julia Wright both draws on and extends the romantic logic of poetic *inspiration*, wherein poetic wholeness is granted as a gift to the poet through the intake of a whole breath; her father's broken breaths are formalized as disarticulated syllables. The first connection between the haiku and the body was the poem's literal lightness, the second connected the syllable to breath; in the third, Julia Wright connects the unease of the body at the typewriter to the "breadth" of the line of poetry. So it is not the length of the poem that is at issue; rather, the geometrical dimensions of each line reflect an accommodation to a body unable to "sit up," to pay attention, not to slouch.

In this account, the haiku does not precisely emanate from the suffering body, but neither is it mediated by it. The poem is mere, preexisting form that awaits the encounter between an embodied subject and hostile environment—a negotiation of which the only possible end is the death of the poet. In one sense, the haiku furnishes a pungently literal example of textual vaccination: an ("antidote," says Julia Wright) that reenacts ("matched") the action of the poison it was ingested to cure.[65] But here I am interested less in whether this tender and intimate account of the specificity of the haiku form might be more widely applied, than by its similarities and obvious differences from accounts of the Anglophone haiku as irruptive, condensed, and modernist that so frequently characterize its generic history. Ezra Pound offered the first and most influential of these in his essay on "Vorticism," in which he describes composing "In a Station of the Metro" as a "*hokku*-like sentence."[66] That well-known poem, which was first published in the journal *Poetry* in 1913, and appears on the inaugural page of the Norton anthology *Haiku in English: The First Hundred Years,* comprises two lines:

> The apparition of these faces in the crowd;
> Petals on a wet, black bough.

The above version, with a semicolon at the end of the first line, is how the poem is reprinted in *Haiku in English,* as well as in Pound's later versions. In its initial publication in *Poetry,* however, and then again in Pound's discussion of the poem in the "Vorticism" essay, the first line ends with a colon. The colon might extend the line for an extra, unvoiced moment—a reader might, conceivably, slip down to the second line more quickly when invited to do so by the more rapid semicolon. But the opposite might also be true: colons project meaning forward, rather than opening a relation of subordination. So one might imagine the colon as more rapid, or at least more propulsive, than the semicolon.

Might there not be semantic differences too? Pound describes the *hokku* as a "form of super-position, that is to say, it is one idea set on top of another."[67] It would not then be *juxtaposition,* in which the suspension of multiple elements foregrounds the *differences* between them, but neither would it be *apposition,* in which the one element is subordinated to the other in order to identify it. In the "Vorticism" essay, Pound is both tempted by and dismissive of apposition. Translating third-hand an occasional poem apparently written by a Japanese naval officer, he introduces a parenthetical simile between the first line and the second—"The footsteps of the cat upon the snow: / (are like) plum-blossoms"—before adding, "the words 'are like' would not occur in the original, but I add them for clarity."[68] If that truly was the aim, the parenthetical aside was wholly counterproductive: by adding a simile to the poem's altogether adequate syntax, Pound has set two forms of apposition against each other, the colon and the parenthetical simile now both attempting to identify the relationship between the footsteps and the blossoms, with each attempt successful only insofar as the other fails. Further complicating matters is the modal verb in the disclaimer. Pound insists not that the simile does not appear in the original, but that it *would* not: there is something murky about the haiku in English that requires an editorial clarification, but that very supplementation thereby abdicates the very aesthetic effect—the particular haiku mode of super-position—that the translinguistic transcription had sought to import.

In practice, though, Pound resolves these difficulties by recourse to a therapeutic rhetoric, narrating the composition of the poem as a gradual process of sublimation and healing: "I found it useful in getting out of an impasse in which I had been left by my metro emotion." Pound narrates the poem's composition as the overcoming of that impasse through the sloughing off of verbiage and detritus: "I wrote a thirty-line poem, and destroyed it because it was what we call 'of second intensity.' Six months later I made a poem half that length; a year later I made the following *hokku*-like sentence:—" The compositional process maps onto an aesthetic consciousness become lighter and more limber, as though modeling in advance the very mobility that will, eventually, characterize the haiku's formal properties themselves: "one is trying to record the precise instant when a thing outward and objective transforms itself, or darts into a thing inward and subjective."[69] It is this "darting" quality that comes to characterize the mobility and flexibility of the Beat haiku as practiced, for example, by Jack Kerouac, whose work in the field constitutes part of his own, no less than Wright's, late style. In Kerouac's poetry, the haiku is a plastic and portable form, one whose whimsical sense of triumph has left Pound's impasse far behind. In his "Haiku Berkeley," for example:

Haiku Snyder

I hurt the black ink
on your kind book

the only inconsistency sin
I done yet to you
sweet heart

And John Wino anyway
was to blame
Dont kick me out
of your tea
house
great man[70]

Addressing Gary Snyder, another haiku enthusiast, with a winsomely flirtatious wink, Kerouac offsets the potentially weightier aspects of the Orientalist repertoire (the *black* ink; the *kind* book) with a lightness of an entirely different sort to Wright's. This haiku, if it is one, enacts a freedom of movement—indeed, an implied right to occupy Snyder's "tea / house"—as its lines wobble around the page, and its inconsistency transforms into versatility. The lightness of the haiku indexes its cultural portability, as in Kerouac, or its material portability, as in Wright. But the freedom that Kerouac's haiku enacts also indexes something else: his whiteness, which occupies the Orientalized space—the "tea / house"—without troubling itself over whether or not it really does belong to Snyder, or whether John Wino really is to blame. As Richard A. Iadonisi put it in a recent essay on the "masculine urge" of Kerouac's haiku, the forms served him as "a way of capturing immediacy, spontaneity, and, most importantly, freedom."[71] In Kerouac's own understanding, that "freedom" is posed as an ethnicized American characteristic that stands in *opposition* to an orthodoxy coded as Oriental rigor: "The Japanese haiku is strictly disciplined to seventeen syllables but since the language structure is different I don't think American Haikues (short three-line poems intended to be completely packed with Void of Whole) should worry about syllables because American speech is something again."[72] Indeed, within the white avant-garde American tradition, an insistence on numerical regulation resembled those metrical orthodoxies of Victorian poetry that modernists repudiated. The modernist John Gould Fletcher made the case that it was the odd number of syllables that rendered Japanese syllabic conformity so ungainly in an English-language tradition in which lines of poetry contain almost exclusively even numbers of syllables, such that even lines with odd numbers are generally understood as *missing* a syllable—the catalectic that is generally scanned along with the extant syllables. "The only part of [Japanese versification] that we Occidentals could not accept perhaps, with advantage to ourselves, is the peculiarly Oriental insistence on an odd number of syllables for every line and an odd number of lines to every poem. To the Western mind, odd numbers sound incomplete. But to the Chinese (and Japanese art is mainly a highly specialized expression of Chinese thought), the odd numbers are masculine and hence heavenly."[73] Meanwhile, in a context in some ways closer to

Noguchi, that of contemporary prosodics, the so-called "syllabic system of prosody" had been fully discredited. George Saintsbury's *Manual of English Prosody* (1910) briefly discusses the procedure of measuring out poetry by syllables, rather than by stresses or feet. Among the unpleasant effects of counting syllables rather than stresses—a practice "of course, French in origin" (14)—is that the canon of English poetry had to be eviscerated and contracted in order that a verse be seen to contain the correct number of syllables. These contractions far exceeded "elision proper," (16) Saintsbury argued, and included the "utterly hideous" (17) constructions "vi(o)let," "di(a)mond," and "wat(e)ry."[74] The stereotype of the barbaric and bloody-minded French convention shadowed the stereotype of the Japanese imitativeness.

Critics treating the haiku as a genre of sublime modernist condensation mistake Pound's insistence on *his own* compositions' intensity for an attribute of the form itself. Such a history can hardly then explain Julia Wright's theorization of the haiku—which she offers in a recuperative, rather than scornful, mode—as the poetic equivalent of hospital food. In a world as hostile to self-expression as that cohabited by Billy Collins and Richard Wright, the extravagant rigidity of the form provides a shield, a brace around which the expressive drive might grow. Collins's almost Thoreauvian formulation, one of the epigraphs to this chapter, describes *going to the syllables because I wanted to live non-expressively*: his encounter with form "could not be simpler," because unlike the nugget of modernist meaning, the haiku is purely vacuous, its authority crystal-clear, arbitrary, and unimpeachable. In other words, the haiku pervaded twentieth-century American culture not merely as one set of poetic conventions among many, but as the *problematization* of poetic convention itself in a cultural landscape that had only partially absorbed the modernists' demands for objectivity and spontaneity. It therefore proved a singularly useful tool for the very pedagogical and ideological structures that enforce the abolition of self-expression—that require us to keep it inside. Is there a poetic genre more aggressively promoted in schools, or one whose formal properties are more dogmatically patrolled, not merely by avant-gardists or prosodic pedants, but by a broad-based coalition of educators, enthusiasts, and developmental linguists? Two examples: the *New York Times* hosts a website, haiku.nytimes.com, that every couple of days condenses one of its articles into haiku—a story about the financial trials of the Chicago Cubs generated "They kept their money / in their pockets until they / got what they wanted."[75] The poem's wryness depends on the haiku's putative worldliness, or even world-weariness, the sense that the poem indexes more meaning, and retains more knowledge, than it makes apparent; four deictics in this particular example index the same, offstage "them." Its historicity is unspoken but immanent; it draws on a consciousness not merely of the quotidian history it inhabits but another body of knowledge, that which is called "common knowledge," that it doesn't need to, and in fact lacks the syllables to, say. Second, and in a mode both more playful and more critical: a photograph that became an internet meme in 2014. In felt-tip pen, and a handwriting style coded as childish, is written, underneath the word "HAIKU," "Five syllables here / Seven more syllables there / Are you happy now??"[76] Is the resentment so opportunistically articulated here that of a subject unwilling to treat syllabic conformity as a precondition for aesthetic expression? Or might this be an obverse pedantry, in which the apostrophized reader's reduction of the haiku form to such conformity is the satire's object? In either case, this poem evokes something like what Sianne Ngai calls "stuplimity"—the stuttering repetition that indicates an "aesthetic experience in which astonishment is paradoxically united with boredom."[77]

This haiku might be a test case for the hybrid form of exquisite stuplimity, whose grouchy demonstration that poetry can be reduced to mere technique directs its low-grade irritation simultaneously at the arbitrariness of the form and the coerciveness of the institutional structure that enforces it. Yet the outrage at arbitrariness never quite breaks the form's surface. In such a work, the haiku affords a screen onto which a militant engagement with form as such might be articulated: these poems thematize the coercive arbitrariness of form, but one cannot known in advance how that theme will be politicized: as a convalescent acceding to power and time (Wright), an ethnically coded performance of freedom (Kerouac), the dissolution of formal particularity within a naturalized and progressive historical narrative (the *NYT*); and the precisely metadiscursive rehearsal of *ressentiment* ("Five syllables here"). That this last response is tediously familiar, always-already a cliché, only reinforces the sense that the haiku's cultural authority derives from its constant tendency to melt into tedium and decay—a tendency articulated by Donald Richie as a property of "Japanese aesthetics," whose plural forms share, he suggests, a "quality that finds permanence only in its frankly expiring examples."[78]

Ngai dedramatizes the Kantian aesthetic by treating it as an everyday encounter (and in that sense quite unremarkable), but she does not reduce the power of its hold over us. Quite the opposite: Kant's account of the sublime offers a narrative in which a subject's triumph over his disorientation centers him as a more autonomous, and indeed happier, person—hero, obstacle, victory. In the stuplime experience, however, the narrative collapses; victory cannot be taken for granted, and stuplimity simply "holds opposing affects [of, e.g. fear and tranquility] together" (271). The salient difference between the Kantian sublime and the exquisite obtains between their modes of narrative closure, then: the sublime is complete at the moment of subjective reintegration—the reestablishment of control. But the exquisite, keyed as it is to the

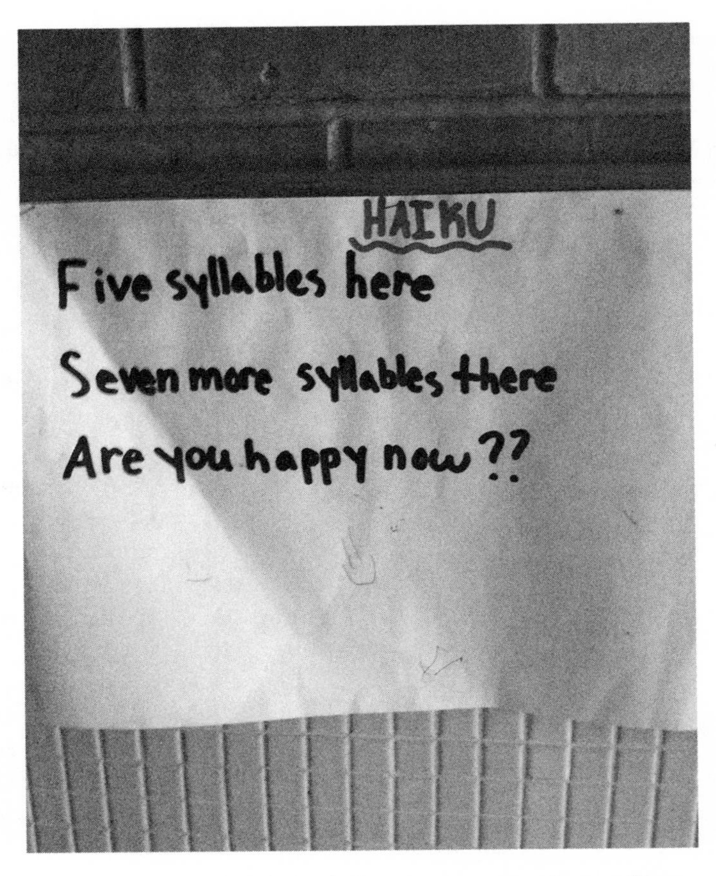

FIGURE 3.2. "*Five syllables here.*" This poem was written by one of the students at Tolson Elementary School in Tucson, AZ, and this image was uploaded to Facebook by their teacher Eric K. Carr on May 27, 2012. For this remarkable discovery, and much else, I am grateful to Mary Mussman. Some visual aspects of its composition are worth remarking: the horizontal trisection of the image into bricks, poem, and tiles has the effect of forcing an analogy between the regular geometric arrangement and the syllables of the poem. The posted poem – here "post" is performed by the meme, and depicted in the image itself – occupies the photograph almost as a flag, vivid red and blue staining the white backdrop. And, lastly, some kind of comparison and contrast is incited by the two smiley faces doodled in pencil, underneath the poem. Both are transcriptions of emoticons, composed from punctuation: a colon and a close parenthesis (the left), and an equals sign and a close parenthesis (the right). The emoticon, fore-runner to the emoji, abstracted from orthographic equipment an affective directness, a minimalist portraiture of a kind analogous to the minimal poetic effect of the *haiku* itself.

judgment of the beautiful, does not close off in narrative terms at all: sustained by a melancholic temporality, the exquisite simply replaces temporal progression with formal synchrony. As does this particular haiku, for all of its defensive stupidity.

Another possibility for a stuplime exquisite emergences from the haiku's kigo structure, the "season-word" that locates any individual composition in a particular time of year, and so produces a sense of the singularity of the poetic event while insisting that the event is repeatable, that its legibility is determined by its position within a typological matrix. It is this aspect of the haiku, a generic deixis connecting the minimalist form to a naively (though no less minimally) organized realism, that Kerouac and the midcentury haiku critics whose work he assiduously read (especially R. H. Blyth) took to typify the haiku's allegiance to "*Zen*." In his magisterial, four-volume book, *Haiku*, Blyth developed a theory of haiku as a spiritual practice "in which we are not separated from other things, are indeed identical with them, and yet retain our own individuality."[79] Blyth's first book, *Zen in English Literature and Oriental Classics* (1942) argued that the most valuable substrate of *world* literature was that which expressed Zen concepts, the genealogy of which, he claimed, ran from *Hamlet* to W. E. Henley.[80] Yet another: does the very exhibitionism of the haiku, its frank avowal of both the arbitrariness and the economy of its form—seventeen syllables—qualify it as a kind of conceptual poetry *avant la lettre*, in the vein of Kenneth Goldsmith's No. 111 2.7.93–10.20.96?[81] In its pure auto-indexicality, "Five syllables here" manifests something of the koan's abstract objectivity, something of Goldsmith's puerile brio. But whereas conceptual poetry attempts to privatize as cultural capital a rational procedure it disingenuously asserts to be independent of any individual subject—a resemblance to finance capital, incidentally, that informs Keston Sutherland's trenchant critique of conceptualism—the haiku's laws inhibit the gestation of an author-function.[82] None of the haiku writers I have mentioned so far are primarily known as such—despite the broad penetration of haiku poetics into Anglophone ideological and institutional assemblages, there is not a single canonical Anglophone author known primarily as a composer in the form. This absence emanates from the hole at the center of the haiku, the programmatic quality of the verse-form: on this evidence, not merely a more vernacular, but a more effective deconstruction of the lyric subject than the conceptualists have mustered.

To treat the avowedly antimodernist form as an ironic pastiche of modernism would be, still, to underestimate the volume of cultural space in which haiku circulates—to treat the Haiku Society of America, for example, as analogous to an avant-garde poetry scene. It isn't: the Haiku Society of America's website describes the "English-language haiku movement" as "refreshingly democratic"; by which it means to indicate to readers that the benefit of the haiku form is that it is more, less, or other than a cultural asset of metropolitan elites. The "HSA Regional Announcements" section of the site in particular draws connections between the pastoral thematics of haiku verse and the provincial settings of the HSA's regional affiliates. From Bangor, Maine, for example: "It has been cold with the snow piling higher each week. / a cold morning / with a ski sweater / cardboard snowman / for Carlos / Bruce Ross."[83] One may question whether the democracy modeled by such an avowedly provincial poetic movement is worth the name, given its snow-white model of collective participation, but an antimodernist removal from the metropolitan centers of avant-garde culture is resiliently figured as the political climate in which the haiku flourishes.

IV. Embarrassing Modernism

I suggested in the introduction that the mythological construction of Japanese postmodernity belongs just as much to the age of Kipling and Fenollosa as it does to the age of Kojève and Barthes. At the level of ideology, Lyotard's periodic inversion, I suggested, holds true: what we might call the Japanese postmodernism *did indeed* predate the Euro-American modernism. Yet much of the best critical work dealing with Japanese influence on the West stresses the modernizing function of Japanese art.[84] The salient question has been *how*, not *whether*, Japanese aesthetics served the interests of modernism. Some, for example, have suggested that although Japonisme may have been primitivist, the purpose of primitivism, after all, is to serve as a first order negation of modernity to be subsumed and sublated. As we have seen with Noguchi's advocacy of the haiku and adoption of specifically Victorian verse, however, the trajectory of the Japanese effect on Western aesthetics strives, at least as much as to modernize, to uphold a peculiar, quaint kind of *traditionalism*. We would only refer to this traditionalism as a *type* of modernism if we had already absorbed the modernist ideology itself. What other options are available?

In his recent book examining the convergence of Japanese aesthetics and queer Western masculinities in modern art, Christopher Reed thoughtfully and persuasively explains this dialectical argument, describing the modernists' Japan as a "hinge between two stages of primitivism: one used depictions of the East to confirm the superiority of the West; the other undermined Western ideas of depiction altogether, fundamentally challenging what Westerners thought they knew."[85] *Bachelor Japanists* (2017) is a breathtakingly thorough reconstruction of the history of ideas and forms that passed between the idea of Japan and the West through descriptions of three avant-garde scenes: Paris at the fin de siècle, the Boston of William Sturgis Bigelow, and postwar

Seattle. The book's narrative divides the history of Japonisme into two phases: a minor Victorian Japonisme during which "a few Victorian discontents used Japan to critique the West," and the more fully or radically absorbed mature phase of Japonisme in which "self-consciously modern deployments of Japan disauthorized Western systems of belief and representation" (10). That disauthorization, nonetheless, was performed by Western artists, drawing on the occasional collaboration of Japanese self-mythologization: Reed's protagonists are the Goncourt brothers, Bernard Leach, Isabella Stewart Gardner, Mark Tobey, and other Western enthusiasts of abstraction. Accordingly, Reed's story of the absorption and diffusion of Japanese art forms in the West is easy assimilated into a dialectical account of Western modernity as the major metanarrative of world history. (1) There exists "the West," with its naively representational art forms; then (2) comes the merely negative "critique [of] the West," whose effects are negligible except that they pave the way for (3) the more radical embrace of abstraction that more adequately conveys or expresses the emerging spirit of the modern age.

How, then, to account for Noguchi's attachment to a poem—"The Blessed Damozel"—that, by 1902, already seemed old-fashioned when placed alongside Noguchi's modernist contemporaries? The question was raised, indirectly, in another influential recent work dealing with the diffusion of Japanese forms, in an essay by Hoyt Long and Richard Jean So entitled, "Literary Pattern Recognition: Modernism between Close Reading and Machine Learning," which seeks to synthesize algorithm-driven distant reading and traditional humanistic scholarship, to identify the essential characteristics of a haiku poem. As the authors put it, "sometimes, it seems, an ineffable sense of haiku-ness can indeed be reducible to statistical patterns of word choice."[86] Deprived of that alarming verb choice, Long and So's analysis might be reducible to a tautology, if it were not a mistake: a cmd+f search of their article reveals that neither "kigo" nor "season" appears in it, and that therefore they do not, evidently, account for the fact that the haiku is written, by design, by dipping into a restricted and conventional semantic field. Long and So *do* discuss Noguchi, and offer several useful descriptions of haiku aesthetics more generally, but what interests them is the genre's proximity or distance to an idea of poetic abstraction developed out of the poetic theories of the modernists: accordingly, their primary archive comprises Pound, Williams, Richard Aldington, Wallace Stevens, and the other white, male Anglo-American usual suspects. Their graph describing the distribution of haiku over time, the "self-identified haiku," begins in 1899. Given that their argument already helpfully detaches haiku poetics from such self-identifications, the question seems inevitable: what would be included if the authors expanded the corpus to include the verse of the previous century—verse that, obviously, cannot be "self-identified haiku" any more than could "The Blessed Damozel," or, to return to the poem I examined at this book's outset, "Gone Were but the Winter"?

In the second chapter, I suggested that British aestheticism's engagement with Japan explored the *limits* of abstraction—which I took to be one Western mode of representation among many, endowed with no greater dialectical force than conventional portraiture. But, more extensively, I have been pushing against one of the premises that Reed, Long, and So share: that the story most worth telling is the major story of Western modernism. Instead, as Noguchi's relation to Rossetti exemplifies, the idea of Japan was in certain respects a thorn in the side of the modernist heralds of abstraction, and as a vehicle for quaint historical attachments I have associated with postmodernity and with the more oblique, antimodernist sense of "modern" I derived from Barthes. The modernist skew of the scholarly treatment of haiku radically diverges, I have suggested, from the antimodernist milieux in which haiku poetics are practiced. Yet its intellectual origins are easy to trace, through the scholars Long and So group "under the name modernism and Orientalism" (244), Christopher Bush, Robert Kern, Eric Hayot, Steven Yao, Zhaoming Qian, and some others they don't mention explicitly: Josephine Nock-Hee Park, Carrie Preston, Christopher Reed, and Haun Saussy.

But the privilege accorded to *modernism* as a grounds for *comparison* between Western and Japanese cultural forms is partly due to the influence of Earl Miner's 1958 book *The Japanese Tradition in British and American Literature*, which established the grounds for many comparative analyses of Western and Japanese literatures, and also sets many of my own intellectual coordinates.[87] Miner's broad work covers the totality of Western writing on Japan from Marco Polo to I. A. Richards, and is remarkably light-footed in drawing conclusions concerning "this consistent appeal of Japan" (267), arguing that the "exoticism" of Japan that draws so many Western artists and writers to the place might be accounted for on the grounds of the relatively *similarity* of Japan to Europe: "Japan, a civilization as highly refined as the West, is familiar and congenial in its modern conveniences, in addition to having the additional grace for a world-weary Westerner of new and idealized forms of behavior and art" (270). One of the *rhetorical* effects of Miner's taste for analogy ("as highly refined as the West") is the blurring of lines between the "British and American" categories that his title, at least, refuses to synthesize either geospatially (as "Western") or linguistically (as "English"). The name for this blurring is, eventually, clear: it is modernism. "The importance of Japan to English literature would comprise but a small chapter of our literary history had not two of the most important modern poets found answers to their poetic and critical needs in Japan." He means W. B. Yeats (an Anglo-Irish poet) and Ezra Pound (an American who spent formative years in Britain and Italy). These two authors, turning to Japan at the moment of Japanese triumph in the Russo-Japanese War, imported the haiku and Noh from Japan much as early modern poets had imported the sonnet from Italian and French (279).

Miner wrote in the context of a Cold War in which American comparative literary studies were themselves positioned as a signal of the capacious liberality of the Western mind: needless to say, modernist studies as it is currently convened would hardly assent to his relatively uncritical celebration of a Western appropriation of Asian cultural forms. In retrospect, his ideological biases provide useful evidence of the schizoid white defensiveness that has proven fully compatible with an embrace of Japanese form. That is to say: Miner's promulgation of the pluralizing effects of Japanese aesthetics on Western art attributes to white modernists a cosmopolitanism against which, in fact, Japan was supposed to inoculate—a misjudgment he makes because he, too, has looked to Japan to perform the same task. The exquisite force of Japanese art, as we have seen, confronted the narcissistic ego of the West with an Other Empire, but it did so, however, not as a preliminary move towards a broader cultural pluralism, but rather simply to install Japan *as the singular exception.* Miner himself is an exemplary case: when he argues that Japan was attractive to Europeans because of its similarity to Europe, the rider he puts on that argument makes clear its racist limits: "it is difficult, after all, to exoticize or idealize the forms of Ubangi culture—or of the Indian and Chinese hinterlands—beyond a certain point, since few Westerners can really imagine themselves happy for a moment in such societies" (270). The formal pleasures attendant on the contemplation of Japanese art stand in marked contrast to the displeasure of contemplating what was still, in Miner's 1958, the Belgian Congo.

A more general objection to Miner concerns the privileged position he accords modernist poetry, as the singular clarifying force of Japanese aesthetics, and the relatively muddiness he ascribes to the Victorian perception of Japan. This objection clearly has less moral significance than the first, but it is in its way no less consequential, and strikes me as a more avoidable error on Miner's part. His historiography is nuanced, and marked by a habitual tendency to exhibit moments of reference and influence, rather than to synthesize or explain them, but nonetheless it is clear that Yeats and Pound, whom he situates in the median position of "imitation and excited borrowing" between "early exoticism" and "mature absorption" (277), articulate the highest degree of Western aesthetic achievement with Japanese forms. The "Victorian sensibility," he thinks, absorbed Japan relatively easily, although "it did bring many uniquely Victorian problems to a significant and illuminating focus" (26–27). It is certainly true that the Japan discussed and theorized by Yeats and Pound strove to produce a more rigorous and coherent aesthetic principle than the less systematic treatments of Japanese form in Gilbert, Whistler, and Wilde. But modernism paid a price for that rigor: the hypothetical, partial, and fragile connections between individuals that Japanese aesthetics had enabled were traduced, and replaced by systems of thought that emphasized concreteness, irruption, decisiveness—that privileged ambivalence over ambiguity. That is to say: Pound and the modernists remasculinized the troping of Japan, attempting and necessarily failing to abolish the quaintness to which so-called "Japanese aesthetics" had already fallen prey.

Pound certainly stands as an outlier to the narrative of haiku as a generic force working to preserve a historical attachment to metrical form that had become quaint. But, since Miner places Yeats alongside him as the two progenitors of modernist Japanophilia, let me admit that I am not at all so sure about the latter. Yeats's troubled relationship to modernism, of course, has generated a good deal of critical attention.[88] Pound himself, for what it is worth, dismissed Yeats as a proto- or premodernist: "I've not a word against the glamour as it appears in Yeats' early poems, but we have had so many other pseudo-glamours and glamourlets and mists and fogs since the nineties that one is about ready for hard light."[89] Although Yeats's "glamourlets" were not, exactly, Orientalized, for Pound, they were certainly *awkward*; they are, in that sense, aligned with what W. H. Auden saw as Yeats's cringeworthiness, which certainly *did* include his Orientalism: "A. E. Housman's pessimistic stoicism seems to me nonsense too, but at least it is a kind of nonsense that can be believed by a gentleman—but [Yeats's] mediums, spells, the Mysterious Orient—*how* embarrassing."[90]

To read Yeats on Japan is constantly to face down such embarrassment. "Sato's gift, a changeless sword" appears as a concrete symbol in two of Yeats's major poems—"Meditations in a Time of Civil War" and "A Dialogue of Soul and Self"—and, in each it is charged with a powerful task: to "moralize / my days out of their aimlessness" and to "protect." Its primary quality is permanence—"a changeless sword"—whose repeat appearance in two Yeats poems marks it, by that very qualification, as a unique object within his oeuvre. (Bees and swans recur—but never the same bee.) How embarrassing to learn, then, that this auratic gift came into Yeats's possession in a hotel room in Portland, Oregon, where it was offered and accepted in the spirit of diplomatic exchange by one representative of a nation state (Funzo Sato) to another?[91] Another example: Yeats writes powerfully of Michio Ito, a Japanese dancer who "made possible" the *Four Plays for Dancers* that Yeats wrote in the Noh tradition, with a scopophilic delight in the mixture of strangeness and intimacy in their encounter: "There where no studied lighting, no stage-picture made an artificial world, he was able, as he rose from the floor, where he had been sitting crossed-legged or as he threw out an arm, to recede from us into some more powerful life. . . . One realized anew, at every separating strangeness, that the measure of all arts' greatness can be but in their intimacy" (153).[92] Essays have been written on the importance of Ito's practice for Yeats's own, and on the reciprocal importance of Yeatsian symbolism to the dramatic work Ito took back to Japan with him. How embarrassing, too—or, I should say, *I* was embarrassed—that, in the typescripts for the *Noble Plays* I examined at the National Library of Ireland, Yeats couldn't even remember the man's name.[93] He had left a gap in the typescript, and filled "Ito" in later by hand—literally couldn't tell the dancer from the dance.

Yeats's final reckoning with Japan appears in the form of a deeply embarrassing short poem entitled "Imitated from the Japanese" (1938):

A most astonishing thing
Seventy years have I lived;

(Hurrah for the flowers of Spring
For Spring is here again.)

Seventy years have I lived
No ragged beggar man,
Seventy years have I lived,
Seventy years man and boy,
And never have I danced for joy.[94]

"Imitated," according to editorial notes, from "a Japanese haiku poem in praise of spring," and yet the praise of spring, sardonically hemmed in by two parentheses and a mordant period, is hardly the poem's matter.[95] Yeats appears here not so much tired by his old age, as tired of his having already recounted it to greater effect elsewhere. In "Among School Children," (1927) eleven years earlier, he frailly self-presented "a sixty year old smiling public man"; in the prefatory poem to *Responsibilities* (1914), he was already desperate to plead with his ancestors their "pardon that for a barren passion's sake, / Although I have come close on forty-nine / I have no child."[96] Here the line "Seventy years have I lived" appears three times, not to recontextualize itself but to prolong its self-evident fatigue: the poem makes nothing happen, and it doesn't even happen until the last line. Like "Pardon Old Fathers" before it, and "The Circus Animals' Desertion" after, "Imitated from the Japanese" is both thematically and formally embarrassing: it describes one embarrassment (of being old and never having danced for joy) and performs another (as vagueness, vacuity, and repetition). Of that sequence, "Imitated from the Japanese" is the only explicitly Orientalist composition. The air of Japaneseness that looms over the poem, albeit above the line of a mimetic "imitation" that marks Yeats's composition as structurally an effect rather than a cause, desublimates form into theme, as though the whole poem could be excused on the grounds of its Oriental oddity. Not merely quaint, then, but strategically eccentric.

I have not adequately conveyed how overwhelmed I am by the image of a body too weak to carry a manuscript on which are written more words than those required to pump out the seventeen syllables of juice. But, at some point since I set down the sentences above, which still seem to do the work they need to do, my relation to the idea of daily practice has changed. Accordingly, what began as writing on the subject of (in the precise and brutal formulation of one of this chapter's early readers) *being too cool for the haiku,* must end by reflecting on what I have learned from it. That there is something one must do every day, but equally that the "day" in that phrase shifts with rhythms beat out in the pit, or offstage; that there is something in banality that cannot be coopted, but which nonetheless obdures and must be endured; that the touch that works, the hand on the knee or the glance, is not merely percussive but also corrosive; that the unfathomable condition of having something to prove will tend to outlast the act of proving, however virtuosically that act is carried out; that one will never know *how* the Other knows, even if one knows *what* it is that is known.

4

Loving John Ruskin

The Japanese never matured, however, and learned that modernization didn't really require maturity, anyway; whether the vertical control was internalized or remained external also didn't matter because there are neither elderly nor adult types; instead, the relativistic competition exhibited by other-oriented children provides the powerful driving force for capitalism.

—FÉLIX GUATTARI, AS RECOLLECTED BY ASADA AKIRA, CITED IN GENOSHKO[1]

Ruskin was one of the most gentle-hearted and peace-loving men that ever lived. Yet he believed in war with all the fervor of a worshipper of the strenuous life.

—INAZO NITOBE, *BUSHIDO: THE SOUL OF JAPAN* (1905)

I. The Styles of Dead People

It takes at least two, for one to feel abandoned. But how to describe that relational dimension of abandonment? After all, it is the defining characteristic of the relationship called "abandonment" that the parties involved do not agree that any relationship whatsoever exists. So to describe abandonment as a relation is already to accept the phantasmatic logic of the abandoned, which may be nothing more than delusion or *resentment*. Classical psychoanalysis offers a number of developmental narratives in which children learn to overcome, and internalize their overcoming of, a *fear* of abandonment: the boy in Freud's *Beyond the Pleasure Principle* who dramatizes parental abandonment (and reconciliation) as a technique for conquering his fear of it; the child in Melanie Klein's essay on "Schizoid Mechanisms" who integrates his ego by splitting the world into good and bad objects, externalizing the divided quality that had structured the child's life hitherto. The effect, Klein goes on to suggest, is both to *escalate* of the fear of abandonment, and to *normalize it* through the child's learning to inhabit "states akin to mourning."[2] The literary critic Eve Sedgwick's essay "Paranoid Reading and Reparative Reading" advances the Kleinian theory of developmental integration as a model for literary criticism, and seeks to integrate the experience of reading as one in which happy surprises, and not simply the instantiation of anticipated loss, are conceivable.[3] These narratives all align loss with anxiety and thereby futurity: though fear of loss derives from the infantile development of the subject, it subsides in adults as an attitude towards the future. Abandonment as it pertains to the experience of the exquisite belongs to the other side of this story; not the anxiety that one might be abandoned, nor the depressive realism that assures one that abandonment is survivable; but the real condition of conspicuous survival that obtains after the Other has turned away.

A prolific theorist, exponent, and survivor of the cultural relations between Japan and Victorian Britain in the twentieth century, the maestro of such exquisite abandonment is Mikimoto Ryuzo; his beloved object, who could not recognize the existence of the relation because he was long dead, the Victorian art critic and social theorist John Ruskin. Mikimoto wanted to transform Japanese society through the dissemination of Ruskin's work, whose work he assiduously collected, translated, and glossed throughout the 1920s and '30s. Mikimoto—the son of Mikimoto Kokichi, a successful Meiji businessman who developed a technique for artificially culturing pearls—founded both a library and a society in Tokyo to assist in the circulation of Ruskin's work, and in 1930 he launched a monthly journal, in which he published his own translations of critical essays about Ruskin by major British scholars, including the socialist anticolonial writer J. A. Hobson and the philosopher R. G. Collingwood, as well as many essays and memoirs and sketches of his own composition, in both English and Japanese. Yet while Mikimoto's careful work in establishing a Japanese readership for Ruskin flourished in Taisho Japan, a place characterized by broad cultural obsessions with labor, aesthetics, and crafts, what remains of that effort is confined to a rarely visited collection in a small Tokyo office, a fragile testimony to the intensity of feelings of an unusually enthusiastic reader of Victorian literature. Mikimoto was a *bricoleur*, experimenting with and recontextualizing Ruskin in the service of new personal and political demands, his library evidence of the capacity of literary writing to shape, and be shaped by, distant acts of reception. His generally insightful and often outrageous writing on Ruskin records the triumphs of a scholarly son of wealth and narrates a relationship with a father whose successful business was a source of a shame freighted with gendered meanings. He always braids his own familial dissent with broad political reflections, reflections on the discomforts of Japanese modernization, on the history of racism, and on the crimes of empires, striving to articulate an immanent critique of capitalism, the theoretical coordinates of which are to be found not only in Ruskinian socialism but also in Marxist commodity theory and in the syncretic anticapitalist writings of his mentor, Kawakami Hajime. What Mikimoto learned from Ruskin above all were the radical possibilities for a life in which emotional and political commitments could be considered part of a single, breathtakingly complex whole, which was reflected in what Caroline Levine calls "the close intertwining of Ruskin's iconoclastic aesthetics with his radical political principles."[4]

Scholarship dealing with Ruskin has often encountered the apparent lack of a singular theme underlying his extraordinarily large and diverse oeuvre, a unifying notion that might yoke together texts as diverse as *Modern Painters* and the *Fors Clavigera* letters. Questioning a long-held dissatisfaction with what early reviewers called his "crotchety contradictions and peevish paradoxes" and "if not insanity, sheer extravagance," the aim has been to recover Ruskin as a systematic thinker after all. Indeed, as we saw in the second chapter, Ruskin's most prized aesthetic—the Gothic—was notable for its formal regularity but lack of "finish." While Ruskin scholars have done much to reveal Ruskin's philosophical sophistication, in doing so they have needfully turned away from the frenzied energy that characterized Ruskin's literary style from his earliest texts through until his last, almost incoherent, letters.[5] Consider the following passage from "The Nature of Gothic," the excerpt of *The Stones of Venice* that was printed as a pamphlet in 1854 and that circulated among working men's clubs:

> And, on the other hand, go forth again to gaze upon the old cathedral front, where you have smiled so often at the fantastic ignorance of the old sculptors: examine once more those ugly goblins, and formless monsters, and stern statues, anatomiless and rigid; but do not mock at them, for they are signs of the life and liberty of every workman who struck the stone; a freedom of thought, and rank in scale of being, such as no laws, no charters, no charities can secure; but which it must be the first aim of all Europe at this day to regain for her children.[6]

Ranging freely between gothic fiction, instructional literature, and art criticism, Ruskin's prose models the liberty that he attributes to the free laborer and picks up most of the qualities he attributes to Gothic architecture: savageness, changefulness, naturalism, grotesqueness, rigidity, and redundancy. Even nineteenth-century critics of Ruskin were quick to note that much of his reputation derived from the intensity of his style rather than from his claims or readings, with one commentator comparing him to de Quincey, who, the commentator cheekily noted, "sought to obtain by prose effects commonly associated with poetry."[7] As the comparison implicitly suggests, the disruptive, aggressive force of Ruskin's prose was not merely purple but pushed against boundaries of acceptable discourse. Such a force is legible without relying on what Raymond Williams called the "almost wholly irresponsible biographical attention" that Ruskin has received, but the affective incoherence of Ruskin's prose is only amplified by his biography, beset as it was by sexual scandals and madness.[8] The work of freedom as Ruskin records verges itself on a kind of hysterical expressiveness, a stylistic practice whose effects are felt as emotions rather than internalized as doctrine.

To treat Ruskin as a dilettante is not necessarily to blunt the force of his social criticism but to relocate it. Ruskin himself understood that the value of a work of criticism did not depend on its engagement with existing sources or its conceptual completeness—indeed, in *The Political Economy of Art*, he explores ways in which such a dependence might itself befuddle a critical insight: "The statements of economical principle given in [this] text, though I know that most, if not all, of them are accepted by existing authorities on the science, are not supported by references, because I have never read any author on political economy, except Adam Smith, twenty years ago. Whenever I have taken up any modern book upon the subject, I have usually found it encumbered with inquiries into accidental or minor commercial results, . . . by the complication of which, it seemed to me, the authors themselves had been not unfrequently prevented from seeing to the root of the business."[9] To engage with the habitual vocabulary of a discipline, even with the intention of displacing that vocabulary or radically undoing the structures of its claims to legitimacy, is inevitably to reinforce many of the structuring assumptions of that discipline.

Mikimoto's engagement with Ruskin circumvented any and all such premises, to the disorienting extent that engaging with it one encounters a Ruskin breathtakingly remote from the ornery sage and repressed fuddy-duddy of critical stereotype. An uncritical reading of Ruskin makes itself known in spasmodic bursts of genre-subverting adoration: in, for example, the middle section of Mikimoto's essay "Ruskin's Views of Economic Art" when Mikimoto recognizes the illegitimacy and excessive emotion of his interest in Ruskin:

> I do not like exaggeration and overestimation. I am criticising Ruskin. I think Masashige Kusunoko was a great man. And I think Napoleon was a great man, too. I think Carlyle was a great man, and that Mr. Kosen Sakai is praise-worthy. I have once wept over Mr. Natsume's *Sore-Kara*, and [have been] deeply moved by Dr. Kawakami's Story of Poverty. Though criticising Ruskin, I feel tears stand in my eyes when I think of his love affairs.
>
> With such a sentiment I keep studying Ruskin. I sometimes wish I would rather be influenced by his personality than by his reasonings. A

> merchant's son should be a merchant. If I am gently engaged in accounting, I can do without Ruskin, and can go to the Kabukiza Theatre or a London comedy month.[10]

Transcribing this prose presents a set of problems, since the texts of his English works have evidently been typeset by a printer with limited experience of setting English writing, and there are infelicities of expression, which perhaps betray Mikimoto's own incomplete knowledge of the language. On the other hand, because there are no extant manuscripts, there is no possibility of resolving the question of who is the source of the apparently strange vocabulary choices. I have corrected obvious mistakes (such as the occasional spelling "Ruskiin") and have maintained British English spelling (such as "criticising"), but I have not corrected the formatting idiosyncrasies, such as the underlining of "Sore-Kara," but not "Story of Poverty." Note also here the unusual reference to Soseki as "Mr. Natsume," which was the novelist's family name rather than his pen name.

Nonetheless, Mikimoto's watery eyes peep through his scrambled prose, transmitters and receivers, formalizing an intense affection that flickers between homosocial, filial, and romantic nodes; the tone of wounded perseverance articulating both a dissent from the scripts of gender patrolled by capitalism, and a desire for greater intimacy with a thinker than the mere act of reading can provide. Casting himself as Dorian Gray and Ruskin as Lord Henry, Mikimoto comes to understand both the scope of and limits on his own experience of textual influence and treats the transcultural counterarchive as simultaneously momentous and incomplete. This jarring confessional moment intrudes into a text that has hitherto restricted itself to a descriptive précis of Ruskin's essay "On the Political Economy of Art" (1857) and returns both Mikimoto and his readers to a set of painful feelings. The poignancy of Ruskin's ill-fated love affairs urgently demands that the author veer off course, necessitating the still-greater confession that even Mikimoto's veneration of Ruskin is the result of a substantial failure to conform to the plot attached to his patronym.

Mikimoto's work thematizes the collector's painful consciousness of his distance from Ruskin—a distance with implications for body and soul. At the heart of "Ruskin's Views of Economic Art" is a desire for intimacy with Ruskin's "personality" rather than his "reasonings." What are the politics of a sympathetic reading that fails to achieve sympathy? Further, how are the sympathetic readings of professional critics interrupted or complicated by the hysterically affirmative readings of the dilettante, the dogmatist, the uncritical acolyte? These questions have begun to surface in our own moment, particularly in Carolyn Dinshaw's moving image of transhistorical reception, the "touch across time," the desire for "partial, affective connection" in the distant past that might ground alternative communities in the present.[11] But when Mikimoto remarks that he wishes to be influenced by Ruskin's personality, he also points to the necessary failure that structures all such attempts to find community. The two are separated by something other than the passage of time: a *history* that disqualified Mikimoto's love for Ruskin. Ruskin's styles—of living, loving, writing, and arguing—appear by Mikimoto's light as compensatory objects, or rather, compensatory channels through which to experience communion with a lost love, even in the face of incontestable abandonment. Style in this context reveals itself as the essential medium of *fandom,* especially the obsessive, nerdish species of fandom that revels most intensely in its object's quotidian effects—the effluvia whose very unremarkableness paradoxically amplifies the object's auratic power by broadcasting the explosive discovery that, after all, *he was just a regular guy*.

In the context of historical abandonment, the apparently minor historiographical energies of such fandom are transformed into practices of affirmative commitment with profoundly radical consequences. Let me populate that argument with two other examples of twentieth-century radicals whose fidelity to Victorian literature derived more from the affect and style of that literature than from any of its propositional content. In the introduction to *Sarvodaya* (1908), his adaptive translation of Ruskin's *Unto This Last,* M. K. Gandhi refers to his work as a "paraphrase": "What follows is not a translation of *Unto This Last* but a paraphrase, as a translation would not be particularly useful to the readers of *Indian Opinion*. Even the title has not been translated but paraphrased as *Sarvodaya* [the welfare of all], as that was what Ruskin aimed at in writing this book."[12] Gandhi's paraphrase invents a syncretic Ruskin who might serve the dual functions of exploiting the veneration of British sage writers in the colonial education system in order to disseminate dissent and of visibly reproving the hypocrisy of such a system that would insist on the applicability of a Ruskinian cultural project to the colonial situation while escalating violence at home and abroad and eliminating even the fragile provisions that midcentury liberalism had afforded the British state. But, no less importantly, the "paraphrase" indicates Gandhi's awareness that fidelity to Ruskin required creative reinterpretation. In his autobiography—whose title, "My Experiments with Truth," indicates its author's capacity for imaginative, nondogmatic criticism—Gandhi records reading *Unto This Last* as a moment of conversion rather than one of persuasion: "I could not get any sleep that night. I determined to change my life in accordance with the ideals of the book."[13]

Gandhi's concept of the paraphrase can be juxtaposed with the theory of "orthodoxy" with which Georg Lukács characterizes his relationship to Marx. Seeking to maintain a viable relationship to Marxism after the successful establishment of the All-Russian Congress of Soviets, Lukács emphasizes that the indispensable part of Marx's writing is his "method" and that the notion of orthodoxy "does not imply the uncritical acceptances of the results of Marx's investigations."[14] So, like Gandhi, Lukács seeks a methodology for reading Marx that is not dependent on any particular Marxist concept. His argument is formulated in fractious, combative prose, and his conclusions are complex and dialectical:

> Great disunity has prevailed even in the "socialist" camp as to what constitutes the essence of Marxism, and which theses it is "permissible" to criticize and even reject without forfeiting the right to the title of "Marxist." In consequence it came to be thought increasingly "unscientific" to make scholastic exegeses of old texts with a quasi-Biblical status, instead of fostering an "impartial" study of the "facts." These texts, it was argued, had long been "superseded" by modern criticism and they should no longer be regarded as the sole fount of truth.
>
> If the question were really to be formulated in terms of such a crude antithesis it would deserve at best a pitying smile. But in fact it is not (and never has been) quite so straightforward. Let us assume for the sake of argument that recent research had disproved once and for all every one of Marx's individual theses. Even if this were to be proved, every serious "orthodox" Marxist would still be able to accept all such modern findings without reservation and dismiss all of Marx's theses *in toto*—without having to renounce his orthodoxy for a single moment.[15]

The desire to strip Marxist orthodoxy of any indicative statement and replace it with a "dialectical method" whose most vital element is "the dialectical relation between subject and object in the historical process" cannot be taken at face value: Lukács did not imagine that this description alone would suffice for describing Marx's unique contribution.[16] The indisputably Marxist character of the passage derives partly from its electric, nervy style, swerving between scare-quote ventriloquism and withering bathos, in a rhetorical escalation no doubt designed to recall Marx's own prose style, which Benedetto Croce called "that note of violent indignation and bitter satire which is felt in every page of *Das Kapital*."[17] Yet in a text whose ostensible purpose is to recover Marxism from literalism, the imitation of Marx's style comports a special meaning, implying that true fidelity to the Marxist tradition is to be sought in the intensification of certain affects. In place of a body of knowledge, Lukács rewrites Marxism as a stylistic relation entailing both parrhesiastical frankness and a distinctive kind of masculine cruelty.

In the ideological sense, such affirmations are neither inherently radical nor conservative. Yet the examples of Mikimoto, Gandhi, and Lukács reflect more than a recumbent idiocy or fandom—they share a desire to theorize without theory, to create new meanings from old literary texts by maintaining contact with a historical subject rather than a text. Mikimoto identifies this proximity as "personality," but Gandhi's "paraphrase" and Lukács's "orthodoxy" speak to it as well, just with a different inflection—each represents a truer bearer of a text's potential than the text itself. From one angle, an overinvestment in style at the expense of content resembles stupidity—a cognitive function that, as Avital Ronell writes, "makes stronger claims to knowledge than rigorous intelligence would ever permit itself to make."[18] Yet these three contexts reveal, too, the ways in which affirmation is a particularly vital strategy for historical subjects excluded from the Enlightenment project of rationalism—non-Western intellectuals, the colonized, and workers, to name the categories each of these three authors examines. Mikimoto himself found pleasure in the very abjectness of his project, aware as he was that his fidelity to Ruskin entailed both risk and glee: "I do not care even if the socialists laugh me to scorn. And if there is any one who laughs at me, I think I will advise him to read G.F.G. Masterman" (2). But such reading is indissociable from the logic of the Other Empire. Mikimoto's response to Europe was a literal but redundant form of expropriation (a material operationalization of Noguchi's engagement with Western form) and, more powerfully, against the abandonment of historicism, the hystericism of the abandoned. The very quaintness of Mikimoto's desire, to express love and to be loved in the face of exorbitant historical abandonment, reconfigured and politicized the major/minor binary that constructed, and continues to maintain, the political question of the archive of Victorian literature. In the spirit of Mikimoto's radical quaintness, I will next explore the convergence of Marx and Ruskin in Japan, contemporary writers on related themes whose historical coincidence in the London of the 1860s neatly frames the problem of historical major/minorness. Marx is generally considered a major writer (a father of discourse!) to the extent to which he is excised from the context of Victorian Britain; Ruskin is a major writer only *within* that context, but rarely treated as major in the intellectual histories of Europe that govern the prehistory of, for example, "theory." Throughout Mikimoto's intellectual formation, and through his own engagements with style, might we begin to glimpse a *minor* Marx and a *minor* Ruskin?

II. Two Victorians

Perhaps not. Mikimoto's own descriptions of his citations from Ruskin were usually counterposed to those of the joyless, mechanistic readers of Marx. He had read at least *Capital* and *The Communist Manifesto* and disparaged Marx himself as a weak counterpart to Ruskin, a vulgar materialist who didn't de-

FIGURE 4.1. *Mikimoto Ryuzo, with a portrait of Kawakami Hajime,* undated.

serve his newfound popularity among Japanese anti-imperialists—the Japanese Communist Party (JCP) was formed in 1922, and remained a focus of public dissent, especially among intellectuals and academics, until many of its members were imprisoned on March 15, 1928. The insistence that Marx and Ruskin were comparable figures, each of whose merits was to be debated against the other, was hardly outside the mainstream of Japanese left thought in the period. Both were read widely and in tandem at Kyoto Imperial University under Kawakami Hajime, who had become one of the most prominent advocates for Marxist critique in Japan.[19] Kawakami's early socialist manifesto *Bimbo Monogatori* (*The Tale of Poverty*), published in 1916, drew heavily on both Marxist and non-Marxist socialisms, citing both Ruskin and William Morris, but in 1919, he began publishing the Marxist journal *Shakai Mondai Kenkyu* (*Studies on Social Questions*), as well as writing articles on Marx in a wider array of radical magazines. Under Kawakami's influence at Kyoto, a left student organization called the Labor-Student Society formed, whose members included Nosaka Sanzo, a founder of the JCP, and Sano Manabu, a leading Communist who in 1933 broke off from the Communist International in favor of the ideology of "Tenko"—a nationalist, pro-imperialist revolutionary theory. The radical context of Kyoto Imperial University is vital to understanding how revolutionary Ruskin seemed to Mikimoto, who frequently aligned him with other, more celebrated, revolutionaries: "Some socialists say that Ruskin is not sufficient. In some respects he may seem illogical. But there is an ideal course or order in things. The society which is idealized by humanitarian economy is a form of society which may bring happiness on mankind. Lenin is great. And Ruskin is great as well" (16).

The implicit comparison to Lenin drew on an essay called "Ruskin the Prophet" by a senior Liberal member of the British Parliament, the aforementioned Masterman, which was published in a collection of essays published by Ruskin's own press, George Allen and Unwin, to commemorate Ruskin's centenary. Prefiguring the old cliché (sometimes attributed to the Labour prime minister Harold Wilson) that the Labour Party owed "more to Methodism than to Marx," Masterman writes enthusiastically of the Russian Revolution as an extension of Ruskinian humanism: "I think when the story is told, and if this great experiment emerges from its present difficulties and succeeds, you will find that Lenin and his ideal community owe less to Karl Marx than to John Ruskin."[20] Wishful thinking, no doubt, but striking in demonstrating the surprising competition between Marx and Ruskin as originary moments for Communist radicalism. Nor was Masterman alone: the American Christian socialist W.D.P. Bliss had already published an anthology of Ruskin's work designed to claim him as the fount of global socialism, under the title *The Communism of John Ruskin* (1891), drawing on volume 7 of *Fors Clavigera*, in which Ruskin declares himself "a Communist of the old school—reddest also of the red."[21] The passage has remained less widely known than the similar formation in volume 10 of *Fors Clavigera*: "I am, and my father was before me, a violent Tory of the old school": whichever political position Ruskin preferred at a given moment, he certainly preferred it to be "of the old school."[22]

Although Mikimoto was aware of the tactical benefits of comparing Ruskin to the more celebrated Lenin and Marx, it is clear that the stronger benefit he derived from Ruskinian thought was its capacity to work on the individual soul: "Now that Marxian political economy is enlightening the populace with an extraordinary power, I have chosen Ruskin as a guide who enables me to settle down" (16). Yet Mikimoto's attempt to separate such a personal, reflective politics from a wider, rabble-rousing one was tested dramatically and repeatedly in his searchingly self-critical texts. The first of such challenges presented itself in the figure of Kawakami Hajime himself, whose reputation as a Marxist firebrand threatened to obscure his debt to Ruskin—which was, naturally enough, far greater than his debt to Lenin. To Mikimoto, Kawakami was emphatically a Ruskinian first and a Marxist second. Before the 1920s, Ruskin had been the subject of articles and monographs by a large number of literary critics and art historians in Japan, including Shimazaki Toson, who translated parts of *Modern Painters*, and the Natsume Soseki, who included a section on

Ruskinian aesthetics in his book *Theory of Literature*.[23] But Kawakami was the first professional economist in Japan to write extensively on Ruskin, and he had also written the preface to Kenji Ishida's translation of *Unto This Last* (1918). Mikimoto discussed his teacher at length in a lecture delivered in front of the International Women's Institute at Girton College, Cambridge, in 1929 called "Ruskin's Influence in Japan," calling his preface "the shortest . . . and most noteworthy" introduction to Ruskinian economics. In it, Kawakami also juxtaposes Ruskin and Marx, though he does so more systematically than Mikimoto. For Kawakami, according to Mikimoto, the critique of political economy had generated two compatible, but discrete, forms of discourse, which he called "socialistic economy," represented by Marx, and "humanistic economy," represented by Ruskin (42). Unacceptable though such a view would appear from the familiar perspectives of Western Marxism, Mikimoto held not only that a unification of romanticism and Marxism was possible but also that Kawakami had ensured that such a unification was uniquely possible in Japan: "In Japan Ruskin has been raised, though temporarily, by Dr. Kawakami to the same level as Marx's throne" (43). Even during his many travels abroad, Mikimoto was keen to emphasize the particular contribution of a Japanese critic to the ongoing project of reading Ruskin. In the same lecture he joked that "it may be an unexpected fact that the greatest Marxian teacher in Japan has once been so Ruskinian that he was called the Japanese Ruskin by his colleagues" (40).

The phrase "Japanese Ruskin" aptly communicates Mikimoto's feeling that being inspired by Ruskin was not just a matter of reasoning but also of personality. Indeed, in neither "Ruskin's Views of Economic Art" nor "The Influence of Ruskin in Japan" are the theoretical differences between Ruskin and Marx explored: the contest is simply one of reputation, and it resolves itself by the power of insistence.

> Was Ruskin an economist? He did not write any consistent book on political economy. So some insist that he ought to have been called a kind of economic reformer more justly than an economist. But I prefer to treat him as an economist. Some of the subjects which he has treated of in his *Unto This Last* (1862) and *Munera Pulveris* (1872) are quite different from those which were hitherto discussed by other economists, but in substance they teem with such pure theories as meet with the approval of modern economists. Though a student of little learning, I am so bold as to believe that Ruskin's worth lies not as an art critic, but as a social reformer—nay, as a Political economist. ("Ruskin's Views," 18)

In calibrating the proper designation for Ruskinian criticism, Mikimoto deploys the word "economist" as an instrument by which to detect intellectual legitimacy. He begins by dispatching consistency as a grounds for establishing the credentials of an economist, treating it as the hobgoblin of the "some" who see Ruskin as a reformer rather than a theorist. Then he goes further, claiming that neither *Unto This Last* nor *Munera Pulveris* would warrant attributing the title "economist" to their author—who, incidentally, begins the latter by declaring it to be "the first accurate analysis of the laws of Political Economy which has been published in England."[24] So if economics is neither a consistent theme throughout Ruskin's work nor a substantially elaborated field of his two most celebrated works of social criticism, what forms the basis of the designation "political economist"? Two factors: an appeal to the unusual *modernity* of Ruskin's thought—more on this shortly—and a simple assertion of boldness on the part of a "student of little learning." This latter strategy, which finds Mikimoto adopting a passive-aggressive tone of deference before asserting his expertise, recurs throughout his writing and is just as frequently addressed to (implicitly Marxist) socialists as to the political economists he reproves in "Ruskin's Views." These moments are painful to read, as the author comes to understand that he is traumatically remote from the groups to whom he most wants to speak—but, in isolation, doomed by a commitment over which he has lost control. Like Adorno's dilettante, Mikimoto feels himself caught between a utopian faith in the life of the mind and a failure to share a vocabulary with potential allies from whom he receives nothing but scorn. Even if the Mikimoto is, like the dilettante in Adorno's epigram "On Marcel Proust," "a secret envoy of the established powers," nevertheless it was Mikimoto who exposes the reality that, insofar as it is institutionalized, even radical thought relies on a narrative of professionalization.

From the earliest moments in the reception of *Modern Painters*, moreover, critics of Ruskin recognized that the quickest way to discredit him was to accuse him of dabbling. James Whistler, in his attacks on art criticism, for example, in which Ruskin joins Sidney Colvin and Harry Quilter among his *bêtes noires*, repeatedly insists that only artists were qualified to discuss the meaning or value of art. With his characteristic taste for hyperbole and wittily apocalyptic tone, Whistler, in the guise of "the Preacher," declares: "And now from their midst, the Dilettante stalks abroad. The amateur is loosed. The voice of the aesthete is heard in the land, and catastrophe is upon us."[25] Whistler's case is scientific: beauty is apparent in a painting or it is not, just as "two and two the mathematician would continue to make four, in spite of the whine of the amateur for three, or the cry of the critic for five."[26] Yet the hostility toward art criticism found in Whistler's attacks was substantially less widespread than the sense that Ruskin's turn from the art criticism of the 1850s to the social criticism he wrote from 1860 (when the first installation of *Unto This Last* was published) onward was a deep blunder, with the *Cornhill* magazine famously abandoning publication of *Unto This Last* after four weeks. In the fifty-third *Fors Clavigera* letter, Ruskin furiously and poignantly connects the power of his prose to the skepticism the readers of *Sesame and Lilies* expressed: "In the one volume of *Sesame and Liles*—nay, in the last forty pages of its central address to Englishwomen—everything is told that I know of vital truth, everything urged that I see to be needful of vital act;—but no creature answers me with any faith or deed. They read the words, and say they are pretty, and go on in their own ways."[27] Notice here the gendered polarization of style and substance, the former "pretty," the latter embodying "vital truth." The stylistic reading of Ruskin is here figured as a failure to perform, to make oneself heard.

In spite of Mikimoto's claims that "modern economists" had ratified Ruskin's theories, at other times he pitted Ruskin against modernity and implicitly against Marx. There was no doubt that to do so was unfashionable, although it was an unfashionableness capable of being enjoyed: "Now that Marx is so prevalent, it may seem behind the times to discuss and admire Ruskin" ("Ruskin's Views,"19). Here again, the insistence on Ruskin's supreme virtue is undergirded by neither critical exegesis nor interpretation but by an act of insistence whose tone is elegiac and sentimental.

> Before discussing Marx, we shall find it to be of some service to hold the thought of Ruskin, and that it provides a foundation most necessary to criticise Marx. As a Japanese, and as an inhabitant of that island of Japan which has been left behind in this material civilization, I wish that there may appear in present Japan only one great Ruskin rather than many small Marxes. There are many millionaires in Japan who contribute a million *yen* towards establishing a public cemetery in Tokyo. But, in present Japan, a Ruskin would be able to solve the problem. ("Ruskin's Views," 19)

The architectural metaphor arranges Marx and Ruskin vertically, with the latter not only providing the interpretative solution to problems posed by the former but also offering a deeper critique of social inequity. In a sense, however, the critical distinction here resembles Michael Löwy's influential argument concerning the difference between a romantic anticapitalism focused on reinstituting premodern forms of belonging and a Marxist critique of modern civilization motivated by the enthusiastic pursuit of new and more modern social organizations. Ruskin is positioned as the solution to the problems of a Japan that Mikimoto holds to be "left behind in this material civilization," and Marx the modernizer whose materialism has become indistinguishable from capitalism's own incursions into Japanese culture. Following his instinct to defend rather than analyze Ruskin's contribution to the critique of political economy, Mikimoto began to understand capitalism as a metaphysical force, a power whose effects were not limited to poverty and inequality but could also be said to include the problem of death itself—or, at least, the problem of processing mass death in a modern city. To such a problem, orthodox Marxism could only respond like a millionaire writing a check, by addressing material problems in the hope that spiritual solutions would follow. The passage's startling comparison—"one great Ruskin rather than many small Marxes"—indicates that its author is indicting not Marx the theorist but the collectivity that spoke for him. Mikimoto's politics reappears as a radical individualism, encompassing theological and even messianic language. Yet the necessity of reading both Ruskin and Marx was a strikingly personal matter for Mikimoto, embodied above all in Kawakami, to whom he dedicated his published works after the latter's arrest and imprisonment. In Mikimoto's private study, moreover, on the wall adjoining the dresser constructed especially to house his first *Complete Works*, hung a portrait of his mentor; Kawakami was the other constant presence in Mikimoto's private study.

III. My Own Private Exposition

Throughout his texts, Mikimoto contrasts the overcrowded cemeteries and joyless urban grind of modern Tokyo with both the gentle melancholia of London—his "lonely second native place" ("Ruskin's Views," 1)—and the Gothic landscapes of Ruskin's Lake District. The first issue of Mikimoto's *Journal of the Tokyo Ruskin Society* was published in January 1931, a year after the Tokyo Ruskin Society had been formed, and contained a narrative of Mikimoto's tours of England, written in English and directed not at the journal's Japanese readership but at the British figures credited with helping Mikimoto build his collection.

MY OWN PRIVATE EXPOSITION
OF JOHN RUSKIN

I met with Mr. Arthur Severn, R. A. in London and Brantwood, Coniston in 1920, 1923, 1925, 1927, 1929.

I had the "Ruskin tea" with Miss F. Banks of High St., Kensington, visited, sought Maggs Bros., Henry Southeran, and other noted places for Ruskin Relics.

I haunted Ruskin Relics in Coniston and the Lake-district with Mr. J. H. Stephenson, the painter of S.R.A. who is the intimate pupil or the friend of Ruskin.

I am very grateful and thankful to these 3 of them for my own collections of Ruskin.

R. Mikimoto
Jan. 20th, 1931

The document is signed "R. Mikimoto" and introduces the journal, although the curator's description of his note as a "private exposition" is slightly oxymoronic, the conflicting energies of which reflect its author's ambivalence about the privacy and publicity of his collection. "Haunted" should probably read "hunted," but in its present form it neatly fleshes out the Gothic trope, reversing the visitor's interest in the "relics" of Coniston, the sacral objects that nourish the ghostly persistence of the great man, so that it is Mikimoto himself that is haunting England. The reference to J. H. Stephenson as an "intimate pupil or the friend" of Ruskin likewise plays with the reader's expectation, here aligning intimacy with pedagogy rather than friendship. Under this chronology, which also functions as a dedication of the collection to Severn, Banks, and Stephenson, Mikimoto lists the items in his collection. The list contains two manuscripts of Ruskin's—*Munera Pulveris,* which is still in the library's collection, and "On Usury," which is now at the University of Lancaster—but the plurality of the "relics" are related to Ruskin only at a remove.

Much of the desire for proximity to "relics"—his personal effects, manuscripts, and other items imprinted with Ruskin's personality—was deflected by Mikimoto onto the childless Ruskin's nearest surviving relative, his distant cousin Arthur Severn, who had been living at Brantwood since before Ruskin's death in 1900 and had maintained it as a heritage site in the intervening years.[28] The Severn family had come to live at Brantwood, Ruskin's Coniston home, in the late 1870s and was already involved in mythologizing Ruskin nationally in Britain. Arthur, an academician, prepared lithographs and sketches of Ruskin's home for R. G. Collingwood's important double-decker biography of Ruskin, the first volume of which was published in 1893, whose dedicatee was Joan Agnew, Ruskin's niece and Severn's wife. Among the three items in the list headed "[Ruskin's] birth and his childhood" is "collection of sea plants and cuttings and Etc. by Arthur Severn," with Severn's childhood serving as a stand-in for his uncle's. A couple of items listed are described only vaguely: "Other important things of Ruskin at his age of 9 presented to R. Mikimoto by Prof. Faunthorpe the president of [the] London Ruskin Society, and by Arthur Severn Esq." and "the important writings of his love episodes and his married life" ("My Private Exposition," 65). Love and childhood, themes to which Mikimoto returns in his writing, are the notable grey areas in the archive. Mikimoto's trips to Britain were all coordinated with Severn, who formed a relatively unbroken link between the dead and the living. Among the front matter of the *Catalogue of the Tokyo Ruskin Library* is a photograph of a young Mikimoto and an elderly Severn, taken in the last of Ruskin's three bedrooms at Brantwood—today it is called "the death room" because Ruskin died on the bed on which Mikimoto is sitting.[29]

FIGURE 4.2. *Mikimoto and Arthur Severn in the "death room,"* undated. Mikimoto's hands are behind his back, either resting or propping him up on the site of Ruskin's death. The space in the middle of the photograph is occupied by a kind of absence; perhaps a shadow or an imprint. What kind of ghost could separate these two men?

The five trips Mikimoto made in the 1920s yielded the large majority of his collection; some texts were procured by mail order, but since the original library was closed, and the records with it, the provenance of many of the texts is unclear. One at least (a New York printing of *The Crown of Wild Olives*) was bought at Maruzen, the largest bookstore in Tokyo. Many of the texts are inscribed to this Faunthorpe, a teacher of classics from London who had been charged by Ruskin with the interminable task of providing a workable index to all of the *Fors Clavigera* letters. Faunthorpe had produced a five-hundred-page list of entries published in running editions by Ruskin's own publisher, George Allen, up until 1887, with topics related to England alone running for over fifty pages, including the following entry: "what Americans have and have not learned from, *ib*; flesh-eating, 42, 130, unsentimental, 42, 131, notion of civilizing China, 42, 135." It also lists: "JAPANESE, we are afraid of, January 1st, 1871, 1, 4; screens, 26, 18; 48, 267; inlaid work, gift by Mr. Willett to S. George's Museum, 64, 125; horticulture 66, 183."[30] The index reproduces the

FIGURE 4.3. *Mikimoto and Stanley Unwin*, undated. The observation can hardly be avoided that Stanley Unwin, settling into his armchair while serenely closing his eyes behind round spectacles, calls to mind the father of psychoanalysis himself. Yet if Unwin is an analyst in this image, he is ours, rather than Mikimoto's – the guest looks happier here than in other photographs, cheerfully making eyes at the camera and matching Unwin's serenity with a frank enthusiasm.

haptic structure of *Fors Clavigera* in an abbreviated form, stripped of all syntagm—only the main topics are in alphabetical order; the subjects themselves are neither alphabetically nor chronologically arranged. Mikimoto's mania for Ruskin thus found a kin in another eccentric practice of collation.

By the end of the 1920s, the collection was complete and Mikimoto set about writing the commentaries, initially as occasional essays for a lecture at Girton College, Cambridge, and eventually in the *Journal of the Tokyo Ruskin Society*. In the late 1920s, a teashop modeled on Ruskin's Drury Lane café was opened in Ginza, and a few blocks away, in 1934, the Ruskin Library of Tokyo opened at last. It is in the context of the library's initial success that Mikimoto began to reflect on his own complicity, and that of his family, in the social structures he had sought out Ruskin to ameliorate. A particular source of concern—and malice—is his father's pearl farm, the very model of a Meiji-era business:

> Moralists and educationalists may negatively advise us not to be extravagant. But so long as there exists the merit of my father who has been invested with a decoration for producing pearls with the help of five hundred employees, we cannot extirpate the bacteria of poverty, which are the social disease. ("Ruskin's Views," 14–15)

Almost as startling as his appeals to the reader's sympathy or his intense sentimentalism, Mikimoto's aggressive, sullen attack on his father again disrupts the fragile tonal equanimity of the essay. The text wears its symptoms on its surface, interweaving political and personal feelings. Accordingly, Mikimoto Kokichi is figured as both a barrier to progress and a partisan of a corrupt system, one that is to be eradicated in the struggle to overcome the "social disease" of poverty. This is a struggle inflected by the language of eugenics—the passage is motivated by a desire to "extirpate." Mikimoto goes on to cite *Time and Tide,* in which Ruskin had differentiated between good and bad forms of luxury by stipulating that while "you may have Paul Veronese to paint your ceiling, if you like, . . . you must not employ a hundred divers to find beads to stitch over your sleeve."[31] In Mikimoto's paraphrase, though, the attack on his father's trade is spelled out more clearly, as he changes "a hundred divers to find beads to stitch over your sleeve" to "a hundred divers to seek for pearls" ("Ruskin's Views," 15).

The passage places the affective life of family at the heart of the struggle for social justice, which is in turn reconfigured as a generational clash over the life of the nation. The complex of associations—justice, nation, family—resonates within the broader literary climate of Japanese modernity. The generational character of revolutionary struggle, which turns on the figure of the young scholarly man, is one of the most frequently recurring thematic structures within the novels of Natsume Soseki, the greatest of the late-Meiji generation of Japanese novelists. In "Ruskin's Views of Economic Art," Mikimoto acknowledges his appreciation of Soseki, especially his 1909 novel *Sore-Kara* (*And Then*).[32] In that novel, as throughout his comparatively brief but extraordinarily productive career—he published twenty novels over a career that spanned only eleven years, 1905–16—Soseki investigates both the opportunities afforded to and limitations imposed on the scholarly scion of wealth. In *Sore-Kara,* an aesthetically sensitized and cosmopolitan young man named Daisuke struggles with his lack of productivity in the capitalist empire and rues, over two hundred pages, his reliance on his wealthy but barbaric father and the feelings of shame and deracination such a reliance generates. His imaginings of the future, as the novel's title suggests, are always stuttering and incomplete but, for all that, utopian and optimistic. Like Daisuke, Mikimoto does not treat his displacement by the enthusiastic libertarianism of the Taisho era as itself evidence of greater investment in the nationalist project of Japanese modernization: "My father was born and brought up in the ago of individualistic economy. The rising generation should make it their mission to fix their eyes upon the world of socialistic economy. . . . To be faithful to one's country is not merely to fight bravely in battle and defeat one's enemy" ("Ruskin's Views," 16).

This important assertion—that Ruskinian moralism itself might be coopted to serve the Japanese imperial mission—is posed as a formal problem in Soseki's second novel, *Kofu* (*The Miner*), published in 1908. *The Miner* has often been dismissed as a great novelist's juvenile experiment in metafiction—it ends by declaring of its narrative that "every bit of it is true, which you can tell from the fact that this book never did turn into a novel."[33] But its failure to resolve a *Bildung* plot might also be taken to designate a wider failure for which Soseki could hardly be held responsible: the difficulty of imagining futures for individual subjects outside the structure of the modern nation. In the story, a lonely, unnamed intellectual young man, who has violated some unknown taboo involving a fiancée, leaves Tokyo by foot and finds himself outside the city. Oscillating between indolent passivity and a desire to escape the strenuous expectations imposed on him by his family, he is recruited by an unscrupulous wandering gang master as manual labor in a local mine. He wanders around the mine as various laborers try to prove to him that the work is too menial for somebody of his particular skill—an idea he repeatedly repudiates, so full is he of self-disgust at his never-revealed transgression. He accepts every instruction and follows every rule until, deep in the mine, he encounters one of very few named characters—an older miner named Yasu. Yasu reveals that he too was once a student in circumstances very like the narrator's and that he stayed in the mine for similar reasons, with the result that he has become the degenerate that others had always thought him to be:

> It's a terrible thing to cause the degeneracy of an individual human being. Just killing him would be less of a crime. The degenerate goes on to cause harm, to hurt others. I know what I'm talking about because that's just what I have done. It's the only thing I *can* do—now. And all the screaming and crying in the world isn't going to change that. Which is why you have to get out of here fast. For the others. It's not just you who'll suffer if you become degenerate . . . Tell me, are your parents living?[34]

The consequence of this degeneration—of failing to live up the intellectual capacity that the young man has within him—is the impoverishment of the empire. Yasu's next question—"And you're a Japanese, aren't you?"—leads to the following disquisition: "If you're a Japanese, you should take a profession that will benefit Japan. For a man of learning to become a miner is a great loss to the nation. That's why you should get out now. If you're from Tokyo, go back to Tokyo. And do something decent—something that's right for you and good for the country."[35] Even in the place where the narrator had most hoped to avoid pegging his own fortunes to the national will, such a moral imperative is inescapable. Most post-1945 readings of *The Miner* have agreed that this late advice is not meant to be taken literally, that Soseki's tone is satirical—and indeed the narrator himself is suspicious of the staginess of Yasu's appearance: "For me to meet Yasu at a time like this was something right out of a novel."[36] But Soseki's *Theory of Literature* reveals that satirizing the claims of the nation is easier than doing without them and that despite a desire to retain a writerly conscience independent of the state, "I must face without shrinking whatever measure of unhappiness may prove necessary when it comes to upholding the honors and privileges due a sovereign subject of Japan."[37]

It remains unknown whether, after the collection was stowed in 1937, Mikimoto had given up on the idea of having a Ruskin library altogether or whether other circumstances prohibited him from reopening the library or teashop in a different location after the war. The precise date of the removal is not established either, but it certainly occurred later than May 1937, because in that year the library printed a *History of the Ruskin Library*, which makes no mention of its closing. This book was written by Uemura Ryuzo, a contributor to the *Journal of the Tokyo Ruskin Society*, and in the midst of a scrapbook of various photographs and images from the collection's history, it outlines in Japanese, as Mikimoto had already done in English, the history of Ruskin's reception in Japan and situates the library's own history within wider narratives of Japanese anticapitalism and Victoriana. A commentary on Mikimoto's counterarchival practice, the *History of the Ruskin Library* adopts many of Mikimoto's habits in its assembly of material and bears textual traces of Mikimoto's work: a menu from the teashop, photographs of the staff of both the teashop and the library, and a group photograph of the Ruskin Tennis Club in Tokyo, taken in April 1937. It reprints a facsimile of R. G. Collingwood's family tree, which shows the relation of Ruskin to Arthur Severn and Joan Ruskin Agnew, and photographs of the various items Mikimoto had had made to adorn the library: his *meeshi*, which bore the slogan "A JOY FOR EVER" underneath a Beardsley-style image of roses (for Rose La Touche, perhaps), for instance, and the welsh dresser he had had specially constructed in order to perfectly suit the dimensions of the *Complete Works*. One encounters on each page both the fragility of transhistorical intimacy and the possibility of its archival persistence in the recurrence of the slogan, attributed to Ruskin, "a thing of beauty is a joy for ever."

Ruskin adapted the line from Keats's *Endymion* as a name for the 1868 edition of *The Political Economy of Art*—adding the cruel rejoinder "and its place in the market." The title evokes the familiar distinction between art and commerce that aestheticism's practitioners habitually made (in however bad faith). The distinction here appeared to favor the commercial, and indeed Ruskin was hardly an optimist when it came to the transformative power of art. In fact, as his critique of the 1857 Great Britain Exhibition in Manchester—the largest collection of art ever amassed anywhere in the world—stresses the problems of accessing art just as much as the benefits of doing so.

> [The] fury of the sight of new things, with which we are now infected and afflicted, though partly the result of everything made a matter of trade, is yet more the consequence of our thirst for dramatic instead of classic work. For when we are interested in the beauty of a thing, the oftener we can see it the better; but when we are interested only by the story of a thing, we get tired of hearing the same tale told over and over again, and stopping always at the same point—we want a new story presently, a new and better one—and the picture of the day, and novel of the day, become as ephemeral as the coiffure or the bonnet of the day. Now this spirit is wholly adverse to the existence of any lovely art. If you mean to throw it aside to-morrow, you can never have it today. If any one had really understood the motto from Keats, which was blazoned at the extremity of the first Manchester exhibition building, they would have known that it was the bitterest satire they could have written there, against that building itself and all its meanings—"A thing of beauty is a joy for ever." It is not a joy for three days, limited by date of return ticket.[38]

The local reference is to the special edition train tickets that train companies offered to bring people from across Britain to Manchester. But what is more striking is Ruskin's treatment of the Keats line, which stems from his division of objects of aesthetic appreciation into "the thing" and "the story of the thing"—a division that perhaps owes some genealogical debt to the Kantian aesthetics in which apprehension of beauty depends on the free play of cognitive forms, from which it follows that a particular experience of beauty cannot be strictly described, except by reference to the general form. But, unlike Kant's, Ruskin's concerns are deeply bound up with questions of public policy: how can access to beautiful things be as wide as possible, given the necessary commercialization of art that accompanies increased access? Ruskin's view is not, strictly, antiegalitarian—he would prefer beauty to be available to all. But it is structured according to a familiar double bind: to encounter art is to achieve a lifelong pleasure, but the mediating structures that allow for such encounters to occur—the train, the story, the exhibition—nullify such pleasure before it is achieved. Only a set of serial encounters with the thing itself is any guarantee that beauty will evade mere narration and endure in a new future.

The lecture gives voice to some of Ruskin's many doubts concerning art's ability to morally improve those who consume it—but it was delivered in a context that may be obscured if it is simply related to the Great Britain Exhibition. In one sense, Ruskin's anxiety over art's capacity to improve people and peoples is nothing new: it is, indeed, a fundamental premise of the exquisite logic whose historical elaboration I have been tracing back to Kant. But for Ruskin, whose interest in the public appreciation of art was shaped by national and racial concerns, doubt over the ameliorative power of art was grounded in the epochal violence of the imperial enterprise. As is well known, Ruskin spent the latter half of 1866 working on behalf of the Eyre Defense Committee, established by Thomas Carlyle to provide funds for a legal defense of the governor of Jamaica who had ordered the judicial murder of hundreds of Jamaicans in the wake of the Morant Bay Rebellion. What is less known and more important for understanding Ruskin's aesthetics is that his response to the Sepoy Rebellion of 1857 was even more uncompromising and troubled. In a lecture delivered at the Kensington Museum in January of 1858, Ruskin explained that the rebellion had disproved the notion that a race's capacity for artistic appreciation, such as he accorded the Indians, could be morally improving:

> Since the race of man began its course on this earth, nothing has ever been done by it so significative of all bestial, and lower than bestial degradation, as the acts [of] the Indian race in the year that has just passed by. Cruelty as fierce may indeed have been wreaked, and brutality as abominable been practiced before, but never under like circumstances; rage of prolonged war, and resentment of prolonged oppression, have made men as cruel before now; and gradual decline into barbarism, where no examples of decency or civilization existed around them, has sunk, before now, isolated populations to the lowest level of possible humanity. But cruelty stretched to its fiercest against the gentle and unoffending, and corruption festered to its loathsomest in the midst of the witnessing presence of a disciplined civilization,—these we could not have known to be within the practicable compass of human guilt, but for the acts of the Indian mutineer. And, as thus, on the one hand, you have an extreme energy of baseness displayed by these lovers of art.[39]

The absolute mutual indifference of art and morality that would become, from Ruskin through to Wilde, the cornerstone of aestheticism's politics is here represented as a historical rather than metaphysical truth—one resulting from the sheer incommensurability of anticolonial violence with the concept of "civilization" that hinges aesthetics and policy.

Critics as different as Paul Gilroy, Ian Baucom, and Raymond Williams have argued that Ruskin's version of aestheticism provided a cultural context for British imperial ambitions, reconfiguring the cultural heritage of the race as an implicit justification for the civilizing mission.[40] But while Ruskin's pieces on the Sepoy Rebellion and his personal participation in the Morant Bay scandal reveal him to be an enthusiastic imperialist, each configures the relationship between aesthetics and imperialism quite differently from that generally assumed. Both insist on the essential incompatibility of aesthetic and imperial modes of civilization. The exhibition's sheer ambition and array fades quickly into trivial vulgarity, proving nothing more than that the state is not a fit provider of art. And the escalation of imperial violence in India is defended precisely on the basis that the aesthetic nature of the Indian race had only precipitated the uprising. Treating aesthetic pleasure as both an object to be desired and an insurgent force to be resisted, Ruskin reveals the unresolved ambivalence of Victorian aesthetics. Such an ambivalence might also account for Ruskin's surprising lack of interest in Japanese art. Other than generalizations about Asian cultures and a briskly generous response to a book of woodblock prints he had been given by William Michael Rossetti—"the sea and clouds are delicious, the mountains very good"—I have not been able to find anything he wrote about specifically Japanese art anywhere.[41] In a lecture delivered in 1906, the art dealer and Japan-enthusiast Marcus Huish offered an anecdotal explanation for Ruskin's lack of interest, recounting a conversation with a friend who was asked to stop sending Ruskin Japanese art books, "as they disturbed him, and it was too late for him to enter into those matters."[42]

Disturbance and belatedness: two aestheticized affects that connect Ruskin to Mikimoto through the mysticism of the archive. One of Mikimoto's names for such a connection was "love": "In the case of Ruskin, morality was love. Apart from love, there was neither beauty nor virtue. Beauty was virtue, and virtue was love" ("What Is Ruskin in Japan?," 57). His most systematic treatment of the subject occurs in a short piece written in English but published inside the Japanese-language *History of the Tokyo Ruskin Library* titled, "On Ruskin's Loves: In Loving Memory of Rosie." Unlike his other Anglophone texts, "On Ruskin's Loves" seems less designed to attract an English-speaking readership than to avoid a Japanese-speaking one, so much more candid and personal is it than the rest. It largely comprises a schematic account of Ruskin's doomed love affair with Rose La Touche, the young girl with whom he was scandalously infatuated. But Mikimoto moves between third-person narration, first-person confession, and interior monologues in the person of Ruskin with disorienting verve, seeming cheerier than usual and returning to the theme of dancing with optimism tinged with melancholy: "Last autumn, I felt sadness in gladness, with my young tennis-mates, finding men and women dancing, lonely at the Florida dance hall, Tameike, Akasaka. A lady had a dance with me cheerfully as if she had been the camellia of early spring; and another girl seemed to be a fading cosmos. But I, as a disciple of Ruskin, happily could play [and] dance in tunes from [the] Moulin Rouge" (2). Mikimoto's dancing recalls for him the discussions he had with the gravedigger at Coniston during his seven trips to Ruskin's grave, in which the gravedigger (echoing Miss Coward of Brantwood) often referred to Ruskin's joy at the English waltz and distaste at the Scotch trot. Mikimoto recognizes that it may seem odd to imagine the old sage dancing but concludes that "by regarding any ancient sage too morally, sometimes we young generation would have bad influences from him. Therefore I am afraid of making [my account of] Ruskin [an] extraordinarily poeticalized one. But I cannot help believing him one who essentially appreciated the dance and was a solitary philosopher" (5).

Mikimoto's redemptive "poeticalization" of Ruskin through the dance worked to find an afterlife to a "marriage [that] was too distressful a tragedy to be mentioned and of which we cannot find anything about his opinions in the 'Praeteritia' " (7). And the poeticalization of Ruskin comes at a moment in the text where Mikimoto himself feels complexly drawn to Ruskin's tragic love of Rosie and also repelled enough to feel old: "Readers, I thank you for reading this poor lecture in the waste of the precious sheets of this book. It is just five in the morning. Now I am in my forties and father of my two children. And I am a dry man, unable to love another woman. [But even] to such a man as I am, the portrait of Rosie drawn by Ruskin is enough to make him tearful" (9). Even Ruskin's celibacy, which Mikimoto knows all too well was enough for him to have been treated with contempt, is a sign of Ruskin's virtue and of his lovability: "If a man . . . abstain from conjugal relations for a long time, he may be a hero who has been able to perform one of the highest deeds in humanity. I am in wonder on this subject as a disciple of Ruskin, for his does not enter into the physiological laws. But I believe in the destiny of love through Ruskin's experiences. One sometimes may find a profound love in the conditions of one's lasciviousness, but one must be careful lest such things shall fall into ugliness and deadness" (10). It is finally in celibacy that Mikimoto finds an apt figuration for his ideal relationship with Ruskin—a connection of intimate friendship and discipleship. The final name for a transtemporal, transcultural relationship that had hitherto lacked one, celibacy affords Mikimoto a model of aesthetic sociality capable of sustaining, however briefly, the fragments of affect that had comprised his own habitual practice of fidelity.

In *An Archive of Feelings*, Ann Cvetkovich describes queer counterarchives—by which she means, in general, repositories of ephemera connected to gay and lesbian histories of oppression in North America—as social externalizations of the psyche's need to process trauma, "the desire to collect objects not just to protect against death but in order to create practices of mourning."[43] Such archives pose an implicit challenge to positivist historiography because "they are composed of material practices that challenge traditional conceptions of history and understand the quest for history as a psychic need, rather than a science."[44] The needs that one finds in the Ruskin Library of Tokyo—for beauty; for Ruskin; for a life plot outside of family expectations; perhaps, casually, for some kind of revolution—are hardly submerged; they comprise his archive as such. Like the affective labor of the queer archives Cvetkovich describes, which have more broadly become a focus of contemporary queer theory, Mikimoto's collection paradoxically preserves not just the flotsam of an intimate relationship but the desire that necessitated searching for such materials in the first place. The queerness of the archive, if it reasonable to refer to such a thing, derives not from the sexuality or identity of either its superintendent or its subject, but exists somewhere in the gap between them. The parts of the archive most central to its functioning are also those furthest from it: personality, intimacy, reciprocity. Even the small number of manuscripts of minor works that Mikimoto assiduously amassed point out all the more clearly the huge number of major manuscripts he didn't find or couldn't afford. Despite his successes, Mikimoto's affirmation remains asymptotic and repetitive: failing to convene a substantial *proportion* of Ruskin's manuscripts or rare editions under the same roof, he went for *quantity*, buying the same books over and again. Sixteen years dedicated largely to his Ruskin collection yielded seven sets of the *Complete Works* but manuscripts of only *Munera Pulveris* and "On Usury," along with a few letters purchased from Faunthorpe. The tone of J. B. Bullen's review of the collection (the only notice the library's reopening received in the British academic press) may have been patronizing, but his claim is substantively correct: "They are all rather impersonal, public pieces, . . . not major contributions to our knowledge of Ruskin and his ideas."[45] On the contrary, it is that exquisite *im*personality of the work that ensures its value in the currency of love.

5

The Sword and the Chrysanthemum

The more acute stages of the mimetic process are more obviously compulsive and self-destructive than the earlier ones. But they are only the full development of what was present as a germ before. That is why these stages are, among other things, caricaturally mimetic. Everything obscure and implicit until then becomes transparent and explicit. Normal people, so-called, must resort to the "madness" label in order not to perceive the continuity between this caricature and their own mimetic desire. In front of Hamlet's outburst inside the grave, a well-informed psychiatrist must diagnose the type of symptom that belongs to "histrionic schizophrenia," or some such disease. He cannot see anything there but pure pathology, completely divorced from all rational behavior, including his own, which he does not perceive as mimetic. The writers of genius never share that illusion. If schizophrenia often imitates "with a vengeance," if it turns to spectacular "histrionics," the reasons may be not that the patient is particularly eager to imitate, or gifted for imitation, but that he is less gifted for the unconscious imitation that is being silently pursued at all times among the normal people all around him.

—RENÉ GIRARD, *A THEATER OF ENVY* (1991)[1]

I felt as though I had been knocked flat. The person I had thought a *he* was a *she*. If this beautiful knight was a woman and not a man, what was there left? (Even today I feel a repugnance, deep rooted and hard to explain, toward women in male attire.) This was the first "revenge by reality" that I had met in life, and it seemed a cruel one, particularly upon the sweet fantasies I had cherished concerning *his* death. From that day on I turned my back on that picture book. I would never so much as take it in my hands again. Years later I was to discover a glorification of the death of a beautiful knight in a verse by Oscar Wilde:

Fair is the knight who lieth slain
Amid the rush and reed

—YUKIO MISHIMA, *CONFESSIONS OF A MASK* (1949)

I. No Cuts!

In 1997, the animator Miyazaki Hayao, buckling in advance at demands for edits to *Princess Mononoke* from the film's American distributor, Miramax, sent in the mail, c/o Harvey Weinstein, a katana, captioned in the characteristically abrupt English of the movie samurai: "no cuts!"[2] What is the utility of an anecdote that so perfectly—perhaps *too* perfectly—associates the samurai sword with the exquisite logic of aesthetic autonomy? First, obviously, that the anecdote (which may be apocryphal) also demonstrates the limits of that association, in at least a few ways: (i) the practical sense that any threat of violence implied by the sword was surely offset by the sense that Miyazaki had disarmed himself before Weinstein; (ii) the campy inefficacy of the threat in a more general sense; (iii) the fact that the gesture, if it happened, drew together a few senses of "cut" generally thought quite distinct from each other: an abrasive cut (as with a sword), an internal cut (for example an excision), and a delimiting cut (the removal of an object's edges).

These senses of cut are, of course, not exclusive of each other. Nonetheless, the katana's aesthetic function was, and has often been, to render for consummate contemplation the play of a boundary, to turn an object's mere edge into the bolder form of *edginess*. The last chapter will argue that representations of the Japanese sword—whose presence has already been felt in Koko's axe, the haiku's kireji, Yeats's evocation of Sato's sword, and throughout the entire book—exhibit that distinctively feminized type of exquisite aesthetics. Feminized, because although Victorians were already interested in swords by the publication in France of Pierre Loti's story *Madame Chrysanthème*, it was through Anglophone revisions of that story that the play of the sword, as an instrument of internal and external violence, has become most deeply entrenched. This chapter will follow the Chrysanthème story's mutation into the Americanized story of Madame Butterfly, the Anglo-Chinese-Canadian auto-Orientalizing revision of the Butterfly stories in the work of Onoto Watanna/Winnifred Eaton, and then to cinema: a Japanese body-horror movie named *Audition* (1999) and a couple of American blockbusters made by Quentin Tarantino.

The particular form of body horror that psychoanalysis refers to as "castration anxiety" inevitably permeates Western concern with the samurai sword. But it will only seem strange for a moment that such an object as a sword is here understood as both feminine, and *feminizing*, rather than as a kind of phallic auxiliary. Nothing could be less phallic—except, perhaps, a penis. (As Judith Butler puts it, "[a]lthough Lacan explicitly denounces the possibility that the phallus is a body part . . . , that repudiation will be read as constitutive of the very symbolic status he confers on the phallus.")[3] Rather, the katana as an emblem of exquisite violence becomes, in the *Madame Chrysanthème* stories and their revisions, a formal principle concerning the limits of aesthetic judgment. In this sense, although some of the stories discussed below don't depict swords directly—Eaton's stories don't entail swords and *Audition* doesn't involve blades at all, both the minimalist satire of the Onoto Watanna stories and the weaponization of a piece of piano wire in *Audition* perform the aesthetic role accorded to the samurai sword. So, because the aesthetic function of the samurai sword formulated within Western culture primarily by the *Madame Chrysanthème* stories, that function depends upon a particular form of feminine heterosexual abjection, a theme that certainly connects the chapter's four objects. In some ways, the social relations we will see convened around the katana resemble the kinds of abandonment that we witnessed in the previous chapter, whereas the haunting poignancy of Mikimoto's desire for Ruskin derived from a kind of homosocial abandonment, the female abjection and male absence that characterizes *Madame Butterfly*, the Watanna stories, *Audition*, and especially *Kill Bill* is distinctively feminine, and distinctively heterosexual. The fantasies of castration in these stories—fantasies whose eventual target is not a man's but a woman's body—both aggravate and compensate the pain of women abandoned by beloved men.

Yet these swords also point towards a problem that they can represent but hardly make sense of: how is it possible to fetishize an object one takes to be an agent of one's castration? It should not, if Freud is to be believed, be so. It would be possible to *desire* castration, either for oneself or another, but since the fetish object remains, for the fetishist, "a token of triumph over the threat of castration, and a protection against it" (Freud, 1927), it occupies the psychic place vacated by that threat. And since the threat is absolutely singular and asymmetrical, it would make no sense to diagnose castration fetishism as merely an extreme presentation of masochism, which Freud understood as an "extension of sadism turned round upon the subject's own self" (Freud, 1905).[4] Deleuze attacks Freud's theory of sadomasochism precisely as too neatly symmetrical, but the catholicity of his own, which treats masochism as the multiform "combination" and "defusion" of multiple psychic procedures, limits its applicability to a psychoanalytic theory of the *fetish*—a singularity of a different kind, but a singularity nonetheless (Deleuze, 1971, 95–96).[5] To fetishize the agent of castration would require renouncing the singularity of both the fetish and the castrated penis; it would amount, in other words, to renouncing the singularity of the phallus altogether.

The sword is the point at which force and grace converge: it is, in the words of Inazo Nitobe, a Japanese writer and diplomat who lived in the United States and Canada in the late nineteenth century, and writing in 1900:

> Perfect as a work of art, setting at defiance its Toledo and Damascus rivals, there was more than art could impart. Its cold blade, collecting on its surface the moment it is drawn the vapour of the atmosphere; its immaculate texture, flashing light of bluish hue; its matchless edge, upon which histories and possibilities hand; the curve of its back, uniting exquisite grace with utmost strength;—all these thrill us with mixed feelings of power and beauty, of awe and terror. Harmless were its mission, if it only remained a thing of beauty and joy! But, ever within reach of the hand, it presented no small temptation for abuse. The abuse sometimes went so far as to try the acquired steel on some harmless creature's neck.[6]

Flickering too close to the hand, the sword tempts its bearer into a degrading act; an act that not only degrades the one who performs it, but (almost as an afterthought) decapitates and murders the "harmless creature" to whom it is done. The thought is too much for Nitobe to bear—"it was a great pity that this high ideal was left exclusively to priests"—so he abruptly ends the chapter to "devote a few paragraphs to the subject of the training and position of women" (131). Accordingly, although Edwin Arnold, in his 1891 book *Japonica*, wrote of "the pride felt in these exquisite instruments of rage or revenge,"[7] the fate of the Japanese sword, for Western Orientalists, has been rather to produce an enduring and provocative theory of *shame*. Ruth Benedict's ethnography of Japanese internees, entitled *The Chrysanthemum and the Sword* (1946), famously boils down Japanese cultural patterns to a dialectic of aestheticism and militarism, limned by "the primacy of shame in Japanese life" (Benedict, 1946, 224).[8] Nineteenth-century writers were likewise fascinated by the notion of a weapon that was also an artwork. An 1896 article in *The Far East*, an English language periodical primarily written by Japanese Anglophone journalists and scholars towards the ever-popular end of "explaining" Japan to American visitors, goes further: "It is not too much to say that the very back bone of Japanese art is found in these weapons" (Negishi, *FE.I.9*, 1896, 32).[9] As that spine-stiffening description already hints, the katana served to remind readers of English that the liquefacient "free play" of the aesthetic faculties operated only under condition that the object of contemplation bound itself to rules of hard steel—that aesthetic pleasure, indeed, takes place under perpetual threat of a kind of castration. The sword, in other words, materializes and formalizes the interdependent relationship of beauty and violence that Benedict calls "shame," but whose exquisite effects we have been following throughout under different names. But the sword, as we shall see, is already implied by the *Chrysanthème*.

II. Suicide as One of the Fine Arts: *Madame Butterfly*

Much of the work delineating the textual histories of these texts can be found in Christopher Reed's edition of Félix Regamey's *The Pink Notebook of Madame Chrysanthème, a pastriche of the "Madame Butterfly" genre.*[10] Reed's meticulous reconstruction of the textual history of the "Madame Chrysanthème" / "Madame Butterfly" trope brings into view a complex intertextual history into a web of mutual citation and influence. Together, these texts comprise a genre in the sense proposed by Lauren Berlant in *The Female Complaint*, "an aesthetic structure of affective expectation, an institution or formation that absorbs all kinds of small variations or modifications while promising that the persons transacting with it will experience the pleasure of encountering what they expected" (4).[11] Madame Butterfly, and her consistent recurrence in a variety of different media, indicates the presence of an unsolved problem—of what Berlant calls the "unfinished business" of sentimentality. It is nonetheless a genre with a distinct origin: Pierre Loti's novella *Madame Chrysanthème* was an extraordinarily quick success. Printed first in serial form in *Le Figaro* in 1887, it was published the following year in a lavish illustrated edition edited by Calmann Lévy (including a hundred "exemplaires sur Japon, numérolés") and bearing an ostentatious dedicatory epistle to the Duchesse Richelieu. It was translated into English in 1889, and reprinted 222 times before Loti's death in 1923.[12] A first-person narrative detailing a French naval officer's marriage to the eponymous Chrysanthème, Loti's text delights in both the visual spectacle she presents, and the aestheticized environment into which she had been ensconced, as though the marriage contract had pulled the narrator into a work of art that he could inhabit at first comfortably, and eventually with nothing more than a desire to escape. "In our home, everything looks like a Japanese picture," the narrator confides a few days after his marriage; but eventually the aesthetic pleasure goes sour as Chrysanthème's condition appears to her more and more abject as she realizes her husband is about to leave. Her sadness is a matter of irritation to Loti's narrator, who would "infinitely prefer that this marriage should end as it had begun, in a joke."[13] Within a few years, Loti's novel had produced both pastiches and adaptations; had been, indeed, adapted into an unsuccessful opera by André Messager in 1893—eleven years before the debut of Giacomo Puccini's opera *Madame Butterfly*, which was based on the play by David Belasco, an adaptation from John Luther Long's 1898 novella, which was, indeed, deeply indebted to Loti.

Yet if the casual cruelty of Loti's narrator was brutally apparent to many of his contemporary readers—including to his contemporary Félix Regamey, who published in 1893 a version of the events told from Chrysanthème's side—then the structural cruelty of Long's novella, transposed into a third-person narrative from which the husband is almost entirely absent, proves almost unbearable. For the majority of the plot, the reader is locked with the eponymous Cho-Cho San into the same room in what Long, in the introduction, calls "the little, empty, happy house on Higashi Hill, where she was to have had a honeymoon of nine hundred and ninety-nine years!"[14] That designation, "honeymoon," is a horribly apt description of the plot's span, which takes us from Cho's marriage to B. F. Pinkerton up, asymptotically, to the commencement of a "normal life" when he returns from America. Yet it is a honeymoon without a husband, a temporal suspension played out in isolation barely mitigated by a child by whom she seems irritated (and names "Trouble," with an irony that grows increasingly menacing), and a series of mannered conversations with various bureaucrats and meddlers attempting to resolve her situation. Cho's friendship with her nurse Suzuki is an important exception to these formulaic and routinized conversations—to which we will return. When Pinkerton is finally spotted in the harbor, he is arm-in-arm with a blonde woman—who will later be revealed to be his wife—which sets in motion a series of melodramatic tableaux. First, Cho and Suzuki return home to hide behind a screen (with Trouble) awaiting Pinkerton's return; they wait all night, though, and he never shows up; they repeat this scene for "the next day" and "many after." Next, Cho seeks advice from the American consul, who graciously hands over a wedge of cash left for her by Pinkerton, and dishonestly (the narrator is very generous towards his "compassionate lying") informs Cho that her husband has been called away by the navy. Before she can leave, however, he gets another visitor, and hides Cho behind a screen—the second time she is screened in a few pages—so that he can receive the second visitor. It is Adelaide, the blonde woman seen with Pinkerton who is—as a marriage broker had predicted early on in the novella—Pinkerton's new American wife, who has come to ask the consul to send her husband a telegram: "Just saw the baby and his nurse. Can't we have him at once? He is lovely. Shall see the mother about it to-morrow. Was not at home when I was there to-day. Expect to join you Wednesday week per *Kioto Maru*. May I bring him along? Adelaide."

There follows a scene of subtle homosocial sadism whose complexity, I think, has been underestimated by Long's critics, which mobilizes against Cho the compulsory performance of carefreeness that comprised her primary sense of wifely duty—a kind of domestic labor, that is, whose sole purpose is the invisibilization of labor itself. After dictating the telegram to the consul,

Adelaide spots Cho, and (without, seemingly, recognizing her as the mother of the child she is trying to adopt), is arrested in a moment of scopophilic desire: "How very charming—how *lovely*—you are, dear! Will you kiss me, you pretty—*plaything!*" Cho demurs, prompting the observation from Adelaide that "They say you don't do that sort of thing—to women at any rate. I quite forgive our men for falling in love with you." On the one hand, Adelaide reduces Cho to the status of "plaything"—a smart that wounds its victim enough that it is repeated to Suzuki a few pages later. But, still more brutal is the outrageous breeziness of Adelaide's request for a kiss, a successful performance of playfulness that casts a pall over Cho's all-too-infelicitous playacting with which the reader has become familiar. Standing in the position of power, Adelaide is able to reduce Cho's body to an object of mere play, while proving her own superior fitness for that role. Mari Yoshihara argues that Adelaide's role here is to demonstrate that "white women don't take Asian women seriously, that they are in alliance with American men rather than with Asian women, and that they are more concerned with their own womanhood at home than with the lot of women across the Pacific."[15] Which is clearly true, but the inverse is true too: in this performance of carefreeness, Adelaide—whose blondeness seems itself to be a superfluous, and thereby self-negating, performance of carelessness—engages Cho in the contest of heterosexual women to determine who is the *most* carefree, the *most* plaything-like.

Yet this moment of dramatized cruelty relieves the tension from the novella's more punishingly sadistic element: the distension of time over a plot that, for the most part, dwells with a young woman in a single room, as she waits with increasingly animated desperation for the return of her husband. The framing bears comparison with Charlotte Perkins Gilman's story "The Yellow Wallpaper," published six years prior to Long's *Madame Butterfly*, which narrates a young wife's mental dissolution as a result of her confinement to a single room, and her eventual psychic incorporation within the walls that bind her.[16] Yet there are important differences, too. Cho-Cho San is first introduced to the reader in the same sentence as the house; both thematically and formally, her imprisonment is taken as constitutive of her character.

> With the aid of a marriage-broker, [Pinkerton] found both a wife and a house in which to keep her. This he leased for nine hundred and ninety-nine years. Not, he explained to his wife later, that he could hope for the felicity of residing there with her so long, but because, being a mere "barbarian," he could not make other legal terms. He did not mention that the lease was determinable, nevertheless, at the end of any month, by the mere neglect to pay the rent. Details were distasteful to Pinkerton; besides, she would probably not appreciate the humor of this.

> Some clever Japanese artisans then made the paper walls of the pretty house eye-proof, and, with their own adaptations of American hardware, the openings cunningly lockable. The rest was Japanese.
>
> Madame Butterfly laughed, and asked him why he had gone to all that trouble—in Japan!
>
> "To keep out those who are out, and in those who are in," he replied, with an amorous threat in her direction.
>
> She was greatly pleased with it all, though, and went about jingling her new keys and her new authority like toys,—she had only one small maid to command,—until she learned that among others to be excluded were her own relatives. (8–10)

The "amorous threat" of Cho's imprisonment is thus presented to the reader as a transnational collaboration between American and Japanese men; Pinkerton's foreignness, far from impeding his marital strategy, endows it with a most fitting sigil—a jail sentence far beyond the span of a human life. The Bluebeard mythos underpinning the plot is instituted as its premise. In reprintings of *Madame Butterfly* after its initial appearance in the *Century*, the shared immobilization of character and reader is felt in the punishing sameness of sixteen awkwardly lifelike illustrations, each of which presents Cho-Cho San in some melodramatic pose, in the same room, on the same mat.

"Tragically sudden," underneath the illustration of a body lying prone but not, evidently, dead, beautifully performs the suspension of narrative sequence by *tableau* that, in the final vignette, we will retrospectively associate with suicide. The exorbitant feeling of narrative suspension (at two scales: the millennial scale of the lease on the building, and the more attenuated scale of the distended honeymoon) lands hard on the body of the novella's heroine, who morphs her whole body into a mass of folds. In *Audition*, the heroine's *slump* in the final sequence contrasts with her earlier taut pose, while we watch her waiting by the phone.

While "The Yellow Wallpaper" was written in order to illustrate a very specific polemic—that women should not be treated with rest cures when experiencing mental disturbance—the politics of *Madame Butterfly* are far harder to determine. Long himself seemed baffled by the novella, though inevitably delighted at its success after the relative commercial failure of *Miss Cherry-Blossom of Tokyo* in 1895.[17] "Concerning the genesis of the story," he writes in the preface to the reprint, "I know nothing. I think no one ever does. What process of the mind produces such things? What tumult of the emotions sets them going? I do not know. Perhaps it is the sum of one's fancies of life—not altogether sad, not altogether gay."[18] For a number of readers, *Madame Butterfly* was simply an exhibition of the charms of Japanese womanhood:

FIGURE 5.1. *It was tragically sudden*

"daintily told and full of local color," according to the *Book Buyer*; "dear and beautiful," according to the *Delineator*.[19] On the other hand, Long did find readers prepared to think a little harder about the novella's complex narrative treatment of marital abuse, albeit in terms that implicitly or explicitly blamed Cho-Cho San herself for the plot. Reviewing a reprint of *Madame Butterfly* alongside four of Long's other Japanese stories, the *Critic* noted that his plots often "turn upon the facility with which divorce is still obtained in the island empire, and the wrong which is thus done to the awakening consciences of the women."[20] Cho does indeed complain to Suzuki about the difficulty of obtaining a divorce in the United States ("if one is marry one got stay marry" [38]), but it is by no means obvious that the narrative blames her for doing so. For which reason it is even more difficult to accept the guileless assessment of the *Delineator* that Japanese women's "naïve admissions of wrong-doing are in themselves purifications and forgiveness." Rather, the ritualized performance of abjection extorted from Cho is the fulcrum at the middle of Long's balance between sympathy and sadism, between the generic demand that the reader *pity* the sentimental heroine, and the Orientalist opportunity to *delight* in the suffering of the Other.

The phenomenology of containment mediated by *Madame Butterfly*—the feeling that one is shut in—is produced, likewise, in "The Yellow Wallpaper," though the difference between Gilman's first- and Long's third-person narrators modulate the experience differently. Gilman's tale is premised upon its narrator's pathology—"temporary nervous depression"—which she then gradually reframes as a problem of narrative unreliability. When a first-person narrator begins to inform us that she can see "a strange, provoking, formless sort of figure, that seems to skulk about behind that silly and conspicuous front design," we are added to the ranks of whose ministrations have caused, and are exacerbating, the very conditions they (and we) are attempting to diagnose. Yet unlike Gilman's narrator, Cho-Cho San is not rendered pathological by her imprisonment, and though increasingly desperate, she never loses the plot, partly because the task of narrating what plot there is falls to two assuaging and self-possessed male voices—the narrator and the consul—both of whom are quite open about their unreliability. Through the long nights in which Cho and Suzuki are waiting for Pinkerton's return, both are physically exhausted—"finally Cho-Cho San could no longer hold the glass"—but mentally intact. Cho's decision not to seek Pinkerton out directly, on the grounds that "the only woman who seeks a male is a yujo, a coutezan," enforces a hard limit to her abjection. The narrative force counteracting Pinkerton's "amorous threat" consists of the equally oxymoronic (i.e., not) mode in which Cho (successfully) negotiates for visitation rights for her family, glossed by the narrator as "weak remonstrance" (12).

The distinction qualifies an ending whose ambiguity is flattened in Belasco's and Puccini's adaptation: does Cho kill herself? Unambiguously so in the Belasco, whose final stage direction—"(*She dies.*)"—leaves no room for doubt. Yet the Long offers no certainty on this point:

> Then she placed the point of the weapon at that nearly nerveless spot in the neck known to every Japanese, and began to press it slowly inward. She could not help a little gasp at the first incision. But presently she could feel the blood finding its way down her neck. It divided on her shoulder, the larger stream going down her bosom. In a moment she could see it making its way daintily between her breasts. It began to congeal there. She pressed on the sword, and a fresh stream swiftly overran the other—redder, she thought. And then suddenly she could no longer see it. She drew the mirror closer. Her hand was heavy, and the mirror seemed far away. She knew that she must hasten. But even as she locked her fingers on the serpent of the guard, something within her cried out piteously. They had taught her how to die, but he had taught her how to live—nay, to make life sweet. Yet that was the reason she must die. Strange reason! She now first knew that it was

sad to die. He had come, and substituted himself for everything; he had gone, and left her nothing—nothing but this.

The maid softly put the baby into the room. She pinched him, and he began to cry.

"Oh, pitiful Kwannon! Nothing?"

The sword fell dully to the floor. The stream between her breasts darkened and stopped. Her head drooped slowly forward. Her arms penitently outstretched themselves toward the shrine. She wept.

"Oh, pitiful Kwannon!" she prayed.

The baby crept cooing into her lap. The little maid came in and bound up the wound.

When Mrs. Pinkerton called next day at the little house on Higashi Hill it was quite empty. (149–51)

Has the maid successfully treated Cho's wound, and absconded with her and Trouble? Or is the house empty because Suzuki has disposed of Cho's corpse, and taken Trouble off on her own? In his preface, Long supports the first of these interpretations: "And where has she gone? I do not know. I lost sight of her, as you did, that dark night she fled with Trouble and Suzuki" (xii). Yet he also speaks with pride about the Belasco adaptation, and excitement about the forthcoming Puccini. Despite Long's use of "fled," then, one derives the sense that Cho's fate is a matter of little concern to her author, and that the singular gesture of terminating a plot of interminable waiting was, for him, a violent gesture in itself, an unacceptable violation of a character whose function was, all along, to remain in limbo.

Within the novella, however, the knowledge of whether Cho's wound is treatable is coded as specifically Japanese: she has wounded "that nearly nerveless spot in the neck known to every Japanese." A delicate procedure, whose erotic vividness reaches the verge of pornography in its climactic image—blood congealing between the breasts—the precise nature of Cho's paradoxically painless act of self-harm is obscured from the reader. Yet if the nature of Cho's puncture is hazy, the reader is all too aware of another kind of incursion: in those descriptive sentences the perforation of the narrator's style by Cho's thoughts, in the form of free indirect discourse, feels intimately apparent. "She now first knew it was sad to die": these awkward and simple monosyllables seem to construct a paratactical effect without being, in fact, paratactical, but merely very simple. There is a temporal distortion ("now first knew") but it is easily resolved, and barely even warrants the designation of "free indirect discourse" that, this being a third-person narrator mimicking the affective intensity of a character it is representing, we might be tempted to ascribe to it. The quantum mechanics of simplicity mimic, here, those of parataxis.

Cho-Cho San is not the supine and passive object variously celebrated by Long and denounced by his critics. Rather, her strategy was a purposively weak remonstrance whose effects are registered, first, through their limited (but real) intradiegetic success, and then much more dramatically at the larger scale of genre, where in the hands of the author known as "Onoto Watanna," the figure of the abandoned woman became a focal point for a generic revisionism whose strategic value will resonate even more forcefully in the climactic sequence of *Audition*. Although in the case of Watanna, we will depart from depictions of *swords*, we will nonetheless see the aesthetics of feminine abjection deployed forcefully against a masculine adversary—in this case, the affective structure of sexual difference that organizes the Butterfly genre itself.

III. Me; Butterfly: Onoto Watanna

Winnifred Eaton was an Anglo-Chinese Canadian whose novels and short stories penned under the name "Onoto Watanna" engaged, in various ways, the *Madame Butterfly* genre. Two of her fictions draw on it explicitly—"A Half Caste" and *Miss Numé of Japan*—and many more of her stories and novels participate in the Butterfly ethos, and draw explicitly or implicitly on its assumptions and codes. The plot of "A Contract," for example, has little to do with *Madame Chrysanthème* directly: a Japanese clerk asks his (white) boss to permit his marriage; it is revealed that the marriage is to the boss's own intended lover; eventually the clerk is defeated through the agreement of the boss and the girl's father.[21] A first reading will doubtless emphasize the collusion between capitalist modernity and traditional Japanese patriarchy, across the lines of racial and cultural reproduction represented by the clerk (Ito) and the daughter (Kiku). Symptomatically, such a reading might suggest, the boss is named "Masters"—plural; no less that in his first, failing appeal to Kiku, Masters demands to be recognized as Japanese by virtue of having been born there. Kiku's resistance to this idea distinguishes between an abstract notion of Japaneseness that white people are capable of obtaining, and a property conferred by citizenship from which Masters is barred: "Am I or am I not Japanese?" he demands; "Japanese citizen, yes" . . . "Japanese man, naever" (56). Yet this reading will persuade only if it is prepared to make a determination about the ending of the story that Watanna stubbornly, and indeed perversely, resists, concerning Kiku's true feelings towards the two men. To everybody's surprise, after having been forced into this marriage apparently against her will, Kiku declares that her true love is not Ito but Masters, and that she has concocted this whole situation in order to be rid of an unscrupulous suitor. Such a conclusion seems thoroughly unlikely—Masters is clearly no less unscrupulous, and Kiku has denounced his proposal both to his face and to her father. Nonetheless, by stepping to the side of the plot as it has been advancing, Kiku's semantically indeterminate declaration throws the story, and its male protagonists, onto the floor.

Onoto Watanna's complex position has proven less than amenable to both Orientalism-critique and feminist criticism: daughter of a Chinese immigrant, Winnifred Eaton nonetheless exhibits (and claims authority for) a staggering yellowface Japaneseness with less sensitivity, and less first-hand experience of Japan, than even the boorish Pierre Loti. Yet her writing possesses an uncanny knack of using the Butterfly genre's strength against itself. Unlike explicitly anti-Orientalist treatments of the same theme, most famously David Henry Hwang's *M. Butterfly* (1988), her stories do not invert the characters of the plot, but imagine deviously miniature methods for enforcing that the plot fails on its own terms.[22] In "A Half Caste," the white lover is thwarted when he realizes his intended is his own daughter from a previous adventure: if it is a "sequel" to *Madame Chrysanthème*, it is again one in which it is the very momentum of the plot of courtship—that which the genre convention assumes—that stages the male protagonist's, and reader's, exquisite shame in the final tableau.

Winnifred Eaton confuses readers, however, and approaches to her work have remained ambivalent and allusive. Her compositions perform the same naivety she ascribes to her characters, and, like them, they delight in rerouting sentimental attachment into scenes of mild, uncomprehending horror. The problem has often, and with good reason, been understood as analogous to the question of her background and identity: an Asian woman writer, subject inevitably to the stereotyping and exclusion thereby entailed; she nonetheless adopted a no-less-ruthless Orientalist writing persona from a culture she approached solely through literary and artistic representation. Amy Ling has described the connection between her writerly persona and her embodied identity as a kind of "fight" distinct from the open engagement with racism associated with her sister, Edith, who wrote stories under the Chinese American pseudonym of Sui Sin Far: "Edith's response to racism was a frontal assault, direct and confrontational. Winnifred's response, however, was indirect, covert, and subversive—like the Trojan Horse, an ambush from within the walls." That Winnifred (I refer to the historical individual by this name, rather than "Eaton," solely to distinguish her from her sister; I will refer to the writing persona as "Onoto Watanna") used her fictions to explore the complex relationship between embodiment and stylistic practice in her work was, however, clear from the outset of her career as Watanna.

Since biography is more than usually central to discussions of an author whose work comprises a relentless negotiation of its limits, scholars of Watanna's work are indebted to the thoughtful and thorough biography written by the author's granddaughter, Diana Birchall.[23] Not merely a rich account of Winnifred's life and works, *Onoto Watanna: The Story of Winnifred Eaton* even more helpfully assembles a trove of family lore, drawn piecemeal from interviews with surviving members of the family. As Birchall frankly admits, many of the stories that the Eatons told each other are unpersuasive on their face, but depict a family for whom fictive biography forged important and productive bonds of kinship. In one such early moment, Birchall recalls her cousin being told that his grandmother (Winnifred's mother) was the daughter of "a Mandarin lord" and "was kidnapped by circus performers at the age of three. Too scared to ask for ransom, they put her to work in the circus. One year later the Mathesons (Sir Hugh Matheson), Scottish missionaries, rescued her and brought her to England as their ward" (8). A story of such picaresque dimensions hardly requires debunking, and Birchall is careful to note merely that "it is what family members believed." But one point of interest might usefully be annotated: that Hugh Matheson, appearing here in the picaresque guise of a rescuer, was a director of Jardine Matheson, the largest opium trading firm in China. The family story, in other words, both claimed kinship with a titan of British colonial power and euphemized the nature of that power. The biography itself performs a related kind of effacement, informing the reader that "perhaps the likeliest Matheson candidate to have been Grace's benefactor is not Sir Hugh (though the family would 'love a lord' in the retelling) but Donald Matheson"—a judgment advanced seemingly on the grounds that Donald left Jardine Matheson to become chairman of the Committee for the Suppression of the Opium Trade (and, one presumes, therefore more likely to take pity on a young Chinese woman indentured to a circus). Yet such wishful thinking requires nonetheless that parenthetical qualification, whose propositional content is as difficult to decipher as its affect is palpable. The fanciful story enabled a collective love for a British establishment that singled *this* family out for rescue.

Notwithstanding such a familial context, the breadth and originality of Winnifred's fictive biography stands out dramatically. Accounts differ on when she first began writing in a Japanese voice; in the Calgary archives, Birchall finds an undated story entitled "A Japanese Girl," which Winnifred has signed "this is the first Japanese story I wrote"; another fragment names a lost story entitled "The Old Jinrikisha." These were likely written around 1896 during Winnifred's few months spent in Jamaica in 1896; the following October, however, she was living in Chicago when the literary periodical *Current Literature* published the following notice:

> Kitishima Kata Hasche is the real or family name of the clever Japanese girl who is living in Chicago at present and winning fame by writing for the

> magazines and newspapers of Chicago and the East under the pen name of Otano [*sic*] Watanna, while more dollars come from her work as a ethnographer. Miss Hasche, or, as she prefers to be called, Miss Watanna—the two names meaning the same thing, but in different Japanese dialects—though scarcely past her twenty-first birthday, has seen more of life and experience than the average woman of twice her age.[24]

As has been frequently pointed out, neither "Onoto Watanna" nor "Otano Watanna" is a Japanese name; it is a collection of graphemes that, to certain ears, *sound* Japanese. On the other hand, "Onoto Watanna" *could* be rendered in katakana without distortion; unlike, for example, "Winnifred Eaton," which would require the interjection of an extra syllable between the 'f' and the 'r'. The same cannot be said of "Kitishima Kata Hasche," whose final word entails a Germanic word ending quite remote both from Japanese speech and its stereotyped representations. ("Hasshe" would work.) What is the relationship between these two fake nonsense-names? In a careful discrimination of Lewis Carroll's "Jabberwocky" from its partial translation into French by Antonin Artaud, Jean-Jacques Lecercle has recourse to the category of phonotactics: the quality of a phoneme or phonemes that endows it with the phonic quality of sounding like a real word.[25] According to Lecercle's typology, "Otano/Onoto Watanna" would be an example of "*baragouin*": unwritten rules governing the perception, within one group of language users, about the phonic qualities of *another* language. The syllables of "Onoto Watanna" feel, if anything, *underdetermined*, mere vacant sounds in which echoes of meanings might be discerned but which add up to less than the sum of their parts: "oh no"; "to what"; "an"; "na"; vague and half-formed negations, occasional prepositions, but no "latent content" out of which to forge interpretation. Reading between the two, one might perhaps catch a glimpse of katakana itself, the Japanese syllabary in which English and other loan words are conventionally transcribed. Or perhaps more simply katana, the Japanese sword. (Yuko Matsukawa adds another: "Onoto" is the brand name of a Japanese pen manufacturer.)[26] But the primary effect of "Otano/Onoto Watanna" is not felt in semantic units, but in the hollowness between them; the sound of Japanese, by these lights, is hollow.

Winnifred's own narration of her career took the form of another fictionalization: her memoir *Me: A Book of Remembrance* (1915) was published anonymously, and its protagonist bears another pseudonym, in this case Nora Aycough.[27] Birchall suggests that this "Aycough" refers to another family myth: that the Eatons were descended from the line of Isaac Newton—who married Hannah Ayscough. Whether or not, it is clear that the memoir's narrator is keen to emphasize her British (more specifically, English) heritage, at the expense of any reference to a Chinese mother. Nora's father is introduced as a romantic gallant of the old school: "a young and ardent adventurer (an English-Irishman) [who] had wandered far and wide over the face of the earth." Her mother, on the other hand, appears in quite a different guise, as "an excitable, temperamental creature from whose life all romance had been squeezed by the torturing experience of bearing sixteen children. Moreover, she was a native of a far-distant land, and I do not think she ever got over the feeling of being a stranger in Canada" (3). No further details about the "far distant land" are ever supplied, and while Nora's mother appears melancholic as a result of her displacement, her father's mobility is a source of heroic inspiration to the young protagonist: "was I not the daughter of a man who had been back and forth to China no fewer than eighteen times, and that during the perilous period of the Tai-ping Rebellion?" (5).

Nora's paternal Englishness recurs throughout the memoir as a source of personal and cultural authority, a bulwark against the "race prejudice" that otherwise governs her erotic and social experiences. In the midst of one of the wordy and flirty affairs that take up the majority of the book's narrative, Nora asks one Roger whether, had she been educated formally, she might be admitted to the ranks of high-society women from whom he is supposed to draw a wife. He initially panders: "You are in a class all by yourself, Nora. . . . That's a foolish question." But, sensitive to the rejection she is about to experience—and manipulating Roger with her characteristic verve—Nora persists: "No, it isn't. I just want to know. Now, supposing I got all that culture and everything, and I had nice manners, and dressed so I looked pretty and everything and you wouldn't be a bit ashamed of me, and we could say my people were all sorts of grand folks, they really are in England, my father's people, well, suppose all this, and then suppose that you really loved me, just as I do you, then wouldn't I be good enough to be your wife?" Roger at once excuses himself from the conversation, declaring that he "can't" marry her, without supplying a reason—though, given that he subsequently induces a promise that she will break off her other three relationships (she is engaged to three separate men) and "in no circumstances let any man kiss or touch me, or make love to me in any way," the reader is inclined to suspect him of a kind of sexual possessiveness—that is, unless we are able to read what Nora cannot, but which will be clearly anticipated by readers of Victorian fiction: that Roger is a married rake. We later learn, too, that he has harbored precisely the kind of prejudice of which she suspected him, describing her as a "mongrel by blood, but a thoroughbred by instinct."

The affair between Nora and Roger makes use of a Victorian style in two ways, then: intradiegetically, as the source of cultural authority with which Nora endows her father (and her phantasmatic self), and metadiegetically, as a guide to the generic clues that Nora cannot bring herself to interpret. In a memoir however (albeit one in which important details are omitted and names are changed) this form of generic emplotment has a rather perverse dimension, and requires of the reader a split attention, in which generic clues must be noted, but must also be put into abeyance. Symptomatically, perhaps, Nora occasionally tries to represent her affairs as echoes of recognizable plots: shut in during a Chicago snow-storm, Nora assesses the state of her relationship with Roger in language straight out of the period's sentimental fictions: "I was with Roger, alone, this time, never to be parted again. All the barriers were down between us. All we knew was that we loved each other. What did anything else matter? My work? Ah, it was a poor, feeble little spark that had fluttered out before this vast flame in my heart. I had no room, no thought, for anything else."

At another key moment of the plot of *Me*, the cultural authority of Victorian prose is called upon to provide Nora with employment and security. Shortly after arriving in Jamaica, she is interviewed by a potential employer, Mr. Campbell, "who looked exactly like the pictures of Ibsen." A little irascible, but likeable enough for all that, Campbell is busy considering letting her write for his newspaper, when Nora finds herself distracted by his library:

> He caught me doing this, and asked me gruffly if I had ever read anything. I said:
>
> "Yes, Dickens, George Eliot, and Sir Walter Scott; and I've read Huxley and Darwin, and lots of books on astronomy to my father, who is very fond of that subject." As he made no comment, nor seemed at all impressed by my erudition, I added proudly: "My father's an Oxford man, and a descendent of the family of Sir Isaac Newton."

Her associations sliding between patriarch and *patria*, Nora associates the canon out of which she builds her writing with the body of her father, who appears first in an unfamiliar setting as the beneficiary of his daughter's domestic labor (reading) and then in his more usual guise as a virtuous and storied Englishman. We might wonder, however, what precise form of metalepsis occurs, though, when (in the midst of a scene in which Nora is attempting to pitch *stories*), she describes this fictive familial biography, in an aside to the reader, as a "legend," while "in fact, the greatness of my father's people had been a sort of fairy-story with us all, and we knew that it was his marriage with mama that had cut him off from his kindred." Mama is doubly abjected, then: blamed for the marriage that cut Father's familial ties to greatness, she is perforce absented from the "we" that "knew" the fairy-stories. The father, on the other hand, is placed beyond reproach, but also implicitly beyond repair: an "Oxford man" in exile.

A year after the publication of *Me,* Winnifred published *Marion: The Story of an Artist's Model,* which appeared with the beautifully quizzical subheading "by Herself and the Author of 'Me.'"[28] Though readers may have found this degree of fictionalization impenetrably baroque, "Herself" refers to the book's coauthor, Winnifred's older sister Sara Bosse [née Eaton], with whom Onoto Watanna had authored *The Chinese-Japanese Cook Book,* published in 1914: the first multiethnic Asian cookbook published in the United States. But despite its dual (and multiply layered) authorship, *Marion* continues with the story of Nora Aycough, though it is Sara—in guise as the eponymous Marion—that furnishes the memoir with a protagonist and a narrator. The treatment of (male) Englishness is strikingly distinct. Faced with a French suitor, whose attentions and grace in ice-skating she nonetheless enjoys, Marion confesses "I did prefer the English type. However . . ." (20). It is that English type himself, the pleonastically named "Reggie Bertie," who quickly supplants the French "St. Vidal" in Marion's early affections, and with whom Marion spends the majority of the memoir's plot. He is impervious equally to her preference for the English type and to her growing resentment of it. When she eventually bursts that she is "sick and tired of your old English prejudices and notions, and you can go right now," he first blanches, but quickly recovers himself well enough to grant her what she has requested—permission to continue working for a man he dislikes. Yet in the exercise of that patriarchal authority (and Marion connects her English lover with her English father a few times), Reggie oversteps the bounds of proper English decorum, and so becomes a child. Following Reggie's outburst that "if you ever deceive me, I will kill you and myself too," Marion pledges, indeed, never to deceive him, but confides in her reader that "Somehow, as I spoke, I felt as if I were pacifying a spoiled child" (81).

Reggie is, inevitably, supplanted in turn—in the book's climactic tableau—by the "vitally alive" Franco-German Paul Bonnat. The setting of French against English that provides the memoir with its distinct erotic configuration pivots on Marion's seduction of Paul, in which she recites the entirety of Kipling's poem "When Earth's Last Picture Is Painted," to his delight. The recitation ends in a moment of qualified recognition, with Paul first calling out Marion's lisp (which has not been graphically transcribed along with the Kipling poem that takes up the majority of the page), before offering a reconciliation: "I believe we speak the same language after all. We *think* it, anyway, don't we?" (276). That an erotic connection can breach the boundaries of ethnicity that govern both *Me* and *Marion* is, in the end, the pair of memoirs' conclusion, hard-won from the repetitive and confusing circulation of lovers known by ethnic soubriquets or ethnicized pseudonyms.

"Ethnic shame": that unforgiving diagnosis of Winnifred Eaton's performance as Onoto Watanna has been a persistent theme in critical works dealing with her decision to play Japanese, rather than Chinese: those words appear, for example, on the dust jacket to the 1997 edition of *Me* published by the University Press of Mississippi. And, indeed, the language of shame permeates these memoirs: by Nora on arriving in Jamaica, at her wearing heavy, Canadian clothes in a warm climate; by Marion, after stealing some strawberries; by the various models that appear nude in front of male and female artists in both books. The strongest feelings of shame occur, however, when the author reflects on having used a Japanese pseudonym—though, it must be said, this reflection happens indirectly and allusively:

> A few years later, when the name of a play of mine flashed in electric letters on Broadway, and the city was papered with great posters of the play, I went up and down before that electric sign, just to see if I could call up even one of the fine thrills I had felt in anticipation. Alas! I was aware only of a sad excitement, a sense of disappointment and despair. I realized that what as an ignorant little girl I had thought was fame was something very different. What then I ardently believed to be the divine sparks of genius, I now perceived to be nothing but a mediocre talent that could never carry me far. My success was founded upon a cheap and popular device, and that jumble of sentimental moonshine that they called my play seemed to me the pathetic stamp of my inefficiency. Oh, I had sold my birthright for a mess of potage!

The "cheap and popular device" mentioned has been broadly construed to be the creation and maintenance of a fake Japanese identity. "That," writes Birchall, "was her real shame—not her ethnicity but the lie—and despite the many interviews she gave in her life and her numerous confessional writings, she never once spoke about her past pretense" (xvii). Yet even that more generous assessment misses the theatricality of shame as it appears throughout the memoirs, in which ethnic shame appears intimately connected with the gendered shame of reverse-Oedipal desire, and is as often tied to Englishness as to the "far distant land" whose nonappearance does not, quite, count as absence. These memoirs are populated by scenes where the thematic appearance of Englishness raises the disturbing image of the wounded father: the English lover who becomes fatherlike, only to collapse into a tyrannical little boy; the father himself whose dignity is compromised by his marriage; the English culture that freaks out Roger.

Perhaps, then, the "birthright" that Nora has sold is not, as has generally been deduced, the birthright of Chineseness associated with the mother, but the birthright of Englishness accorded to the father: perhaps, that is, Nora-as-Esau is not regretting her rejection of China, but ruing the failure of her Japanese ruse. The narrator here is no more Chinese than is "Onoto Watanna"—

indeed, the primary difference between the conceits of the memoirs and the Japanese tales is that a putatively Japanese-sounding name has been replaced with a putatively British-sounding one. Lest that assessment seem even less charitable than the "ethnic shame" argument, let me suggest that it is the unique and powerful gift of this author to convert shame—whether of racial stigma or "feminine" passivity—into a powerful and subversive weapon. It is on that level that the memoirs perform the same kind of activism one sees in her energized engagements with the Butterfly genre.

IV. Love and Torture Porn: *Audition*

What, other than their shared capacity for blunt, broad emoting, connects the genre of sentimental romance with that of the horror flick? Western responses to Takashi Miike's 1999 genre-fusing horror movie *Audition* (オーーディション, *Ōdishon*) bore one of the trademarks of exquisite experience: delight in the formal elegance of a torture sequence.[29] Implicitly aligning the sadistic machinations of the film's female lead Asami (Eihi Shiina) with the landscape gardens described in this book's introduction, Peter Bradshaw called *Audition* "an intricate torture garden of a film, lovingly maintained and manicured, with trickling water features and green spaces of pleasingly geometric design."[30] Sublimating an account of violent content into one of aesthetic form, the very hyperbole of Bradshaw's prose dignified what would come to be called "torture porn," not merely as an art form, but more sumptuously as one of the fine arts; appealing to the rarefied taste of a class fraction for which world cinema, and not slasher flicks, would be the relevant context in which to assess *Audition*.[31] The film's impact in the West was multivalent, inspiring an emerging cohort of domestic torture porn directors—Eli Roth described it as a "beautiful movie" that explicitly inspired the creation of his breakthrough 2005 picture *Hostel*—while revealing the existence of a market in the United States and United Kingdom for ultraviolent thrillers from East Asia.[32] Though Miike himself declared "I have no idea what goes on in the minds of people in the West and I don't pretend to know what their tastes are," the film scholar Daniel Martin sees the surprise global success of *Audition* as the inaugural moment of the market in "extreme" Asian cinema, the name he gives to a crop of crossover movies that blended highly formalized cinematography with pungently graphic depictions of violence—among which *Battle Royale*, *Oldboy*, and *The Handmaiden* are some of the better known.[33] At the same time, the exquisite delights that *Audition* evidently unleashed produced a compensatory emphasis on its ethical value, as a narrative about a female "avenging angel" wreaking havoc on the ambient, misogyny of contemporary Japan.[34]

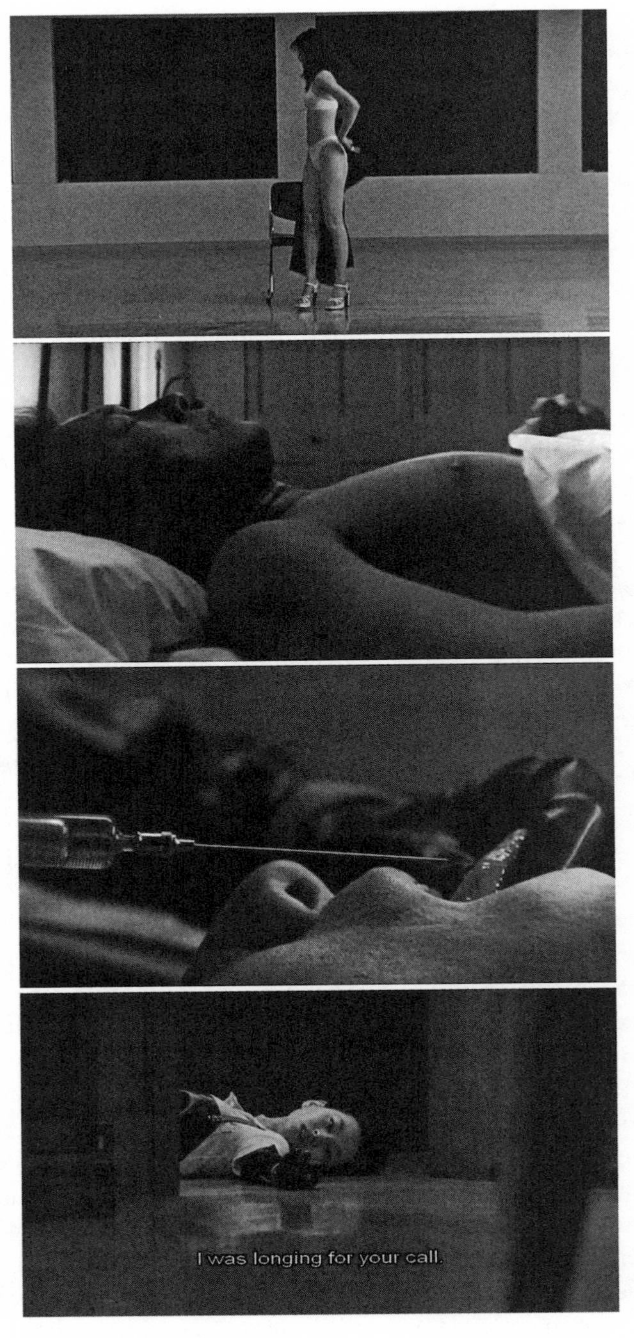

FIGURE 5.2. Takashi Miike, *Audition* (1999). "'I was longing for your call.'"

A parodic high-femme lover who turns out to be a conveyance for genre-deforming violence; an erotically charged set of weapons that function as strange analogues for the work's own medium; a plot whose operational specifics are rendered functionally irrelevant in the denouement; a depiction of self-centered male sexual pleasure precipitating female abjection and eventual self-destruction: these are some of the properties *Audition* shares with the genre that Bradshaw surely has in mind when comparing the movie to a Japanese landscape—the stories of Madame Butterfly. And as with Long's story, if *Audition* is a revenge plot, however, it is of a very strange kind—in this case one that operates at the scale of cinematic genre, rather than at the scale of the film's own story. That story, detached from its generic identifiers, is fairly unremarkable. A middle-aged widower named Aoyama Shigeharu (Ryo Ishibashi) is encouraged by his son to seek a new wife; he turns to a friend for advice. The friend, Yoshikawa Yasuhisa (Jun Kunimura), encourages Aoyama to hold auditions for a romantic lead in a fake movie, and to interview the auditioning women to see if there is one he would like to date. (It will be noted that "audition," in the movie's title, thus refers *literally* to the charade, and *metaphorically* to the dating process.) Aoyama finds a potential partner in Yamazaki Asami, and overrules Yoshikawa's objections to go on three dates with her: to a café, to a restaurant, and finally to a seaside hotel where he plans to have sex with her. Perhaps he does so—a well-timed cut, one of the movie's most complex shots, spares the viewer confirmation on the point—but the next day, Asami has disappeared and is untraceable. Aoyama tries to follow a couple of leads to retrieve her, which leads him to her cackling wheelchair-bound former ballet instructor who, unprompted, tells Aoyama that he maimed Asami when she was a child; and to a music studio, where he is told that the man Asami had given as a reference was recently found dead and dismembered. Dispirited, Aoyama returns home, drinks a glass of whiskey, and (after a ten-minute hallucinatory sequence) wakes to find that Asami is there, and that she has drugged him. The remainder of the movie comprises a twenty-five minute torture sequence, in which Asami paralyzes Aoyama (but leaves his capacity to feel pain intact), inserts a slew of needles into his torso and eyes, and gleefully amputates his foot with piano wire. Finally, Aoyama's son returns home, prompting a brief secondary hallucination of Aoyama's to the effect that, perhaps, he and Asami are still in the seaside hotel, but the son successfully subdues and kills Asami. In the film's final frames, Asami is dying, and a maimed Aoyama is awaiting the police. The question of whether or not Asami was acting out of feeling wronged, or simply out of mad caprice and cruelty, is unanswered. In any case, although Aoyama has certainly acted unscrupulously by feigning the existence of a movie in order to obtain a wife, that transgression is, on its own terms, matched by Asami's own deception:

the reference she had given Yoshikawa was not only unavailable, but dead, presumably by her own hand. Revenge for what?

What the above account of the movie fails to convey, however, is the decisive, almost convulsive, force with which *Audition* shifts genres in its final act. As if disgusted at its own generic development, the movie turns sharply from a sentimental and gently comic erotic thriller into a grisly body horror, repudiating its own aesthetic and narratological premises in an act of generic violence as remorseless as Asami's own plot. Within the story, one of the implements of torture in the final scene, the piano wire, evokes the cruelty of aesthetic creativity: we are meant to take Asami's choice of weapon as a symptom of her abuse by her piano-playing ballet teacher. The wire also performs a similar role at a metadiegetic level, however, as one of the techniques by which *Audition* requires that its viewer consider the flesh of a body as a two dimensional plane, bisected and intersected by lines. The wire (a straight line) "cuts through bone and flesh easily"; Asami's scars (two lines) were left by the ballet teacher's red-hot pokers; the needles (lines) are inserted orthogonally into Aoyama's flesh and eyes. These images, in which aestheticized violence is meted out by a minimalist (and miniaturized) form, will recur towards
e end of this chapter, as an important aesthetic component of Quentin Tarantino's psychoanalytic travesty.[35] For now, I simply wish to observe that *Audition*'s turn to the aesthetics of body horror involves *redoubling*, rather than desublimating, the movie's commitment to a minimalist aesthetic: its representation of very simple abstract shapes, its very limited color palette (black and white, red and blue), and a formal association between the tools used cruelly on bodies and the composition of the movie itself.

Audition has a fulcrum, and both its story and genre change quite dramatically two-thirds of the way through. In that sense, Miike's movie attempts to put into narrative form the exquisite sense of arrest that we have seen operate in the haiku poem's kireji, which there as throughout we have associated with the act of cutting. Turning away from the stilled temporalities of the haiku, however, *Audition*'s peculiar effect is the suspension of narrative time. At a certain point, the protagonist is immobilized, after which neither Aoyama nor any of the other characters *leave* the room that we have seen him enter with half an hour still on the clock; and the hallucinatory sequences—poetic fragments ranging free from the narrative frame we had been inhabiting—seem to perform, even somewhat sadistically, a kind of mobility of which both character and audience have been deprived. Frequently, viewers of *Audition* complain that the experience of watching the final sequence is profoundly unpleasant—"almost as unwatchable as the news reels of Auschwitz," according to one—as though it were the Western (re)viewer, and not a fictional character, that was being subjected to torture.[36] Yet the apparent dissolution of narrative is, conversely, an effect of narrative, not merely in the sense that the suspension depends on the foregoing narrative section in order for its difference to be felt, but in the more radical sense that the very shift between progressive narrative and synchronic arrest establishes those two conditions in a sequence. Rather than close its plot in the same genre as it was opened, then, *Audition* achieves narrative closure at a second order of abstraction, by becoming a movie *that tells the story of* the supersession of narrative progress by an exquisite configuration of beauty and violence, the shared victory of art and pain over time.

In *Audition*, the audience's condition of narrative suspension is closely aligned with a related form of anticipation: the (hetero)sexualized female abjection of *waiting for him to call*. From the outset of the movie, Asami is depicted in a set of tableaux familiar as the poses of libidinal negation: several times, before we have any reason to suspect that the plot is going where it is going, we see her crouched in a dingy apartment, waiting by the phone. As she is dying, in the movie's last moments, she seems to return to what she exposes as a primal condition: "I've been longing for your call." She is "damaged" physically—"you damaged your hips," Aoyama recalls to her during her audition—and the older man self-servingly tells her that, despite her youth (she is twenty-four), "I think you live your life in a very mature way." The scars on her thighs are external, even her bones, jutting out of her skinny frame, are presented as monstrous (47.01)—an anticipation of anorexic body horror of Darren Aronofsky's *Black Swan*. The characteristics that make her an appealing prospect for Aoyama (her seriousness, her capacity for survival) are the skills that the film will eventually bring crashing down, with brutal force, on Aoyama's own body—but they are also fraudulently construed. This is, as Aoyama belatedly realizes after Asami's disappearance, an altogether simpler story of a middle-aged man falling for a beautiful younger woman on the grounds of her perceived beauty and sexual availability.

And she has *baggage*. In Asami's dingy apartment, other than a phone, there is only a large sack, whose hulking, inert masculinity occupies more of the screen than she does. In the movie's most gory sequence, it will turn out that the bag contains a mutilated man, deprived by Asami of both feet, his tongue, one ear, and the fingers on one of his hands. Further, we will be forced to observe that this body, whose abject masculinity, wholly denuded of the cinematic male body's phallic power by wires and needles, finally lurches onto the screen at the moment of Asami's coup, and is nourished on her vomit, served to him in a chrome dog bowl. The liturgical dynamics of the scene are punishingly clear; the recitation of the psychoanalytic category of abjection *textbook*.[37] (Textbookness: the kitsch form of exquisite congruity.) Before the contents of the baggage have been exposed, however, it has done something less dramatic, but in a sense even more consequential: at 48.11, it darts across the screen at the sound of the telephone. The movie's only "jump scare," this shot is one of only three depictions of moving objects in *Audition*. The first (which comes seven minutes before the bag flies across the screen) is an uncharacteristically goofy allegorical composition: Aoyama tossing, fumbling, and finally dropping some golf balls. The third, however, is the fascinating moment at which the central couple may or may not have sex. Miike carefully shoots the scene to show the couple ensheathed by a bed sheet while Aoyama is on top of Asami, then (almost imperceptibly) cuts to a close shot moving slowly up the same sheet to find Aoyama on the *bottom*, smiling and raising his chin as if receiving a blow job. The camera then returns down to the sheet to reveal that there is nobody there, and that Aoyama is alone.

This is a necessarily cumbersome way of describing a shot whose force depends on its brutally economic condensation of a three-act drama: (1) sheet enshrouds bodies; (2) man gets head; (3) there is nobody there. This shot comes at the movie's halfway point, and, especially the imperceptible cut that pulls off the trick, formally bisects *Audition*, both recalling the flying baggage and setting up the hallucinatory sequence in which Aoyama eventually *does* receive the oral sex of which he has been, so to speak, deprived, from both Asami and his son's girlfriend. (Among the effects of the editing is to formalize precisely that dimension of male entitlement: that Aoyama has been *deprived*.) By that point, however, the physical enjoyment of any penetrative, phallic sex—let alone the kind close to the teeth—has been detached from the promise of intimacy that hung between Aoyama and Asami in the seaside hotel. The truest sense of heterosexual intimacy, according to *Audition*'s understanding of female abjection, is the dismemberment and mutilation of the male body in the scene of torture. Following which, and only following which, Aoyama and Asami can speak to each other in a language that is both honest (neither has illusions about the other) and sweet. *Sweetness*, the exquisite feminine substrate of heterosexual abjection, is wrung out of Asami's body at great expense: Aoyama's phallic wholeness and her own life.

V. The Exquisite Art of Castration: Quentin Tarantino

The opening scene of Quentin Tarantino's directorial debut *Reservoir Dogs*, which depicts a group of men bickering and discussing pop music in a diner, contains a very brief reference to Japan that turns out to have prefigured much of the plot.[38] One of the older men, Laurence Tierney's Joe Cabot, who (we learn quickly enough) is the boss of this haphazardly assembled criminal gang, has been distracted while the others have been discussing Madonna, and keeps muttering the name "Toby"—having just found it in an address book.

He is a little alarmed: "Toby . . . who the fuck is Toby? Toby . . . Toby . . . think . . . think . . ." Eventually, a thought strikes him—"Oh fuck, Toby's that little china girl," [*sic* in screenplay]—and so he starts muttering through a series of Chinese names: "Chew? Toby Chew? No." His perhaps performatively mysterious mumbles eventually rouse one of the other older men, Harvey Keitel's Mr. White, into grabbing the book out of Joe's hand, and complaining animatedly, "For the past fifteen minutes now, you've just been droning on with names. 'Toby . . . Toby . . . Toby . . . Toby Wong . . . Toby Wong . . . Toby Chung . . . fuckin Charlie Chan.' I got Madonna's big dick outta my right ear, and Toby Jap I-don't-know-what, outta my left."[39]

It is, in one sense, a provocatively inconsequential moment, one of the casual displays of aggressive masculine wit that quickly came to define Tarantino's oeuvre—"a free-form adaptation of an off-Broadway play," as the *Guardian* reviewer put it.[40] Toby, in any case, never turns up; nor does his surname; and this first of the movie's many jarring uses of racist language hardly prepares the viewer for the dramatic escalation to come. Yet Joe's inability to place the "china girl," and Mr. White's frustration at it, *does* replicate itself in the plot's denouement, in which it turns out that among the robbers Joe has assembled for this bank job is an undercover cop, Det. Freddie Newandyke, appearing here as Mr. Orange. Joe, that is, has been sloppy in his prep—perhaps, as his inability to place Toby indicates, his (doubtless, once great) intuition is abandoning him. The *ethical* crux of the film, however, is the relationship between the younger Mr. Orange, fatally wounded while stealing a getaway car, and Mr. White, who refuses to believe that his younger, injured friend could have been the snitch. In the film's final moments, Mr. Orange, cradled in Mr. White's arms, confesses and apologizes; Mr. White kills him and is then killed himself by cops storming the warehouse where they have been hiding out. If Joe has been *ruined* by his poor planning, Mr. White is *wounded* by the trust he placed in somebody whose identity he mistook. Mr. Orange may as well have been Toby.

Another aspect of the "Toby Jap I-don't-know-what" figure bears further exploration: his apparent contamination by a racialized form of queerness, a "china girl." Mr. White's relationship with Mr. Orange, if it is not pulsating with the kinds of unspeakable desires that, at least since the incest plotline of *The Godfather* (Paramount, 1972), provide the gangster genre with much of its erotic interest, does quite clearly violate the professional codes that, at other points, Mr. White is proud to embody.[41] Mr. White told Mr. Orange his real name. He shouldn't have, as Mr. Pink makes clear: the latter so called, Joe jokes, "cause you're a faggot," though the irony of the joke will mystify an audience watching Steve Buscemi, as Mr. Pink, scrabble around the screen lacking *any* coherent identity principle. "Oh, I don't doubt it was quite beautiful––"

he jibes, before Mr. White rears up in panic. In the diner, meanwhile, Mr. White had been motivated to grab Joe's book and join in the Toby digression because he had "Madonna's big dick outta my right ear," and so gravitated towards the left. The Toby parapraxis was set up to avoid some kind of phantasmatic penetration. The effect is intensified by the heavy citationality of the moment on screen: Harvey Keitel, as Mr. White, is all but replaying the opening scene of *Mean Streets* (to which *Reservoir Dogs* was, entirely reasonably, compared); and Laurence Tierney, whose breakthrough role was the title role in the roughhouse 1945 picture *Dillinger*, appears both as Joe Cabot and as one of the dedicatees of Tarantino's screenplay—among other "sources of inspiration" such as Roger Corman and Chow Yuen Fat [*sic*].[42]

What is there to say about Tarantino's violent repudiation of the male body, in a homosocial set-up designed, above all, to position hyper-masculinity as both the rule and the exception, that has not been preempted by the classical diagnosis of homophobia? What can it mean that Tarantino chose to appear on screen *himself* as Mr. Brown to tell the story of "Madonna's big dick" (it was Pink in the screenplay), and so to get to say "dick" eleven times in a row? (Uniquely among the lines written in the screenplay, these eleven words are lineated, as if in verse.) I think this: that Tarantino's manic ambivalence concerning phallic representation—by which I mean both representations *of* the phallus and his phallic *mode* of representing—was, from the start, intimately connected with the ambivalence facing Japan that he exhibits in the above epigraph, and that it would be brought to a crisis (rather than sublimated) in his deployment of the figure of the sword.

The alien sword plays a vital role in *Pulp Fiction* (1994), one of the movie's climactic moments entails a samurai sword calling to Bruce Willis's character, Butch, and then leading him down the stairs into a primal scene where two men are beating and raping his adversary, Marsellus Wallace.[43] Butch has tried to make use of the tools around him—a baseball bat and a chainsaw, each gripped with an alarmingly playful expression—but none feels right; it is the glistening Oriental splendor of the samurai sword that enables him both to rescue his mortal rival and to comprehend the nobility of his decision to do so. Fittingly, our gaze is directed to the sword by a jump cut, Tarantino launching into practice the connection Miyazaki (if indeed he sent the sword to *Pulp Fiction*'s producer Harvey Weinstein) drew between the editorial technique and the fetishized sword.

Or is it not, perhaps, that Tarantino is deploying against the critics his intuitive grasp of the logic of psychoanalytic film theory—specifically the idea that "fetish," in the Freudian sense, serves as an alternative name for the cut?[44] Psychoanalysis has provided many of this book's hermeneutic tactics, but in a sense it is useless in relation to Tarantino, both because (as is revealed in his

FIGURE 5.3. *Pulp Fiction* (1994). LOAN[S].

interviews) he seems impervious to any notion that he possesses psychic interiority and lacks any capability for self-conscious reflection, and because his movies (and, again, his interview-persona) are gratuitously, even defensively, familiar with psychoanalytic modes of reasoning, if not with psychoanalytic theory itself. Accordingly, though one encounters the presence of psychoanalytic categories in Tarantino's movies (especially fetishism), its presence remains essentially thematic, its critical edge blunted in advance by its intradiegetic representation. Fetishism is the central problematic around which

Tarantino's films organize this question. The fetishist, it will be remembered, chanced upon his object through the redirection of his gaze, but more importantly through the necessary redirection of attention precipitated by his having encountered "an unwelcome perception" (Freud, 1927) of the castrated penis of his mother, which reminds him that he too may be castrated under paternal authority. Tarantino himself explores such a connection in characteristically unselfconscious language in an interview in a 2004 documentary about film editing entitled *The Cutting Edge*: "when I was doing my first movie, the only thing I knew is, I wanted a female editor, [because] I just felt a female editor would be more nurturing, to the movie and to me. They wouldn't be trying to win their way just to win their way, alright, they wouldn't be trying to shove their agenda or win their battles with me. They would be nurturing me through this process."[45] Afraid that an older man might "win," and impede the development of both *Reservoir Dogs* and its auteur, the director hands the scissors to a maternal figure who might enable him to be a better mother to his own movie.[46]

The *Pulp Fiction* sequence is a masterpiece of the art of castration. The Oedipal resonances of the basement behind the green door—where a big daddy is being fucked by two skinny boys—have not been lost on Carolyn Dinshaw, who sees the dungeon, and thereby the "medieval" that it will "get," as an abject space in which masculinities unravel and interact. Her reading depends on an account of the sword as a surrogate dick—"the largest weapon the pawnshop has to offer" (Dinshaw, 185); "his giant, uh, sword" (189).[47] But to the extent that it is one, it is surrogate first and dick second. Tarantino carefully shoots the scene to distinguish between the phallus as incorporated appendage (the hammer, the Louisville slugger) and the sword as an unincorporated, indeed wholly alien, subject. As Butch walks down the stairs behind his weapon, his expression is one of dispossession and estrangement; he knows, so we know, that this isn't his blade, but one stolen from a pawn shop—doubly, triply removed from its intended bearer.

This poignant deprivation is a midpoint in a sequence densely populated with castration images: the sensorially deprived gimp; the rape of Marsellus Wallace; the belittling "step aside Butch" with which Marsellus, and his shotgun, take control of the situation; the literal castrations and murders of Maynard and Zed; and then the theft, by a newly emboldened (though "LA privilege"-less) Butch, of Zed's chopper whose adornment with the word "grace" promises his spiritual, no less than material, salvation. Yet this too is a substitution, a grace that, abjected out of his butchness, Butch can no longer inhabit. He rides off to the right of the screen leaving behind two mementoes of the fragility of his remasculinization: the word LOAN in bright yellow, and another racialized figure, who like Marsellus clasps his weapon with confidence and assurance. Such a procession of simulacra more broadly both defines and partitions the "dick thing" that around which, in bell hooks's account, Tarantino's entire aesthetic is organized (hooks, 1996).[48]

Yet Tarantino's most striking treatment of the theme of castration is organized not around a dick, but around an avenging angel—it might not be going too far to imagine that the pitch for *Kill Bill* entailed some related pun on *Charlie's Angels.* Beatrix Kiddo, credentialing herself before her new master Pai Mei, declares herself skilled in "the exquisite art of the samurai sword."[49] Tarantino's reviewers picked up the word. Echoing reviews of *Audition,* Roger Ebert rhapsodized about the "exquisite formal garden" of the first movie (Ebert, 2003); Peter Bradshaw declared the pair of movies "exquisitely modern" (Bradshaw, 2004).[50] Kiddo's sword—which as the movie goes to pains to tell us, is an absolutely singular object, handcrafted by the master craftsman Hattori Hanzo in breach of a blood oath—feminizes violence itself, silencing the blam-blam of *Pulp Fiction* with an eerie swish, supplanting the black blocks of *Reservoir Dogs,* visually continuous with the tuxedoed arms that bore them, with a glittery reflectivity. Tarantino has been criticized for "aestheticizing violence"—by hooks, for example, who describes his movies as "the ultimate in sexy cover-ups of a very unsexy mind fuck" (hooks, 1996)—and defended in the same terms, in a *Harvard Law Record* article that credits him with the ability "to transform an object of moral outrage into one of aesthetic beauty" (Morales, 2003).[51] But the dualism of these positions ("cover-ups"; "transform") presupposes a premise that the sword, no less than psychoanalysis, seeks to reprove: that beauty and violence are psychically, ethically, and representationally discrete categories.

The plot of *Kill Bill: Volume I* and *Volume II* is deceptively complex, despite the title's disclosure of its ultimate aims; it progresses indirectly and tortuously through a screwy diegesis comprised of more flash-backs and flash-forwards than continuous action. Uma Thurman's Kiddo, an operative of the Deadly Viper Assassination Squad (the DeVAS) has left the group and fled to El Paso, Texas, where she has found a gormless gent delighted to wed her and bring up her child, fathered by the DeVAS' leader, the eponymous Bill. Outraged—though whether at her erotic or professional betrayal remains unclear—Bill instructs the DeVAS to murder all participants in the wedding rehearsal, and shoots Kiddo herself in the face, putting her in a coma for four years. When she awakes, she hunts down each of the DeVAS: first O-Ren Ishii; then Vernita Green; then Bill's brother Budd, whom she finds already murdered by her next victim, Elle Driver; when she finally arrives at Bill's apartment, she finds their daughter B. B. alive and well, kills Bill, and takes B. B. away.

That B.B. is alive and well is one of two heavily hit pieces of plot that the movies withhold; the other, its formal inverse, that "Kiddo" is in fact the

FIGURE 5.4. *Kill Bill, Vol. I* (2003).

central character's name, and not merely the infantilizing moniker Bill has given to a figure known to everybody else as "The Bride." So although the appearance and salvation of her daughter is, of course, a happy outcome for Kiddo, who has spent much of the foregoing movies attempting to play the role of mother—offering stern advice to Gogo, O-Ren's bodyguard; spanking one of the Crazy 88 on the bottom and telling him "this is what you get for fucking around with Yakuzas"—B. B. nonetheless deprives the revenge plot of its *raison d'être*. Kiddo's motivation for the murders of hundreds of people, over the course of the two movies, has been vengeance for her daughter; neither she nor anybody else sheds any tears for the others of Bill's victims, whom he dismissively calls in his opening monologue, "these other jokers." Despite the brightness of its colors, the revenge narrative collapses into the same neurosis René Girard diagnoses in the protagonist of *Hamlet*, whose father's murderousness complicates the morality of his own murder: "the crime by Claudius looks to [Hamlet] like one more link in an already long chain, and his own revenge will look like still another link, perfectly identical to all the other links" (273). Three obvious candidates emerge to take their own revenge against Kiddo, possibly in the long-deferred *Kill Bill: Volume III*: (1) Nicki Bell, Green's daughter, to whom (in one of the first appearances of her mimetically maternal desire) Kiddo apologizes for Nicki's witnessing her mother's murder and promises, "when you grow up, if you still feel raw about it, I'll be waiting"; (2) O-Ren's lawyer, Sofie Fatale, whose name alone is enough to warrant the spin-off Tarantino has occasionally promised her, and who is allowed to "keep [her] wicked life" in order to tell Bill the details of O-Ren's murder; and (3) Elle Driver, who is blinded but alive when the camera leaves her in Budd's trailer.

To protect against the limitless expansion of a narrative that, as Girard puts it, "extends in all directions beyond the limits of its action [and so] has no beginning and no end" (274), Kiddo compiles her own plot into a "death list five," a numerical sequence, written in red and black felt-tips on the plane to Tokyo: the name, and the order, in which she will take down her targets. It is not the first time we have watched at least some of these names written—Hattori Hanzo engrafts "Bill" into the condensation on his window, carefully scratching the top of "i" as though composing a kanji; Kiddo here imitates his "B"—but here, arranged neatly (though getting increasingly large) in a list, we are invited to reflect on them as fragments of language, strophically formed with the names of "deadly vipers." We notice, perhaps, the visual prominence of the initial letters of each name, O, I, V, G, B, E, and B again; perhaps too that "Elle," like the character we will eventually know as "Bea," and who is named in one of the chapter titles as "I," sounds as a homophone of a letter. Character, organized around the orthographically minimal instance of a letter, might then serve to hold in place the various elements of *Kill Bill* after even its most simple plot had failed to do so. Yet this too fails, and perhaps still more dramatically. The "B" pairing, reformulated as the name of Beatrix and Bill's daughter, betrays Tarantino's debt here to the author of *Billy Budd*, the titular character of which is the last entry on the list of Melville's double-B antiheroes: shorter than Kiddo's, rounded out by "Bartleby" and "Babo."[52] Bill's singularity, preserved fastidiously until the moment of his encryption in Kiddo's list, now collapses under the weight of intertextual reference and intratextual doubling.

The Melville scholar Richard Chase writes that "Billy Budd is seeking his own castration—seeking to yield up his vitality to an authoritative but kindly father."[53] If Bill *y* Budd are understood as divided echoes of the unlucky midshipman, their deaths might be likewise ascribed to a sentimental desire to succumb to the sword. Budd's death at the hands of Elle Driver, whose first appearance in a nurse's uniform en route to poison Kiddo pairs the two as bad and not-good-enough mothers, results from a strange and possibly suicidal plot of his own concoction. He has planned to sell Kiddo's sword to Driver for a million dollars, having already told Bill that the sword given by his brother had raised no more than $250 at the pawn shop (a callback to *Pulp Fiction*); the black mamba that kills him is submerged within the cache of money Driver has brought to make the trade. In fact, we learn after his death, he has kept the sword from Bill in a bag of golf clubs in his bedroom, where its homoerotic inscription—"To My Brother Budd, The Only Man I Ever Loved,—BiLL"—rather gives the lie (as is Tarantino's wont) to the hammy heterosexuality of the porn mags all over the place. Bill's masochistic motivations for setting the plot in action are advertised loudly before the opening credits have rolled: "I'd like to believe, even now, you're aware enough to know there isn't a trace of sadism in my actions . . . No, Kiddo, at this moment, this is me at my most masochistic."

To reiterate, masochistic *desire* for castration would not be the same as *fetishism* of castration; *Kill Bill* is not interesting because of its sophomoric diagnoses of defective and murderous masculinities but, as hooks rightly says, those that are ultimately vindicated. The point is not that Bill and Budd *want* to be castrated, and neither in fact falls prey to the movie's castrating agent, the Hanzo sword. (Budd dies from snake venom; Bill's heart explodes after Kiddo has performed the magical "Ten-Point Palm Exploding Heart Technique.") The exquisite art of *Kill Bill* is not masochistic in the least; is not, indeed, characterological at all, but formal. At the level of character, the act of castration that is promised in every frame is withheld: nobody is, in fact, castrated. Yet its symbolic manifestations abound everywhere—or, rather, its symbolic manifestations are *themselves defaced and cut off everywhere*, as though each attempt to sublimate the threat of castration produced its own immediate desublimation. A brief and profoundly incomplete roster: both Elle's eyes are removed, the first by Pai Mei, the second by Kiddo; the hospital rapist Buck's ankle is sliced open; Kiddo cuts off Fatale's arm; Gogo, who has stabbed a would-be suitor ("is it I that has penetrated you?") is deprived of a blade in her confrontation with Kiddo, and fights instead with a ball and chain; the young member of the Crazy 88 has his sword chopped down, piece by piece, to a tiny stub, etc. In one comic flourish, a *reverse* castration almost takes place: Kiddo kicks Pai Mei in the groin and gets her foot stuck, allowing the ancient master to display the uncanny knack of being able to break it off at the ankle.

The most vividly fetishistic image of partial castration occurs at the end of the first movie, at the moment of the Hanzo sword's greatest triumph—the scalping of O-Ren. Something flies, left to right, across the screen; a close-up on O-Ren's thigh reveals a damp red patch on the still largely immaculate white; O-Ren's sword falls gracefully into the snow at her feet; Kiddo, facing away, holds her katana like a conductor's baton. Then, a close-up on O-Ren's face crops out the top of her head, and she intones liturgically, "that really was a Hattori Hanzo sword," before we zoom out to see that the top of her head is missing, and her brain exposed, at precisely the line on her forehead where the shot had stopped, cutting off from the body what had been cut out of the shot. Lucy Liu's brain is unconvincingly rubbery and plastic (or perhaps "plastinated" like one of the corpses exhibited in Gunther von Hagens's *Body Worlds* exhibitions) but the fine line traced out by sword and shot fetishistically disarticulates the actor only as far as she has already, for the previous hour, been fetishized. Indeed, the unpersuasiveness of the shot is all the more surprising given that the effect was achieved with make-up and prosthetics, rather than (as it looks to have been) in postproduction: the very two-dimensionality of the cinematic body that Tarantino exposes with Kiddo's sword is vitiated by the camera's movement out from Liu's face; if this *were truly* a two-dimensional body, we wouldn't be able to see the brain at all. The perfect sublimation-desublimation of the castration anxiety is delineated on the face of *Kill Bill*'s most prominent Asian star, whose big break was playing the ferocious and hypersexual lawyer Ling Woo on *Ally McBeal*. That Tarantino's deployment of the samurai sword draws on long-held Orientalist stereotypes is, for sure, not news; nor is it surprising that, in a medium for which psychoanalysis has supplied such powerful analytic tools, such a deployment is cut across by such Freudian analytic categories as fetishism and castration anxiety. What may be more surprising is the difficulty with which Tarantino is faced when trying to realize the aesthetic potential of the katana. The samurai sword's defining characteristic is a thinness that tends towards infinity; it is in this sense an object whose third dimension defeats its second in order to produce the theoretical form of pure linearity, no more capable of being rendered cinematically than discursively.

Kiddo's *sprezzatura* bisection of O-Ren Ishii's face leaves exposed, impossibly, the seat of O-Ren's intellection, but here that estimable organ is nothing more than an abject, blobby intrusion into a visual space otherwise organized as exquisitely as a Mondrian composition. The aesthetic promise of the sword encounters simultaneously two limits it cannot breach: the material limit of the body and the cognitive limit of subjective perception. In this way, *Kill Bill* violates the principle categorical claim that I have been prosecuting: that the place within Western aesthetics granted to "Japan," a place I have designated "exquisite," has served as a phantasmatic resolution of the melancholic condition of Kantian subjective universality. The narcissistic condition on which that notion of Kant's depends, in which a phantasmatic presence compensates for a real absence, will itself break itself upon those limits: it will break, as Wilde's body did under the conditions of hard labor imposed as his punishment for an aesthete's life. (I take it as axiomatic that Wilde was sentenced for an *ontological*, rather than *behavioral*, transgression.) It will break, as Noguchi's playful appropriation of Victorian tropes will disintegrate into the stream of surging militarism; as the gamesome patter of "I am so proud . . ." will turn morbid on the "big black block." The exquisite, in so far as it represents a moment at all, is necessarily a prologue to events that establish their historicity through rendering their antecedents quaint and queasy. In this sense, the melancholia of the subjective universal, even if it be mitigated by social and cognitive practices in the present, is not precisely *grievable*, by history or by us.

At some point, though, one has to stop. The week that I finished editing the text of this book I went to see *Isle of Dogs*, Wes Anderson's 2018 stop-motion film about a group of dogs escaping from an artificial island in a dystopian, futuristic Japan. *Another* one. Why not a dystopian, futuristic China, or Finland, or Cameroon, or Argentina, or Azerbaijan, or Benin, or Tibet, or New Zealand? Yet despite the over-familiarity of the setting, the movie's relation to dystopia registered something new, a hint that the relation to political authority that undergirds, I think, all of the objects in this book had collapsed. Whereas in from *Kill Bill* all the way back to *The Mikado*, the beautiful violence of the blade was logically associated with the beautiful violence of the authoritarian state, in *Isle of Dogs*, the elegant brutality of, for example, a carefully crafted sequence in which poisonous sushi is compiled is presented as sharp contrast to the rough, masculine edges of Mayor Kobayashi, the gangster capitalist who has stolen the seat of executive power. This seemed to me a distinctively post-2016 type of dystopia, one that (like *The Leftovers* but unlike *The Hunger Games*) takes the collapse of democratic institutions as a premise, and works outwards from there towards the establishment of new institutions. For that reason, I felt a curious sense that this movie was outside my jurisdiction, and not merely because I was, through strange coincidence, wrapping up a manuscript at exactly the moment of its release—and, evidently, that turned out to be negotiable anyway.

Still, other parts of the movie's reception felt very familiar. *Isle of Dogs* was praised by some for being—yes—"undoubtedly exquisite," and criticized by others for its casual deployment of Orientalist stereotypes.[54] It was vaguely dispiriting to feel such a debate unfurl just as I was putting the lid on a decade of research on the topic. Had I somehow talked myself out of taking a position on *either* of those assessments? Personally, I very much enjoyed the dogs (and I'm not usually a dog person), and answered "yes" when asked whether I thought the movie was offensive. People who were familiar with my work seemed surprised by both of those takes —perhaps they thought that my goal was to blunt the force of anti-Orientalist critique by universalizing Orientalism? Or, if not universalizing, at least proliferating examples of so many different kinds (knives, emoji, movies, light opera, portraits, novels, libraries, sonnets . . . etc.) that a certain Orientalist habit of thought would appear absolutely inescapable. And I suspect that some version of the habit of thought described in this book *is* inescapable, if one holds with the Kantian account of aesthetic judgment, which I do. On the other hand, I think the various species of exquisite experience presented here indicate a profoundly variegated aesthetic category, which, though all generative of the same kind of feeling, are not Orientalist in the same way, and interact in different ways with ethical judgments. What this variegation might demonstrate, in the end, is that once separated *from* the sphere of ethical judgment—that is, once one can acknowledge that enjoyment of the dogs operates wholly separately from taking offense at the Orientalism—aesthetic judgment can be returned to the sphere of ethics, to complicate our apparently naïve judgments, and to prove those we make in bad faith. The psychoanalyst Adam Phillips suggests, quite movingly, that the shared purpose of psychoanalysis and literature is to "inspire us to live more justly pleasurable, more morally intriguing lives."[55] If either ever succeeds, it is because both psychoanalysis and literature are enterprises whose essential logic is melancholy, subjective, and universal—enterprises whose fruitless appeal to a world that turns away, nonetheless brings a new world into being.

NOTES

Preface. Another Empire: Victorian Japan

1. Roland Barthes, *Empire of Signs*, trans. Richard Howard (New York: Hill and Wang, 1982), 3.

2. Robbie Collin, "Quentin Tarantino: 'The Confederate Flag Was the American Swastika,'" *Telegraph* (January 2, 2016), accessed online March 31, 2018.

3. To take a powerful and persuasive deployment of the term "exquisite" in quite another register: Claire Jarvis's book *Exquisite Masochism: Marriage, Sex, and the Novel Form* (Baltimore: Johns Hopkins University Press, 2016) aligns "exquisite" with the realist detail, an erotically charged technique for zooming in and out of domestic spaces. Although the present work assesses different genres towards different ends than Jarvis, her analysis of the power of the "asymptotic relationship to pain" that organizes both aesthetic contemplation and sexuality, resonates throughout.

4. Barthes, *Empire of Signs*; Carrie Preston, *Learning to Kneel: Noh, Modernism, and Journeys in Teaching* (New York: Columbia University Press, 2016); Christopher Reed, *Bachelor Japanists: Japanese Aesthetics and Western Masculinities* (New York: Columbia University Press, 2017); John Whittier Treat, *Great Mirrors Shattered: Homosexuality, Orientalism, and Japan* (Oxford: Oxford University Press, 1999).

5. Future Bible Heroes, "How to Get Laid in Japanese," from *Lonely Days EP* (1997).

Introduction. Analytic of the Exquisite

1. Sadakichi Hartmann, *Japanese Art* (Boston: LC Page, 1903), 160.

2. I. A. Richards, *Practical Criticism: A Study of Literary Judgment* (London: Kegan Paul, Trench, Trübner, 1929).

3. Elizabeth S. Bates, "Some Breadwinners of the Fair," *Overland Monthly*, April 1894, 375–76.

4. George Nicholson, *1900 Supplement to the Dictionary of Gardening: A Practical and Scientific Encyclopedia of Horticulture for Gardeners and Botanists* (London: L. Upcott Gill, 1901), 453.

5. Toichi Tsumura, "Dwarf Trees," *Transactions and Proceedings of the Japan Society, London*, vol. 6, twelfth session, 1902–4 (London: 1904), 3.

6. Oscar Wilde, *The Picture of Dorian Gray* (Philadelphia: Lippincott's, 1890), 35. The cigarette is one of dozens of exquisite items threaded through the novel. Basil's first encounter with Dorian persuaded him that "fate had in store for me exquisite joys and exquisite sorrows" (7); at their first meeting Lord Henry commends youth's "exquisite temptations" (17); Dorian, once

Lord Henry's influence upon him has been felt, feels "an exquisite poison in the air" (24). Sybil Vane, Dorian's spurned lover, rues an exquisite "knowledge" bestowed upon her when they met (40); he matches her plaint with "lips curled in exquisite disdain" (41). Later, Dorian's imitators are referred to, scornfully, as "the young exquisites of the Mayfair balls" (66). Books, poems, costumes, and, three times, "life" are exquisite to Dorian, and in the end, in the novel's final paragraph, the word is called on to suture Dorian's dead body (now magically decayed) to his portrait (now magically restored to its original condition): "a splendid portrait of their master as they had last seen him, in all the wonder of his exquisite youth and beauty" (100).

7. Michel Foucault, thinking in 1982 about the inaptitude of "seduction" as a modality for naming homosexual romances, remarks to an interviewer that "[a homosexual today] would say something like: 'the best moment of love is when the lover leaves in a taxi.'" (Foucault, 1982). This taste for retrospection, he elaborates, is the result of a "homosexual imagination . . . for the most part concerned with reminiscing about the act rather than anticipating it," such anticipation having been denied to homosexuals through an "interdiction" on open courtship. The cigarette may be, and may even be for Lord Henry, one of Western literature's most powerful symbols for post-coital reflection; more important for these purposes, however, is that the exquisite dimension of sex, for Foucault, is found only after a certain kind of loss. This version of queerness—delightful, sad, and wounded—suffuses *The Picture of Dorian Gray*, and many of the other literary texts I discuss.

8. A. C. Swinburne, *The Complete Prose Works of Algernon Charles Swinburne*, ed. Edmund Gosse (London: W. Heinemann, 1926), 23. Swinburne made this remark in response to J.A.M. Whistler's "Ten O'Clock" lecture on art, which had concluded that art required no criticism because "the story of the beautiful is already complete—hewn in the marbles of the Parthenon—and broidered, with the birds, upon the fan of Hokusai—at the foot of Fusi-Yama." J.A.M. Whistler, "Mr. Whistler's Ten O'Clock," (Chicago: Old Dominion, 1904), 34.

9. Edward Said, *Orientalism* (New York: Vintage, 1978).

10. An important counterexample is "japanning," which had attracted Western attention since the seventeenth century, and which had been understood as a symbol of impermeability and (racial) inscrutability. See Chi-Ming Yang, "Asia Out of Place: The Aesthetics of Incorruptibility in Behn's *Oroonoko*," *Eighteenth Century Studies*, 42.2 (Winter 2009), 235–53.

11. Laurence Oliphant, *Narrative of the Earl of Elgin's Mission to China and Japan in the Years 1857, '58, ' 59* (New York: Harper and Brothers, 1860), 407. Oliphant, who was Elgin's private secretary, mentions a number of other exquisite aspects of Japanese culture, including, twice, "form" (155, 355).

12. A. B. Mitford, *Tales of Old Japan* (London: Macmillan, 1871), 231.

13. Isabella Bird, *Unbeaten Tracks in Japan: An Account of Travels in the Interior, Including Visits to the Aborigines of Yezo and the Shrines of Nikko and Isé* (London: John Murray, 1880), 78, 99, 105–6, 132, 134, 159, 171, 178, 222, 262.

14. Richard Knolles, *The Turkish History, Comprehending the Origin of that Nation, and the Growth of the Othoman Empire, with the Lives and Conquests of Their Several Kings and Emperors* (London: Isaac Cleave, 1701).

15. E. L. James, *Fifty Shades of Gray* (New York: Vintage, 2011), 281. Throughout the novel, "it," usually designating some sensation within the protagonists' sadomasochistic sex play, is called "exquisite" a further eight times.

16. Michel Foucault, *Fearless Speech*, ed. Joseph Pearson (Los Angeles: Semiotexte, 2001), 74.

17. Thomas De Quincey, *On Murder*, ed. Robert Morrison (Oxford: Oxford University Press, 2006). De Quincey's translation of a short piece entitled "The Last Days of Immanuel Kant" by E. A. Wasianski, finds a kind of morbid levity, too, in the image of Kant's death. De Quincey's reading of Kant—at once responsible to the letter of the *Critiques* and wildly disrespectful of their spirit—helped to found the suspicion of aesthetics in the Anglophone world as a morally suspicious branch of inquiry, keen on rationalizing and elevating pleasure in a nonmoral sense. For a full exposition of this position, and a detailed description of De Quincey's effect not merely on the emergent cultural discourses of modernity, see Alina Clej. See De Quincey, "The Last Days of Kant," *Blackwood's Edinburgh Magazine*, 21:122 (1827), 133–57; Clej, *A Genealogy of the Modern Self: Thomas De Quincey and the Intoxication of Writing* (Stanford, CA: Stanford University Press, 1995).

18. See Guyer, "Beauty, Freedom, and Morality: Kant's Lectures on Anthropology and the Development of His Aesthetic Theory," in *Values of Beauty*, 163–89. Note also that Guyer sees Kant's anthropological turn in the 1770s as an important precursor to the third critique.

19. Immanuel Kant, "Letter 67, to Marcus Herz, June 7, 1771; 10; 123," quoted in Paul Guyer, *Values of Beauty: Historical Essays in Aesthetics* (Cambridge: Cambridge University Press, 2005), 163.

20. Immanuel Kant, *Observations on the Feeling of the Beautiful and Sublime*, trans. John T. Goldthwait (Berkeley: University of California Press, 1960), 97.

21. "To make psychological observations (as Burke does in his book on the beautiful and sublime), and thus to gather material for rules of experience that will be systematically connected in the future, without yet seeking to comprehend them, is certainly the only true obligation of empirical psychology, which only with difficulty could ever lay claim to the rank of a philosophical science." Immanuel Kant, *Critique of the Power of Judgment*, trans. Paul Guyer (Cambridge: Cambridge University Press, 2000). (Guyer further notes that Kant's zinger, "without yet seeking to comprehend them," was inserted into the fair copy at a late stage of composition.)

22. Kant, *Observations*, 110.

23. Kant, *Critique of the Power of Judgment*, 89.

24. Ibid., 123.

25. See Jean-François Lyotard, *Lessons on the Analytic of the Sublime*, trans. Elizabeth Rottenberg (Stanford: Stanford University Press, 1994). Nor will the word "affect" do, precisely, since Kant uses that word to designate an especially intense kind of feeling capable of sustaining, on its own account, aesthetic judgments. For Paul de Man, that latter caveat affords evidence that Kantian affectivity (and aspects of his aesthetics more broadly) begins outside the body—that is, in the world of objectivity: "Kant's discussion of the affects does not start out from the inner experience of a subject, from the sort of interpretive sensitivity, the affective cogito that one can capture in Montaigne, in Malebranche, or in the Romantics." Paul de Man, "Kant's Materialism," in *Aesthetic Ideology*, ed. Andrei Warminski (Minneapolis: University of Minnesota Press, 1997), 123. The claim I am making here does not require that I take a position on this provocation of de Man's, but his consequent discussion of the impossibility of *apatheia* (of feeling nothing in a moment of aesthetic judgment), and Rei Terada's gloss on it in *Feeling in Theory*, find their counterparts in many of the evocations of "exquisite" I have been citing, which for all their pathos, sometimes trope towards absolutely minimal expressions of pleasure.

See Rei Terada, *Feeling in Theory: Emotion after the "Death of the Subject"* (Cambridge: Harvard University Press, 2000).

26. See Hannah Arendt, *Lectures on Kant's Political Philosophy*, ed. Ronald Beiner (Chicago: University of Chicago Press, 1992).

27. We will encounter, over the course of this book, many people and characters in the position of postulating the assent of their fellows to an aesthetic judgment, and being ruinously rebuffed: Oscar Wilde in court; Yone Noguchi late in his correspondence with Rabindranath Tagore; Cho-Cho San in her relationship with Lieutenant Pinkerton.

28. Sigmund Freud, *Mourning and Melancholia, Standard Edition of the Complete Psychological Works of Sigmund Freud,* vol. 14, trans. and ed. James Strachey (London: Hogarth, 1957), 247.

29. Robert Esposito, *Terms of the Political: Community, Immunity, Biopolitics*, trans. Rhiannon Noel Welch (New York: Fordham University Press, 2013).

30. Alan S. Christy, "The Making of Imperial Subjects in Okinawa," in *Formations of Colonial Modernity in East Asia*, ed. Barlow (Durham: Duke University Press, 1997), 158.

31. Yanagi Soetsu, *The Unknown Craftsman: A Japanese Insight into Beauty*, adapted by Bernard Leach (Tokyo: Kodansha, 1972).

32. Stephen Vlastos, ed., *Mirror of Modernity: Invented Traditions of Modern Japan* (Berkeley: University of California Press, 1998).

33. For further examples of work exploring the mutual imbrication of "Japanese aesthetics" and what Barlow calls "colonial modernity in East Asia," see, Leslie Pincus, *Authenticating Culture in Imperial Japan: Kuki Shuzo and the Rise of National Aesthetics* (Berkeley: University of California Press, 1996); Stefan Tanaka, "Imaging History: Inscribing Belief in the Nation," *Journal of Asian Studies* 51.1 (1994); Alan Tansman, *The Aesthetics of Japanese Fascism* (Berkeley: University of California Press, 2009).

34. Kuki Shuzo is an especially important figure in the controversy discussed above, partly because, as a reader, friend, and correspondent of Martin Heidegger, he was among the most prominent intellectual connections between the European romantic tradition, and the emergent Japanese aesthetic nationalism. See Pincus, *Authenticating Culture in Imperial Japan* (1996); also Michael Marra, ed., *Modern Japanese Aesthetics* (Honolulu: University of Hawai'i Press, 2001); Hiroshi Nara, *The Structure of Detachment: The Aesthetic Vision of Kuki Shuzo* (Honolulu: University of Hawai'i Press, 2005).

35. The singular moment of exception, scholars generally hold, was the Russo-Japanese War of 1904–5: after this moment, Japonisme declined, modernist poets turned their attention to China, and Japan was represented increasingly as a threat. One strand of this historiography will be upheld here, in specific relation to *The Mikado*, the reception (and, consequently, cultural semiotics) of which shifted dramatically and quickly in the aftermath of the war. For the most part, however, I will show that the violence attributed to the Japanese national character in the post-1905 period was already implied by the earlier aesthetic exceptionalization of Japan in the west—as early, therefore, as the 1870s—because, indeed, the very act of *aesthetic exceptionalization* entailed a melancholy relation to the exceptionalized object. For a treatment of the effect of the Russo-Japanese War on racial form in the United States, see Colleen Lye, *America's Asia: Racial Form and American Literature* (Princeton: Princeton University Press, 2004). For the British perspective, see Toshio Yokoyama, *Japan in the Victorian Mind: A Study of Stereotyped Images of a Nation 1850-80* (Basingstoke: Macmillan, 1987).

36. "Nothing happened worth mentioning in this voyage." Jonathan Swift, *Travels into Several Remote Nations of the World by Lemuel Gulliver, First a Surgeon, and Then a Captain of Several Ships* (London: Harrison, 1782), 101.

37. *Dublin University Magazine*, 18.103, p. 1.

38. "The United States occupied a different position from all the above named [European] powers, for they had not been brought into such contact with Japan as awakened unpleasant associations. The only effort we had made toward opening friendly relations, (and it scarcely deserves the name,) was in sending two ships under Commodore Biddle, which remained at anchor some eight or ten days, accomplished nothing, and quietly left when the Japanese desired it." Francis L. Hawks, *Narrative of the Expedition of an American Squadron to the China Seas and Japan, Performed in the Years 1852, 1853, and 1854, under the Command of Commodore M. C. Perry, United States Navy* (Washington, DC: Beverley Tucker, 1856), 77.

39. Nathaniel Hawthorne, *Passages from the English Notebooks* (Boston: James R. Osgood, 1872), 140.

40. See Russell Reising and Peter J. Kvidera, "Fast Fish and Raw Fish: Moby-Dick, Japan, and Melville's Thematics of Geography," *New England Quarterly*, 70.2 (June 1997), 285–305.

41. Charles Macfarlane, *Japan: An Account, Geographical and Historical, from the Earliest Period at Which the Islands Composing this Empire Were Known to Europeans, Down to the Present Time, and the Expedition Fitted Out in the United States, Etc.* (Putnam: New York, 1853).

42. *The Spectator*, vol. 14, p. 210

43. Christopher Benfey, *The Great Wave: Gilded Age Misfits, Japanese Eccentrics, and the Opening of Old Japan* (New York: Random House, 2003).

44. Diósy's life and career are detailed in John Adlard, *A Biography of Arthur Diósy, Founder of the Japan Society* (Lampeter: Edwin Mellen Press, 1991). Sir Hugh Cortazzi was the British ambassador to Japan from 1980–84, and has published very broadly on the topics most under discussion here. The *Biographical Portraits* series extended to six volumes under Cortazzi's editorial guidance, in addition to which the following works are of particular interest (from a much longer bibliography): Cortazzi, *Japan in Late Victorian London: The Japanese Native Village in Knightsbridge and "The Mikado" 1885* (Norwich: Sainsbury Institute for the Study of Japanese Arts and Cultures, 2009); *Britain and Japan: 1859–1991: Themes and Personalities* (London: Routledge, 1992); *Victorians in Japan: In and Around the Treaty Ports* (London: Continuum International, 1987); *For Japanese Students of English: Thoughts from a Sussex Garden* (Tokyo: Eichosha Shinsha, 1984). He has also published edited volumes of work dealing with Japan by A. B. Mitford, Sir Alfred East, and Mary Crawford Fraser ("Mrs. Hugh Fraser").

45. Adlard, *A Biography of Arthur Diósy*, 59.

46. Ibid., 59–60.

47. "Hartmann served as secretary to Walt Whitman, and had the dubious distinction of being referred to by Whitman once as "that damn Japanee." Juliana Chang, *Quiet Fire: A Historical Anthology of Asian American Poetry, 1892—1970* (New York: Asian American Writers' Workshop), xvi.

48. Ezra Pound, *Canto LXXX* (New York: New Directions, 1946), 515. A recent exception to this is Andrew Leong, "The Pocket and the Watch: A Collective Individualist Reading of Japanese American Literature," in *Verge: Studies in Global Asias*, 1.2 (2015), 76–114.

49. See Josephine Nock-Hee Park, *Apparitions of Asia: Modernist Form and Asian-American*

Poetics (Oxford: Oxford University Press, 2008). See also Ezra Pound, cited in Carroll Franklin Terrell, *Companion to the Cantos of Ezra Pound, Vol. 2* (Berkeley: University of California Press, 1984).

50. Frank Chin, Jeffrey Paul Chan, Lawson Fusao Inada, Shawn Wong, et al., *Aiiieeeee! An Anthology of Asian American Writers* (Washington, DC: Howard University Press, 1974).

51. Ibid., xxiv.

52. Such is the grim assessment of the field of Victorian studies offered in the "V21 Manifesto" (2015), which begins: "Victorian Studies has fallen prey to *positivist historicism*: a mode of inquiry that aims to do little more than exhaustively describe, preserve, and display the past. Among its symptoms are a fetishization of the archival; an aspiration to definitively map the DNA of the period; an attempt to reconstruct the past *wie es eigentlich gewesen*; an endless accumulation of mere information. At its worst, positivist historicism devolves into show-and-tell epistemologies and bland antiquarianism. Its primary affective mode is the amused chuckle. Its primary institutional mode is the instrumentalist evisceration of humanistic ways of knowing." http://v21collective.org/manifesto-of-the-v21-collective-ten-theses/. My own response to that manifesto, which both describes and advocates a more flexible historicism (that, to be clear, I take to exist already within the field) is published on the V21 blog: http://v21collective.org/joseph-lavery-sex-without-victorians-kate-bush-and-historicism/ (2015). For an account of queer temporality as an attempt to theorize the lived rhythms (quotidian, poetic, and life-long) of queer people, see Elizabeth Freeman, "Queer and Not Now," *Time Binds: Queer Temporalities, Queer Histories* (Durham: Duke University Press, 2010), 1–19.

53. B. H. Chamberlain, *Things Japanese: Being Notes on Various Subjects Connected with Japan* (London: John Murray, 1905), 3.

54. Ibid., 3–4.

55. The specifics of the editorial are lost, but an essay by the politician Y. Ozaki, published in Britain in 1900, calls out Arnold in similar terms:

> Perhaps no country in the world has suffered so much, directly or indirectly, at the hands of the imaginative bookmaker and magazine writer as Japan. Of course, no really great work, whether in literature, science, art or statecraft, can be accomplished without the exercise of constructive imagination. But constructive imagination keeps in touch with realities. However, imagination in the popular use of the word is often synonymous with unrealilty, and it in the sense of the term that Japan has only too good reason to complain of the, no doubt, well-meant but fatal efforts of the imaginative writer. Certain authors, notably Sir Edwin Arnold, have painted Japan as a terrestrial Paradise, inhabited by a race of charming and guileless and perfectly polite angels, endowed with consummate aesthetic taste; as a land where every prospect pleases, without the drawback of even the slightest tincture of vileness among its humanity. This is a well-intentioned but serious misrepresentation; and, naturally enough, we have had to pay for the untruth in the picture. This fashion of writers aroused the spleen of other writers, who have exerted themselves to correct the error by limning Japan and the Japanese in the blackest of colors. Of course, the truth lies midway; in the matter of virtue and vice, average Japanese human nature lies much closer to average European and American human nature than is generally supposed.

Y. Ozaki, "Misunderstood Japan," *North American Review,* 171.527 (Oct. 1900).

56. Thomas Wentworth Higginson, "Unmanly Manhood," *Woman's Journal*, February 4, 1882.

57. For example, Okakura's *Ideals of the East* and Chamberlain's *Things Japanese* were published in the same book series, John Murray's *Wisdom of the East*.

58. Much of the most important scholarly work on British aestheticism has focused on its domestic and national concerns, depending on a contrast (implicit or explicit) between the British or European concerns of Wilde, John Ruskin, and Walter Pater and the period's avowedly imperialist literature in the figures of H. Rider Haggard, Rudyard Kipling, and W. E. Henley. That contrast will be challenged here: in the first place because many of the late- and post-Victorians I discuss could fall into either camp quite easily (Henley, Laurence Housman, and Kipling all wrote interestingly about Japanese art); and in the second place because, in the second chapter, the salient literary-historical discrimination I will make is *within* the aesthetic movement, between the cosmopolitan/global figures of Wilde and Whistler and the nativist/medievalist figures of William Morris and Walter Crane. Yet more important to the present work than either of those arguments is the more categorical case that I outline above: that the *universalist* ambitions of the British aesthetic movement were, perforce, latent theories of globalization in line with the period's other forms of global geometrization. For a theory of that latter term, see Eric Hayot, *On Literary Worlds* (Oxford: Oxford University Press, 2012). For more British-focused work dealing with the relationship between aesthetic universalism and imperial expansion, see Adam Barrows, *The Cosmic Time of Empire: Modern Britain and World Literature* (Berkeley: University of California Press, 2010); Regenia Gagnier, *Individualism, Decadence, and Globalization: On the Relationship of Part to Whole, 1859–1920* (London: Palgrave, 2010).

59. For an historical account of the reception of French philosophy in Anglo-American literary critical cultures in the 1970s and 1980s, see François Cusset, *French Theory: How Foucault, Derrida, Deleuze, & Co. Transformed the Intellectual Life of the United States* (Minneapolis: University of Minnesota Press, 2008). The phenomenon of "French theory," as Cusset calls it (the phrase appears in English in his original, French-language text) is, I take it, partly responsible for the passion sometimes invested in a debate between the "singular modernity" thesis, according to which a singular metanarrative—generally capitalism—adequately describes the historical conditions of increasing global integration in the nineteenth and twentieth centuries; or whether modernities are plural, with capitalism a more-or-less privileged example of a broader category. Japan plays an extremely important part in these questions because of its claims upon a singular narrative of modernization. For an emphatic statement of the singular modernity thesis, see Fredric Jameson, *A Singular Modernity: Essay on the Ontology of the Present* (London: Verso, 2002); for a sociological overview of the debate see Peter Wagner, *Modernity* (Cambridge: Polity, 2012).

60. What one can add is that these infinitesimal adventures (of which the accumulation, in the course of a day, provokes a kind of erotic intoxication) never have anything picturesque about them (the Japanese picturesque is indifferent to us, for it is detached from what constitutes the very specialty of Japan, which is its modernity), or anything novelistic (never lending themselves to the chatter which would make them into narratives or descriptions); what they offer to be *read* (I am, in that country, a reader, not a visitor) is the rectitude of the line, the stroke, without wake, without margin, without vibration;

> so many tiny demeanors (from garment to smile), which, among us, as a result of the Westerner's inveterate narcissism, are only the signs of a swollen assurance, become, among the Japanese, mere ways of passing, of tracing some unexpected thing in the street: for the gesture's sureness and independence never refer back to an affirmation of the self (to a "self-sufficiency") but only a graphic mode of existing; so that the spectacle of the Japanese street (or more generally of the public place), exciting as the product of an age-old aesthetic, from which all vulgarity has been decanted, never depends on a theatricality (a hysteria) of bodies, but, once more, on that writing *alla prima*, in which sketch and regret, calculation and correction are equally impossible, because the line, the tracing, freed from the advantageous image the scriptor would give of himself, does not express but simply *causes to exist*.

Roland Barthes, *Empire of Signs*, trans. Richard Howard (New York: Hill and Wang, 1983), 79–80.

61. For discussions of the miniaturization trope in Kipling's representation of Japan, see Jeff Nunokawa, "Oscar Wilde in Japan: Aestheticism, Orientalism, and the Derealization of the Homosexual," in *Tame Passions of Wilde: The Styles of Manageable Desire* (Princeton: Princeton University Press, 2003); David Pollack, "*A Paradigm*: Kipling and Barthes in the Empire of Signs," in *Reading against Culture: Ideology and Narrative in the Japanese Novel* (Ithaca: Cornell University Press, 1992).

62. See Andrew E. Barshay, " 'Doubly Cruel': Marxism and the Presence of the Past in Japanese Capitalism," in Vlastos, *Mirror of Modernity* (1998).

63. Cited in Nicholas Perry, *Hyperreality and Global Culture* (London: Routledge, 1998), 80.

64. "Michel Foucault and Zen: A Stay in a Zen Temple," trans. Richard Townsend, collected in Foucault, *Religion and Culture*, ed. Jeremy R. Carrette (New York: Routledge, 1999), 111.

65. Kojève first gave lectures from his *Introduction to the Reading of Hegel* between 1933 and 1939; they were published 1947. He visited Japan in 1959, and revised the work substantially. Alexandre Kojève, *Introduction to the Reading of Hegel*, ed. Allan Bloom, trans. James H. Nichols, Jr. (Ithaca: Cornell University Press, 1980), 161. For a detailed treatment of the influence of Kojève's Japan on French modernism, see Jan Walsh Hokenson, *Japan, France, and East-West Aesthetics: French Literature, 1867–2000* (Cranbury, NJ: Rosemont, 2004). Note also the overlapping discourses of modernization and maturation in the writing of the unconventional psychoanalyst Félix Guatarri.

66. Fukuyama, *The End of History and the Last Man* (New York: Free Press, 1992), 320.

67. For a detailed account of Fenollosa's Hegelianism, see Jonathan Stalling, *Poetics of Emptiness: Transformations of Asian Thought in American Poetry* (New York: Fordham University Press, 2010). A thicker history of American Hegelianism, especially concerned with the intersection of Hegelianism with American discourses of race, see Shamoon Zamir, *Dark Voices: W.E.B. Du Bois and American Thought* (Chicago: University of Chicago Press, 1995).

68. See: Warren Cohen, *East Asian Art and American Culture* (New York: Columbia University Press, 1992); Ellen P. Conant, ed., *Challenging Past and Present: The Metamorphosis of Nineteenth-Century Japanese Art* (Honolulu: University of Hawai'i Press, 2006); Ellen P. Conant, Steven D. Owyoung, and J. Thomas Rimer, *Nihonga, Transcending the Past: Japanese-Style Painting, 1868-1968* (St. Louis Art Museum, 1995); Victoria Weston, *Japanese Painting and*

National Identity: Okakura Tenshin and His Circle (Ann Arbor: University of Michigan Press, 2004).

69. Ernest Fenollosa, "The Coming Fusion of East and West," in *The Chinese Written Character as a Medium for Poetry: A Critical Edition*, ed. Haun Saussy, Lucas Klein, and Jonathan Stalling (New York: Fordham University Press, 2008), 155.

70. Michael Barone, "Is America Entering a New Victorian Era?," *Washington Examiner*, July, 27, 2015; Steven Marcus, *The Other Victorians: A Study of Sexuality and Pornography in Mid-Nineteenth-Century England* (New York: Basic Books, 1966).

Chapter One. Not About Japan

1. There are exceptions to the commonplace articulated in my first epigraph: Etsuko Taketani argues that the "not about Japan" myth was an alibi contrived to get British Orientalists off the hook; her argument resembles mine in certain respects. In a much more hesitant way Paul Seeley suggests that the compositional fidelity of the *Miya Sama* march to the Japanese original indicates a more serious engagement with Japanese themes than generally understood. Carolyn Williams's position on the Japan question is "both/and," Japan and the West, but the larger goal of her indispensable book on the Savoy Operas is to exhibit parody (rather than truth-claim) as Gilbert and Sullivan's prevailing method. Josephine Lee's reception history, while both encyclopedic and extremely insightful, joins the consensus that *The Mikado* "defies charges that it is a racist work" (xiv). Josephine Lee, *The Japan of Pure Invention: Gilbert and Sullivan's The Mikado* (Minneapolis: University of Minnesota Press, 2010).

2. For a discussion of the costumes, see *The Complete Annotated Gilbert and Sullivan*, 576. See Seeley's article for an astute formal analysis of the Japanese march, whose provenance remains uncertain, but probably A. E. Mitford played it to Sullivan.

3. G. K. Chesterton, "Gilbert and Sullivan," *The Eighteen Eighties: Essays by Fellows of the Royal Society of Literature*, ed. Walter De la Mare (Cambridge: Cambridge University Press, 1930), 136–58.

4. Roland Barthes, *Empire of Signs*, trans. Richard Howard (New York: Hill and Wang, 1982).

5. Lafcadio Hearn, *Japan: An Attempt at Interpretation* (New York: Macmillan, 1913), 10.

6. Edward Said, *Orientalism* (London: Vintage, 1979), 49.

7. Particularly instructive in these debates have been the signal interventions of: Catherine Gallagher, "George Eliot: Immanent Victorian"; Lauren Goodlad, *The Victorian Geopolitical Aesthetic: Realism, Sovereignty, and Transnational Experience*; Fredric Jameson, *The Antinomies of Realism*; Caroline Levine, *The Serious Pleasures of Suspense: Victorian Realism and Narrative Doubt*; and the special issue of *MLQ* entitled *Peripheral Realisms* edited by Joe Cleary, Jed Esty, and Colleen Lye. In Jameson's recent work, the realist mode is ultimately epistemological—and so any question of its aesthetic would be superfluous. We might adapt his notion of realism as antinomic to explain the relationship between realism's characteristic forms and its implicit claims, the paradoxical entanglement of a representation and an episteme.

8. Gallagher, "George Eliot: Immanent Victorian," 73.

9. Anyone working in gay and lesbian studies, in a culture where same-sex desire is still structured by its distinctive public/private status, at once marginal and central, as *the* open

> secret, discovers that the line between straining at truths that prove to be imbecilically self-evident, on the one hand, and on the other hand tossing off commonplaces that turn out to retain their power to galvanize and divide, is weirdly unpredictable. In dealing with the open-secret structure, it's only by being shameless about risking the obvious that we happen into the vicinity of the transformative.

Eve Kosofsky Sedgwick, *Epistemology of the Closet* (Berkeley: University of California Press, 2008), 22.

10. Sara Ahmed, *Queer Phenomenology: Orientations, Objects, Others* (Durham: Duke University Press, 2006), 112–50.

11. For an initially counterintuitive but persuasive discussion of the Japanese village as a figurative self-representation of metropolitan London, see Joseph McLaughlin, "London's Burning: The Japanese Village and the Metropolitan Construction of Modernity," *RAVON*, vol. 48, Nov. 2007, http://www.erudit.org/revue/ravon/2007/v/n48/017441ar.html.

12. This argument is advanced, in any case, by the editor of the Penguin *Complete Gilbert and Sullivan* (London: Penguin, 2006), 829–30. In Japan the Chichibu theory is most associated with the essayist Rokusuke Ei; see Sumiko Enbutsu, "Playing 'The Mikado' in the 'Town of Titipu,'" *Japan Times*, http://www.japantimes.co.jp/culture/2001/01/28/stage/playing-the-mikado-in-the-town-of-titipu/#.VfySeVzBzRY.

13. For accounts of these performances see Yokoyama, xix and Leiter, 128.

14. Chesterton may indeed be thinking of Sidney Webb's critique of "the pompous inefficiency of every branch of our public administration" in the latter's tract "Twentieth Century Politics: A Policy of National Efficiency," (London: Fabian Society, 1901), 7.

15. Interestingly, though, he returns to the idea in his 1920 travelogue *The New Jerusalem* (New York: George G. Doran, 1921) written to oppose the sending out Sir Herbert Samuel, Britain's first Jewish cabinet minister, as the British representative in Palestine as the action of "a parliament of Pooh Bah" and "quite obviously a flat and violent contradiction to Zionism" (149–50).

16. Among the supporters of the ban were the mountaineer Walter Weston, and the diplomat and Japanologist Joseph Henry Longford. For a wide bibliography of pro-Savoy letters and editorials in the *Times*, the *Daily News*, the *Era*, and elsewhere, see E. P. Lawrence, "The Banned Mikado: A Topsy-Turvey [*sic*] Incident," in *The Centennial Review*, vol. 18, no. 2, Spring 1974. Lawrence also describes in fascinating detail the difficulty of enforcing a ban in provincial theaters.

17. See Sidney Dark, *W. S. Gilbert His Life and Letters* (London: Methuen, 1923), 101. Gilbert writes "I learn from a friend, who had it direct from the King, that the Japs made the objection to The Mikado, and that it was at their instance it was suppressed. A delicate and polite action on the part of a guest towards a host. The rights in the piece do not revert to me for three years; by that time we shall probably be at war with Japan about India, and they will offer me a high price to permit it to be played."

18. Tobias G. Smollett, *The History and Adventures of an Atom* (London: Cooke, 1769), 5.

19. See, for example, Walter Scott, *The Miscellaneous Prose Works of Sir Walter Scott, Bart* (Edinburgh: R. Cadell, 1834). 159.

20. Yuzo Ota, *Basil Hall Chamberlain: Portrait of a Japanologist* (Richmond, Surrey: Japan Library, 1998).

21. Basil Hall Chamberlain, *Things Japanese: Being Notes on Various Subjects Connected with Japan* (London: Kegan Paul, Trench, Trübner, 1891), 4.

22. Douglas Sladen, *Queer Things about Japan* (London: Kegan Paul, Trench, Trübner, 1912), vii.

23. Douglas Sladen and Norma Lorimer, *More Queer Things about Japan* (London: Anthony Treherne, 1905).

24. A queer orientation towards objects underscores the theory of Orientalism underpinning the third chapter of Sarah Ahmed's book *Queer Phenomenology: Orientations, Objects, Others* (Durham, NC. Duke University Press, 2006).

25. The Criminal Law Amendment Act of 1885, it is often suggested, was passed in order to quell public outrage stirred up by W. T. Stead's "Maiden Tribute" campaign against child sex workers in the *Pall Mall Gazette*. Those articles did not equate male homosexuality with heterosexual predation, but the language of "unnatural crimes" was vague enough to be put to the purpose. See Gretchen Soderlund, *Sex Trafficking, Scandal, and the Transformation of Journalism, 1885–1917* (Chicago: Chicago University Press, 2013), 24–66.

26. Quoted in H. Montgomery Hyde, *The Trials of Oscar Wilde* (New York: Dover, 1973), 200–202, 272–73.

27. Sheila K. Johnson, *The Japanese through American Eyes* (Stanford: Stanford University Press, 1988), 89.

28. Oscar Wilde, "Art and the Handicraftsman," in *Miscellanies*, ed. Robert Ross (London: Methuen, 1908), 305–6.

29. Eric Idle, as Koko in Jonathan Miller's *The Mikado* (1987), which has been revived fourteen times by the English National Opera, can be watched here: https://www.youtube.com/watch?v=A-_m6EZ1SUk. Miller's version is set in a ritzy hotel, and each time it is mounted extrudes from a reviewer words like "essential insight that *The Mikado* says infinitely more about England than it says about Japan," in this case from Martin Kettle, "The Mikado Review—Feels as Fresh as Paint," *Guardian*, Monday, November 23, 2015.

30. Peter Lilley's speech to the 1992 Tory Party conference can be watched here: https://www.youtube.com/watch?v=FOx8q3eGq3g.

31. In an important historical discrimination, Gretchen Murphy argues that the rhetorical purpose of Perry's *Narrative* was to quell public doubts about the newly aggressive expansionism of which Perry's expedition was a visible metonym. See Gretchen Murphy, *Hemispheric Imaginings: The Monroe Doctrine and Narratives of U. S. Empire* (Durham: Duke University Press, 2005), 71–98.

32. Frye, 231.

Chapter Two. All Margin

1. Ada Leverson, "Reminiscences," in *Letters to the Sphinx from Oscar Wilde* (London: Duckworth, 1930), 19–20.

2. And reprinted in Whistler's own collection of epistles, epigrams, and tidbits, *The Gentle Art of Making Enemies* (Chelsea: Heinemann, 1929 [1890]), 235.

3. For a formalist analysis of Menpes's and Whistler's adoption of Japanese visual forms, see Ayako Ono, *Japonisme in Britain: Whistler, Menpes, Henry, Hornel, and Nineteenth-Century Japan* (London: Routledge, 2003).

4. Mortimer Menpes, *Whistler as I Knew Him* (London: Adam and Charles Black, 1905), 39.

5. Ibid., 39.

6. Walter Pater, "Conclusion," *Studies in the History of the Renaissance* (London: Macmillan, 1873), 210.

7. Treating aestheticism as a cultural phenomenon, rather than an intellectual disposition or as an ethics, has motivated the most important and interesting work in the field over the last few decades, much of which contests the centrality of men to the aesthetic movement. Richard Dellamora, *Masculine Desire: The Sexual Politics of Victorian Aestheticism* (Chapel Hill: University of North Carolina, 1990); Regenia Gagnier,*Idylls of the Marketplace: Oscar Wilde and the Victorian Reading Public* (Stanford: Stanford University Press, 1987). Regenia Gagnier, *The Insatiability of Human Wants: Economics and Aesthetics in Market Society* (Chicago: University of Chicago Press, 2000); Leela Gandhi. *Affective Communities: Anticolonial Thought, Fin-de-Siècle Radicalism, and the Politics of Friendship* (Durham: Duke University Press, 2006); Talia Schaffer, *The Forgotten Female Aesthetes: Literary Culture in Late-Victorian England* (University of Virginia Press, 2000); Jonah Siegel, *Desire and Excess: The Nineteenth-Century Culture of Art* (Princeton: Princeton University Press, 2000); Margaret Diane Stetz, "Sex, Lies, and Printed Cloth: Bookselling at the Bodley Head in the Eighteen-Nineties," *Victorian Studies* 35.1 (1991), 71–86; Rachel Teukolsky, *The Literate Eye: Victorian Art Writing and Modernist Aesthetics* (Oxford: Oxford University Press, 2009). An important recent counterexample is Benjamin Morgan, *The Outward Mind: Materialist Aesthetics in Victorian Science and Literature* (Chicago: University of Chicago Press, 2017).

8. I would like to distinguish between the "history of ideas" and the "history of thought." Most of the time a historian of ideas tries to determine when a specific concept appears, and this moment is often identified by the appearance of a new word. But what I am attempting to do as a historian of thought is something different. I am trying to analyze the way institutions, practices, habits, and behavior become a problem for people who behave in specific sorts of ways, who have certain types of habits, who engage in certain kinds of practices, and who put to work specific kinds of institutions. The history of ideas involves the analysis of a notion from its birth, through its development, and in the setting of other ideas which constitute its context. The history of thought is the analysis of the way an unproblematic field of experience, or a set of practices, which were accepted without question, which were familiar and "silent," out of discussion, becomes a problem, raises discussion and debate, incites new reactions, and induces a crisis in the previously silent behavior, habits, practices, and institutions. The history of thought, understood in this way, is the history of the way people begin to take care of something, of the way they become anxious about this or that—for example, about madness, about crime, about sex, about themselves, or about truth.

Michel Foucault, *Fearless Speech*, ed. Joseph Pearson (Los Angeles: Semiotext(e), 2001), 74. To this list of topics that interested Foucault specifically, we could add "about Japan" or, in this case, "about aesthetics." It was through the aesthetic movement that aesthetic thinking, though perhaps not "familiar" or "silent" in the mid-nineteenth century, was at least relatively remote from the particular forms of legal, imperial, and affective crises that were brought to bear on Wilde, his circle, and his imitators. Note, too, that while it is tempting to uncover Wilde's queer sexuality (or, at least, his queer sexual practices) as the truly subversive dimension of his career—this, for example, governs Jonathan Dollimore's approach to Wilde's "sexual dissidence"—Foucault's distinction between ideas and thought treats the socially embedded act of *thought*, rather than ontologies of identity or practice, as the motive factor in the "crisis in . . . previously silent behavior, habits, practices, and isntitutions."

9. Oscar Wilde, *Oscar Wilde's Oxford Notebooks: A Portrait of Mind in the Making*, ed. Philip E. Smith II and Michael S. Helfant (Oxford: Oxford University Press, 1989), 164.

10. See Benjamin Morgan, *The Outward Mind: Materialist Aesthetics in Victorian Science and Literature* (Chicago and London: University of Chicago Press, 2017).

11. Walter Pater, "Conclusion," *Studies in the History of the Renaissance* (London: Macmillan, 1873), 211; Oscar Wilde, "The Truth of Masks," in *Intentions* (Leipzig: Heinemann and Balestier, 1891), 212.

12. Oscar Wilde, "Phrases and Philosophies for the Use of the Young," *Saturday Review*, Nov. 1894. For an account of the erotics of Wildean inversion, see Jonathan Dollimore, *Sexual Dissidence: Augustine to Wilde, Freud to Foucault* (Oxford: Oxford University Press, 1991), 64–73; and Alan Sinfield, *The Wilde Century: Effeminacy, Oscar Wilde, and the Queer Moment* (New York: Columbia University Press, 1994).

13. The full title was J. A. Symonds, *A Problem in Greek Ethics: Being an Inquiry into the Phenomenon of Sexual Inversion Addressed Especially to Medical Psychologists and Jurists* (London: Privately Printed for the Areopagitiga Society, 1908). The medical note marks the changing treatment of homosexuality between 1873 and 1908, from historical secret to pathology—a change for which Symonds was partly responsible, having consulted with Havelock Ellis while the latter was composing *Studies in the Psychology of Sex: Vol. 1., Sexual Inversion* (London: University Press, 1900).

14. J. A. Symonds, "Letter to W. J. Courthope, December 28th 1867," quoted in *John Addington Symonds: A Biography*, vol. 2 (London: Nimmo, 1895), 27–28. See Linda Dowling, *Hellenism and Homosexuality in Victorian Oxford* (Ithaca: Cornell University Press, 1994); Whitney Davis, *Queer Beauty: Sexuality and Aesthetics from Winckelmann to Freud and Beyond* (New York: Columbia University Press, 2010).

15. David Kurnick understands novelist representations of sexuality and desire as acts of resistance (one such is "truly heroic," 132), pushing back against the sexological priorities of the late nineteenth century, which asserted that sexual identity defined individuals as individuals. Rather, Kurnick argues, the novel of interiority is a surprising repertory of communitarian impulses, which treat the apparently self-isolating subject of desire as a diffused, multivalent, and social being. Kurnick annotates this process as one of "dethematization," since it locates sexual being in forms, codes, social lives, publics, and communities, rather than in the content of a given anecdote, psyche, or plotline. We have already seen something similar at work with "Japan" in the Japanological Orientalist texts: the strong referential effect of that word will be contested, and its social coding prioritized instead. See David Kurnick, *Empty Houses: Theatrical Failure and the Novel* (Princeton: Princeton University Press, 2012), especially 17–24.

16. Wilde, *The Picture of Dorian Gray*, 8.

17. Oscar Wilde, "The Decay of Lying," in *Intentions* (London: Heinemann and Balestier, 1891), 38.

18. Richard Ellmann, *Oscar Wilde* (New York: Vintage, 1987), 266.

19. William Schwenck Gilbert, *Patience, or, Bunthorne's Bride* (New York: Stoddart, 1881), 44.

20. The extraordinary story of this epigram, Wilde's first public controversy as an undergraduate at Oxford, is detailed in Ellmann, *Oscar Wilde*, 44–45.

21. Oscar Wilde, "Art and the Handicraftsman," in *Miscellanies*, ed. Robert Ross (London: Methuen, 1908 [1889]), 306.

22. Oscar Wilde, "A Note on Some Modern Poets," in *Complete Writings of Oscar Wilde, Vol. 4*, ed. Robert Ross (London: Keller-Farmer, 1907 [1889]), 28.

23. W. E. Henley, "Back-View," in *A Book of Verses* (New York: Scribner and Welford, 1891), 161.

24. Oscar Wilde, "Letter to Theodore Watts, October 1888," in *Letters of Oscar Wilde*, ed. Rupert Hart Davis (New York: Harcourt, Brace and World, 1962), 228.

25. See Rupert Hart Davis, footnote to Wilde's "Letter to W. E. Henley, July 1889," in *Letters of Oscar Wilde*, 248.

26. Oscar Wilde, "Letter to W. E. Henley, July 1889," in *Letters of Oscar Wilde*, 248.

27. Oscar Wilde, "Letter to Will Rothenstein, 14 August 1897," in *Letters of Oscar Wilde*, 631. I am *extremely* grateful to C. Sanders Creasy for drawing my attention to this note.

28. Friedrich von Wenckstern, *A Bibliography of the Japanese Empire, from 1859–1893* (London: Kegan Paul, Trench, Trübner, 1895), 148–71.

29. Otoo Korshelt and Hikorokuro Yoshida, "The Chemistry of Japanese Lacquer," in *Transactions of the Asiatic Society of Japan* (Yokohama: R. Meiklejohn, 1883), 182–220; Lieutenant J. B. Murdock, U.S.N., "The Protection of the Hulls of Vessels by Lacquer," in *Naval Institute Proceedings* (Annapolis, MD: US Naval Institute, 1891), 457–72.

30. For an account of the convergence of racialization and aestheticization as the crystallization of form, see Colleen Lye, "Racial Form," *Representations* 104.1 (2008), 92–101.

31. Percival Lowell, *The Soul of the Far East* (Boston: Houghton, Mifflin, 1892), 10.

32. Anonymous, "Japanese Lacquer Working," *The Architect and Contract Reporter* 14 (August 21, 1875), 103.

33. Christopher Bush, "The Ethnicity of Things in America's Lacquered Age," *Representations* 99.1 (2007), 81–85.

34. Whistler, *The Gentle Art of Making Enemies*, 115.

35. For an overview of Whistler's considerations of, and influence on, the design of books, see Avis Berman, "Whistler and the Printed Page: The Artist as Book Designer," *American Art* 9.2 (Summer, 1995), 62–85; for more detailed investigations of Whistler's interactions with literary culture, see Linda Merrill, *A Pot of Paint: Aesthetics on Trial in Whistler v. Ruskin* (Washington, DC: Smithsonian Institute Press/Freer Gallery, 1992); and Margaret Diane Stetz, "Sex, Lies, and Printed Cloth: Bookselling at the Bodley Head in the Eighteen-Nineties," *Victorian Studies* 35.1 (Autumn 1991), 71–86.

36. Elizabeth Robins Pennell and Joseph Pennell, *The Life of James McNeill Whistler* (Philadelphia: J. B. Lippincott, 1911), 90.

37. See, for example, "Review," *New York Times*, August 24, 1890.

38. Whistler, *The Gentle Art of Making Enemies*, 29.

39. See Jed Esty, *Unseasonable Youth: Modernism, Colonialism, and the Fiction of Empire* (Oxford: Oxford University Press, 2012), 104–14.

40. Oscar Wilde, "Mr. Whistler's Ten O'Clock," in *The Soul of Man under Socialism and Selected Critical Prose* (Oxford: Oxford University Press, 2001), 5.

41. A. C. Swinburne, under Whistler's title of "An Apostasy," in *The Gentle Art of Making Enemies*, 251.

42. Ibid., 252.

43. Robin Spencer, "Whistler's 'The White Girl,'"; Aileen Tsui, "The Phantasm of Aesthetic Autonomy in Whistler's Work"; Nicholas Daly, "The Woman in White."

44. F. T. Palgrave, "The Royal Academy of 1865,'"*Essays on Art* (London: Macmillan, 1866), 106.

45. "We are apt to think of Indian designs as wild and varied in contrast with European. But Japan, further East, carries to still greater lengths the same passion for irregularity. Patterns which, in idea, are common to both countries, in Japan assume a less symmetrical arrangement. In fact, the law of Japanese ornamentation appears to be, that exact repetition of parts, and perfect balance of form, should be reserved for the expression of religious feeling; whilst, in the secular or common-life regions of art, the pains taken to avoid symmetry and evenness are as great as the pains we take to secure them." F. T. Palgrave, "Japanese Art," *Saturday Review*, August 15, 1863.

46. *Spectator*, vol. 38 [June 24, 1865], p. 696.

47. J. Hillis Miller, "The Mirror's Secret: Dante Gabriel Rossetti's Double Work of Art," *Victorian Poetry* 29.4 (1991), 333–49.

48. T. S. Eliot, "Swinburne as Poet," in *Selected Essays* (New York: Harcourt, Brace. 1932), 284.

49. A. C. Swinburne, "Before the Mirror (Verses Written under a Picture) Inscribed to J. A. Whistler," in *Selections from the Poetical Works of A.C. Swinburne* (New York: Crowell, 1884), 476–77.

50. A. C. Swinburne, "To James Abbott McNeill Whistler, Sunday [April 2, 1865]," in *The Yale Edition of the Swinburne Letters*, vol. 1 (New Haven: Yale University Press, 1959), 118–20.

51. Isobel Armstrong sees Victorian mirrors as generally disturbing of subject/object relations: "the I/thou dyad is reversible depending on which 'white sister' is image or substance, reflecting subject or reflected other, and which takes on a blanched, ghostly status." *Victorian Glassworlds: Glass Culture and the Imagination, 1830–1880* (Oxford: Oxford University Press 2008), 112; On the other hand, in a reading of this specific image, Kathy Psomiades sees the redirection from vase to face as a feminist intervention against Whistler on Swinburne's part: "Rather than being a painting about the double nature of the art object, Swinburne's 'little white girl' is a painting about a femininity that constitutes itself as outside heterosexual exchange. The girl takes pleasure in her own image, a pleasure outside heterosexual desire. She is for no man; no ring appears on *her* finger. Enviably self-sufficient, girl for girl's sake, she exists in a pale and shadowy state emotions are felt, but faintly, a state time cannot touch." Kathy Alexis Psomiades, *Beauty's Body: Femininity and Representation in British Aestheticism* (Stanford: Stanford University Press, 1997), 112.

52. Walter Crane, *Of the Decorative Illustration of Books Old and New* (London: G. Bell, 1905), 160, 162.

53. Walter Crane, "Japanese Illustration," in *Of the Decorative Illustration of Books Old and New* (London: G. Bell and Sons, 1921 [1896]), 109.

54. Anonymous, "Japanese Life and Industry," *Furniture Gazette* 22, New Series, January 17, 1885, 56.

55. Ibid.

56. Anonymous, "A Lesson From Japan," *Continent*, vol. 3, no. .22, May, 30, 188, 116.

57. John Ruskin, *The Stones of Venice: Volume the Second: The Sea-Stories* (London: Smith, Elder, 1853), 168.

58. William Morris, "Textile Fabrics," in *Arts and Crafts Essays by Members of the Arts and Crafts Exhibition Society* (New York: Scribner's Sons, 1893), 34–35.

59. Aymer Vallance, *William Morris: His Art, His Writings, and His Public Life* (London: Bell, 1897), 433–34.

60. See John William Mackail, *The Life of William Morris, Vol. 1* (London: Longmans, Green, 1920 [1899]), 90; and Yuko Kikuchi, *Japanese Modernization and Mingei Theory: Cultural Nationalism and Oriental Orientalism* (London: Routledge, 2004), 25 and passim.

61. William Morris, *News from Nowhere; or, an Epoch of Rest* (Boston: Roberts Brothers 1891), 55.

62. Ibid.

63. John Plotz, *Portable Property: Victorian Culture on the Move* (Princeton: Princeton University Press, 2008), 144.

64. Wilde, "The Decay of Lying," 38.

65. Oscar Wilde, "Letter to Helena Sickert, 25 April 1882," in *Letters of Oscar Wilde*, 115.

66. Oscar Wilde, "Letter to Norman Forbes-Robertson, 25 May 1882" and "Letter to Charles Eliot Norton, Circa 15 July 1882," in *Letters of Oscar Wilde*, 120 and 124.

67. Oscar Wilde, "Letter to James McNeill Whistler, June 1882," in *Letters of Oscar Wilde*, 121.

68. Ellmann, *Oscar Wilde*, 186.

69. Wilde, *The Picture of Dorian Gray*, 64.

70. Ibid., 87.

71. I derive this use of the term "format" from Meredith L. McGill, "Frances Ellen Watkins Harper and the Circuits of Abolitionist Poetry," in *Early African American Print Culture in Theory and Practice*, Lara Langer Cohen and Jordan Stein, eds. (Philadelphia: University of Pennsylvania Press, 2012), 55.

72. See Nicholas Frankel, *Oscar Wilde's Decorated Books* (Ann Arbor: University of Michigan Press, 2000).

73. Anonymous, *The Shame of Oscar Wilde: From the Shorthand Reports* (Paris: Privately Printed, 1906), backmatter.

74. Ibid.

75. See James G. Nelson, *Publisher to the Decadents: Leonard Smithers in the Careers of Beardsley, Wilde, Dowson* (College Park: Pennsylvania State University Press, 2000), 173–224; and Rachel Potter, "Obscene Modernism and the Trade in Salacious Books," *Modernism/Modernity* 16.1 (2009), 87–104.

76. Indeed, there is some truth to the claim made too strongly by Sinfield that Wilde personally invented a singular style of male homosexuality. At the end of Havelock Ellis's *Sexual Inversion*, the diagnostician Ellis himself acknowledges that the extraordinary event of the Wilde trials have contributed not merely to the politicization, but to the actual emergence, of male homosexuality. "The Oscar Wilde trial, with its wide publicity, and the fundamental nature of the questions it suggested, appears to have generally contributed to give definiteness and self-consciousness to the manifestations of homosexuality, and to have arouse inverts to take up a

definite attitude. . . . I have been assured in several quarters that this is so and that since that case the manifestations of homosexuality have become more pronounced." Havelock Ellis, *Sexual Inversion* (Philadelphia: F. A. Davis, 1901 [1897]), 212.

77. *The Letters of Oscar Wilde*, 802. For an account of this letter and its context in the relationship between Forbes-Robertson and Wilde, see Holland, "Introduction to the 1994 Edition," in *The Complete Works of Oscar Wilde*, ed. Holland (London: Collins, 1994), 5.

78. See Stuart Mason, *Bibliography of Oscar Wilde* (London: T. Werner Laurie, 1907), 410.

79. See Ellmann, *Oscar Wilde*, 560, for a longer list of recipients.

80. See Leslie J. Moran, "Transcripts and Truth: Writing the Trials of Oscar Wilde," in *Oscar Wilde and Modern Culture: The Making of a Legend*, ed. Joseph Bristow (Athens: Ohio University Press, 2008), 234–58.

81. Anonymous, *The Shame of Oscar Wilde: From the Shorthand Reports*, 2 (emphasis in original).

82. As Bersani writes, expanding on modes of being produced by, but applicable beyond, art: "Our fundamental claim has been that the aesthetic subject, while it both produces and is produced by works of art, is a mode of relational being that exceeds the cultural province of art and embodies truths of being. Art diagrams universal relationality." Leo Bersani, "Psychoanalysis and the Aesthetic Subject," in *Is the Rectum a Grave? and Other Essays* (Chicago: University of Chicago Press, 2010), 142.

Chapter Three. The Pre-Raphaelite Haiku

1. Roland Barthes, "Style and Its Image," in *The Rustle of Language*, trans. and ed. Richard Howard (New York: Hill and Wang, 1986), 98–99.

2. Billy Collins, "Introduction," in *Haiku in English: The First Hundred Years*, ed. Philip Rowland and Allan Burns (New York: Norton, 2013), xxix.

3. Joaquin Miller and Yone Noguchi, *Japan of Sword and Love* (Tokyo: Kanao Bunyendo, 1905). See Amy Sueyoshi, *Queer Compulsions: Race, Nation, and Sexuality in the Affairs of Yone Noguchi* (Honolulu: University of Hawai'i Press, 2012), for an account of the queer friendship between Miller and Noguchi, Noguchi's network of male intimacies in the Bay Area, and his particularly close relationship with Charles Warren Stoddart.

4. Such a Pacific alliance had been frequently touted in both the United States and Japan—often in profoundly interesting ways. Ernest Fenollosa understood the Spanish-American War, for example, as the inauguration of a second Hegelian history. See Ernest Francisco Fenollosa, "The Coming Fusion of East and West," *Harper's Magazine* (Dec. 1989).

5. Yone Noguchi, "Japanese Hokku Poets," marked as "preface" in the Bancroft Collection, CH-127.

6. B. H. Chamberlain, *The Classical Poetry of the Japanese* (London: Trübner, 1880).

7. Ibid., 4.

8. Chamberlain, *Things Japanese*, 377. The word "epigram" was widely used as a description of Japanese poetry—with and without the "poetical" descriptor—until into the twentieth century.

9. Noguchi, "Japanese Hokku Poets," CH-127.

10. Ibid.

11. This book has been dated on the strength of an auction notice, since I cannot find a hard copy: http://historical.ha.com/itm/books/children-s-books/-japanese-children-s-books-new-of-pom-and-song-the-english-and-japanese-ca-1890-twelvemo-text-in-japanes/a/201236-93127.s.

12. A. M. Thompson, *Japan for a Week (Britain for Ever!)* (London: John Lane, the Bodley Head, 1911), 130.

13. Noguchi's reviewer for the *Dial* opined, "we wish he did not feel so terribly lonely" in the *Dial* (1897); Review of "Monologues of a Homeless Snail," *Dial* 21 (1897), 187. But Noguchi himself presented this melancholic sentimentality throughout this period of his career too—not least in the subtitle "Monologues of a Homeless Snail."

14. Noguchi's account of Rossetti's "formalism" appears as this chapter's third epigraph, and comes from a short personal essay entitled "My London Experience" that appeared first in the *Fortnightly Review*. Yone Noguchi, "My London Experience," *Fortnightly Review*, 89.95 (London: Chapman and Hall, 1911), 613.

15. "Newest Thing in Poets," in *Literary Digest*, Dec. 1896, p. 202.

16. Edgar Allan Poe, "Eulalie," in *The Works of the Late Edgar Allan Poe* (New York: Redfield, 1857), 44.

17. Yone Noguchi, "Lines," in *The Philistine*, vol. 3 (East Aurora: Roycroft Printing Shop, 1896), 171–73

18. Yone Noguchi, *The Story of Yone Noguchi, as Told by Himself* (Philadelphia: George W. Jacobs, 1914), 18–19.

19. "Newest Thing in Poets," 202.

20. "Chronicle and Comment," *The Bookman* 4.4 (Dec. 1896), 288.

21. Burgess's "Purple Cow" was printed in a number of literary periodicals at the same time in 1895—in illustrated form, as the identifying sigil of *The Lark*, Burgess's San Francisco-based magazine of comic writing.

22. "Editorial," *Book Notes: A Monthly Literary Magazine and Review of New Books, Volume 2*, Jan.–June 1899, p. 255.

23. Benjamin Rowland, review in the *Nation*, July 18, 1934.

24. Earl Miner, *The Japanese Tradition in British and American Literature*, 187.

25. Hakutani is less persuasive here than critics who point out that the eight words of the first line and the six of the second map on to the conventional arrangement of the sonnet into octet and sestet. Another critic, John Walter de Gruchy, who sympathizes with Arthur Waley's self-presentation as the true authority on the haiku describes the Orientalist's aims as "to challenge the uncritical admiration for Japanese things, and Japanese poetry in particular, that was held by most of Waley's modernist contemporaries who were being influenced by the eccentric and unreliable views of Yone Noguchi" (66).

26. Personal correspondence with gallery.records@tate.org.uk.

27. Translation is the author's own.

28. Suzanne Maureen Waldman, *The Demon and the Damozel: Dynamics of Desire in the Works of Christina Rossetti and Dante Gabriel Rossetti* (Athens: Ohio University Press, 2008), 129–33.

29. Kenneth Yasuda, *Japanese Haiku: Its Essential Nature and History* (Tokyo: Tuttle, 2011), 231.

30. Hakutani bends over backwards to prove the American poet, rather than the Japanese, the originator of the genre. "But there are some differences between Noguchi's and Pound's *hokku*. Noguchi does not as closely adhere to the well-established syllabic measure of five or seven as does Pound. Noguchi's two *hokku* above [Hakutani is not discussing "my love's lengthened hair" here] have 7-5-4 and 4-7-6 measures; Pound's "Alba," "Fan-Piece, for Her Imperial Lord," and "Ts'ai Chi'h" have those of 7-7-8, 7-5-7, and 8-7-7, respectively. If the first line of Pound's metro poem had been reconstructed as two lines, the poem would have had a measure of 5-7-7 ("The apparition / Of these faces in the crowd / Petals on a wet, black bough"), much like a Japanese *hokku*. Noguchi, moreover, tends to ignore the long-established poetic tradition in which a Japanese *hokku* has an explicit reference to a season. Pound, on the other hand, consciously adheres to this tradition as seen in many of his *hokku*-like poems and somewhat longer pieces such as "Heather" and "Society" (*Personae*, 109–11)." Yoshinobu Hakutani, *Haiku and Modernist Poetics* (London: Palgrave, 2009), 79. To be brief: "Alba" has no *kigo*, but "Fan-Piece" and "Ts'ai Chih" do; none of them conform to the haiku's syllabic arrangement as does Noguchi's poem; and Pound did not, in fact, choose to break the first line of "In the Station at the Metro" where Hakutani does. (Any twelve-syllable line could be broken into two lines of five and seven.) Neither "Heather" nor "Society" makes any effort to be recognized as a haiku beyond, in "Heather," a couple of Orientalist images, of which there are none whatsoever in "Society." See Ezra Pound, *Personae: The Shorter Poems of Ezra Pound* (New York: New Directions Press, 1971).

31. I use this phrase "model text" to indicate a mode of borrowing at the level of *form*, rather than *theme*. Barthes writes: "Literary writing must be located not only in relation to its closest neighbors but also in relation to its models. I mean by *models* not sources, in the philological sense of the word (let us note in passing that the problem of sources has been raised almost exclusively at the level of the content), but syntagmatic *patterns*, typical fragments of sentences, formulas, if you like, whose origin is not identifiable but which make up part of the collective memory of literature. *To write* is to let these models come to one and to *transform* them (in the sense this word has acquired in linguistics." Barthes, "Style and Its Image," 97.

32. In *The Preparation of the Novel*, Roland Barthes discusses the kigo, which he calls "the *keynote* of the haiku," as a figure for literariness itself, "trying to do with *that little bit of language* what language can't do" (34–36). He concludes: "It's like the essence of Life, of Memory. This *individual* (for example, aesthetic) investment in the Season (in the Weather) is a continuation of the interest that rural cultures take in the seasons and the weather" (35). Roland Barthes, *The Preparation of the Novel*, trans. Kate Briggs (New York: Columbia University Press, 2011), 34–36.

33. Yone Noguchi, *Selected English Writings of Yone Noguchi*, vol. 2, *Prose*, ed. Yoshinobu Hakutani (Cranbury: Associated University Presses, 1992), 117.

34. Yone Noguchi, *The Spirit of Japanese Poetry* (New York: E. P. Dutton, 1914), 41.

35. This version of Poundian poetics forms the basis of Hakutani's discrimination between him and Noguchi. See Hakutani, *Haiku and Modernist Poetics*, 77.

36. Paul Fussell, *Poetic Meter and Poetic Form* (New York: McGraw Hill, 1979), 116.

37. The pairing of anacoluthon (the rhetorical device of changing syntax part way through

a sentence) and asyndeton (that of omitting lexical units that establish syntactical priority) plays an important twin role in Barthes's understanding of Flaubertian realism. (Quick example of anacoluthon: "One morning, some weeks after her arrival at Lowick, Dorothea—but why always Dorothea?" Quick example of asyndeton: "Signed, sealed, delivered, I'm yours.") Barthes writes: "Of course, rhetoric recognizes discontinuities in construction (anacoluthons) and in subordination (asyndetons); but with Flaubert, for the first time, discontinuity is no longer exceptional, sporadic, brilliant, set in the base matter of common utterance: there is no longer a language *on the other side* of these figures (which means, in another sense: there is no longer anything but language); a generalized asyndeton seizes the entire utterance, so that this very readable discourse is *underhandedly* one of the craziest imaginable: all the logical small change is in the interstices." Roland Barthes, *The Pleasure of the Text*, trans. Richard Miller (New York: Hill and Wang, 1975), 9. Noguchi's work with Rossetti, on the other hand, produces the precise inverse: language in the midst of a generalized *anacoluthon*, in which the forward movement generally guaranteed by any syntagmatic arrangement of language—language's general momentum—is perpetually queried.

38. Fussell, *Poetic Meter and Poetic Form*, 116.

39. See Leo Bersani, *The Culture of Redemption* (Cambridge: Harvard University Press, 1990).

40. D.M.R. Bentley, "The Blessed Damozel: A Young Man's Fantasy," in *Victorian Poetry* 20.3/4 (1982), 34.

41. The online Rossetti Archive provides detailed composition and circulation information of all D. G. Rossetti's published materials: http://www.rossettiarchive.org/index.html.

42. See Jerome McGann, "Rossetti's Significant Details," in *Victorian Poetry* 7. 1 (Spring 1969).

43. See K. L. Knickerbocker, "Rossetti's 'The Blessed Damozel,'" *Studies in Philology* 29.3 (July 1932), 485–504; J. A. Sanford, "The Morgan Library Manuscript of Rossetti's 'The Blessed Damozel,'" *Studies in Philology*, 35.3 (1938), 471–86.

44. Knickerbocker, "Rossetti's 'The Blessed Damozel'" 486.

45. Sanford, "The Morgan Library Manuscript," 471.

46. "Poetic Influence—when it involves two strong, authentic poets,—always proceeds by a misreading of the prior poet, an act of creative correction that is actually and necessarily a misinterpretation. The history of fruitful poetic influence, which is to say the main tradition of Western poetry since the Renaissance, is a history of anxiety and self-saving caricature, of distortion, of perverse, willful revisionism without which modern poetry as such could not exist." Harold Bloom, *The Anxiety of Influence: A Theory of Poetry* (Oxford: Oxford University Press, 1997), 30.

47. Yone Noguchi, *The American Diary of a Japanese Girl* (New York: Frank Leslie, 1902), 28–29.

48. Yone Noguchi, "Noguchi's Song unto Brother Americans," privately printed, August 1897, Bancroft pfPR 6027 03N6.

> Thou, mortal, divorced husband from Lady-Repose, life-sold moneyed-slave to Time,
> Thou, ant, battling for gold-dew, art a demon-child unlike the father-God!
> Gather, mortal, the boundless, boundless gold that bids on abundance adieu––
> The world-illuming gold that kindles mortal's delight!—O gold! not the Klondike gold—

The gold at the proud gate of San Francisco Bay, aye the divine gold of the majestic sun!

49. Sui Sin Far, "Mrs. Spring Fragrance," *Hampton's Magazine*, vol. 24, p. 137.

50. Alfred Tennyson, "The Lotos-Eaters," (New York: Harper and Bros., 1870), 35.

51. For the pro: Edward Marx, Franey, Sueyoshi. For the contra: Halverson, de Gruchy. These debates essentially concern the nature and function of cultural property. As Leslie Pincus writes in her book about Kuki Shuzo (and here she is testing the viability of the claim, rather than asserting it directly): "Japanese travelers *reappropriated Japan from Europe* as an exoticized object" (92, emphasis added). Yet the question for Noguchi, and for the other haiku poets I have been discussing, is what the "proper" might consist of in relation to the disciplining structure of poetic form. See Laura Franey, "Introduction," and Edward Marx, "Afterword," to Yone Noguchi, *The American Diary of a Japanese Girl* (Philadelphia: Temple University Press, 2007); Catherine Halverson, "'Typical Tokio Smile': Bad American Books and Bewitching Japanese Girls," *Arizona Quarterly: A Journal of American Literature, Culture, and Theory* 63.1 (2007), 49–80; Sueyoshi, *Queer Compulsions*. John Walter de Gruchy's critique of Noguchi is especially interesting, since it focuses on the Orientalist Arthur Waley's increasing distaste for Noguchi as the latter began to espouse more aggressively imperialist versions of "the Japanese spirit" from the 1910s onwards. John Walter de Gruchy, *Orienting Arthur Waley: Japonism, Orientalism, and the Creation of Japanese Literature in English* (Honolulu: University of Hawai'i Press, 2003), 78–85.

52. Sueyoshi, *Queer Compulsions*, 76.

53. Mikhail Bakhtin, "From the Prehistory of Novelistic Discourse," *The Dialogic Imagination*, ed. Michael Holquist, trans. Caryl Emerson and Michael Holquist (Austin: University of Texas Press, 1981), 61.

54. Ibid., 60.

55. Rita Felski, *The Gender of Modernity* (Cambridge: Harvard University Press, 1995), 92.

56. Yone Noguchi, "The Wooden Clogs," published in *Eigo-Bungaku* (English Literature), vol. 1, no. 2, Feb. 1918.

57. The imputed masculinity of the haiku was asserted by Noguchi, and affirmed later by Western writers such as J. G. Fletcher and R. H. Blyth. Blyth wrote, "Women are said to be intuitive, and as they cannot think, we may hope this is so, but intuition, like patriotism, is not enough." R. H. Blyth, *A History of Haiku* (Tokyo: Hokuseido, 1963), 207.

58. Rabindranath Tagore, "Letter to Yone Noguchi, September 1st 1938," in *English Writings of Rabindranath Tagore Vol. 8: Miscellaneous Writings*, ed. Mohit K. Ray (New Delhi: Atlantic Books, 2007), 1141.

59. Yone Noguchi, "Letter to Rabindranath Tagore, October 2, 1938," in ibid., 1145.

60. For a liberal defense of the power of modernist literature to defuse the epistemological impasse of emergent forms of propaganda, see Mark Wollaeger, *Modernism, Media and Propaganda* (Princeton: Princeton University Press, 2006). In a sense, Wollaeger is rebutting the strong claims for the immediacy of the propagandistic image made by Susan Sontag in *Regarding the Pain of Others* (New York: Picador, 2004).

61. Noguchi, "Letter to Rabindranath Tagore," in *English Writings of Rabindranath Tagore Vol. 8: Miscellaneous Writings*, 1144.

62. Ibid., 1146.

63. Julia Wright, Introduction to *Haiku: This Other World* (New York: Arcade, 2011), viii.

64. Wright, *Haiku*, §1.

65. For the classical construction of literature as a poisonous cure, see Jacques Derrida, *Dissemination*, trans. Barbara Johnson (London: Athlone, 1981).

66. The haiku is a relatively modern form *in Japanese*, derived from the older *hokku*, which formed the first stanza of a *renga* poem. See Blyth, *Haiku*.

67. Ezra Pound, "Vorticism," in *Fortnightly Review* 96.573 (1914).

68. Ibid.

69. Ibid.

70. Jack Kerouac, "Haiku Berkeley," *Pomes All Sizes* (San Francisco: City Lights, 1992), 43.

71. Richard Iadonisi, "The Masculine Urge of Jack Kerouac's Haiku," *Journal of American Culture*, 37.3 (2014), 292.

72. Jack Kerouac, *Book of Haikus* (London: Penguin, 2003), 5.

73. John Gould Fletcher, *Japanese Prints* (Boston: Four Seas, 1918), 5.

74. George Saintsbury, *A Historical Manual of English Prosody* (London: Macmillan, 1910).

75. http://haiku.nytimes.com/.

76. http://i.imgur.com/gR2yY3Q.jpg. This haiku exhibits, in a single burst, both the haiku's pedagogical and antipedagogical tendencies: it both exhibits the fruit of an act of learning, and rejects the institutional apparatus that enforces, through the syllable, discursive conformity as such.

77. Sianne Ngai, *Ugly Feelings* (Cambridge: Harvard University Press, 2007), 271.

78. Donald Richie, *A Tractate on Japanese Aesthetics* (Berkeley: Stone Bridge Press, 2007), 38.

79. R. H. Blyth, *Haiku*, 52.

80. R. H. Blyth, *Zen in English Literature and Oriental Classics* (Tokyo: Hokuseido Press, 1942). For the zen dimension of haiku, see also Haruo Shirani, *Traces of Dreams: Landscape, Cultural Memory, and the Poetry of Basho* (Stanford: Stanford University Press, 1998).

81. Kenneth Goldsmith, No. 111.2.7.93–10.20.96, an immense, alphabetically organized arrangement of rhymed phrases, can be found at http://www.ubuweb.com/111/contents.html. Goldsmith also coedited with Craig Dworkin an anthology of conceptual poetry entitled, *Against Expression: An Anthology of Conceptual Writing* (Chicago: Northwestern University Press, 2003).

82. The ignorance of technique implies a casual and contemptuous attitude toward the history of work. The antisubjectivist dogma is an optic for ironic theorisation of value alone; its implications for a theory of labour are wholly reactionary. Marx's account of the inhumanity of wage labour was precisely that it extinguishes the individual subject and reduces her to a mere quantity of "socially necessary labour power" and finally to Gallerte. Capital itself is the fundamental "antisubjective" force in the world and the pattern of all the others. Marxist revolutionary theory is about restoring the subject to society and abolishing the coercion that actually and in material reality desubjectivises workers. Conceptual and other antisubjectivist poetries may indeed be colluding with the action of capital in its oppression of individual lives only in an ironic style intended to get that oppression into sharper focus, or to make readers feel agitated or disgusted with their subordination. But if so, the collusion is manifestly nowhere near ironic enough: the

readers of this work are not agitated into fighting against capital but only pestered into moaning about conceptual poetry.

Keston Sutherland, "Theses on Antisubjectivist Dogma," *A Fiery Flying Roule*, online at: http://afieryflyingroule.tumblr.com/post/49378474736/keston-sutherland-theses-on-antisubjectivist (2013).

83. http://www.hsa-haiku.org/regions/archive/regional.htm.

84. For an excellent example of this move, see Christopher Bush, "The Ethnicity of Things in America's Lacquered Age," *Representations* 99.1 (2007), 74–98.

85. Christopher Reed, *Bachelor Japanists: Japanese Aesthetics and Western Masculinities* (New York: Columbia University Press, 2017), 10.

86. Long/So, 263–64

87. Earl Miner, *The Japanese Tradition in British and American Literature* (Princeton: Princeton University Press, 1958).

88. See: Seamus Deane, "Yeats and the Idea of Revolution," in *Celtic Revivals: Essays in Modern Irish Literature, 1880–1980* (Winston-Salem: Wake Forest University Press, 1987); Edward Said, "Yeats and Decolonization," in *Nationalism, Colonialism and Literature* (Minneapolis: University of Minnesota Press, 1990); Declan Kiberd, *Inventing Ireland* (Cambridge: Cambridge University Press, 1996); Gregory Castle, *Modernism and the Celtic Revival* (Cambridge: Cambridge University Press, 2001); Raphael Ingelbein, "Symbolism at the Periphery: Yeats, Maeterlinck and Cultural Nationalism," *Comparative Literature Studies*, vol. 42, no. 3 (2005), 183–284; Richard Ellmann, *Yeats: The Man and the Masks* (New York: Norton, 1978); David Lloyd, *Anomalous States: Irish Writing and the Postcolonial Moment* (Durham: Duke University Press, 1993); Marjorie Howes, "Postcolonial Yeats: Culture, Enlightenment and the Public Sphere," in *Field Day Review*, vol. 2 (2006), 54–73; and *Yeats' Nations: Gender, Class and Irishness* (Cambridge: Cambridge University Press, 1996). For a helpful digest of the debates surrounding Yeats's putative postcoloniality, see Jahan Ramazani, "Is Yeats a Postcolonial Poet?," *Raritan*, vol. 17, no. 3 (Winter 1998). For a survey of contemporary critical debates about Irish modernity's relation to global primitivisms, see Maria McGarrity and Claire A. Culleton, *Irish Modernism and the Global Primitive* (London: Palgrave Macmillan, 1999). Fleshing out the suggestion in Gregory Castle's book *Modernism and the Celtic Revival* (2001) that "the tension between the archaic and the modern . . . characterizes Irish modernism generally," the editors claim in their introduction that:

> It is most likely that owing to Ireland's anomalous position in the British empire during the development of modernism that Irish writers became intrigued with peasantry, common people, and with notions of indigenous cultures, and they inscribed them in their works not to augment distinctions between the high and the low, between the advanced and the elemental, or the modern and the primitive, but to intimate the very unsteadiness of these relational dichotomies. Primitive encounters flaunt each writer's anti-evolutionary rhetoric and his or her intellectual disposition not in fevered religious responses to Darwin but in elaborately scripted rejections of absolute distinctions between primitive and modern realms, and Darwinian theories of a developmental nature for humanity. For Irish modernists outside the revival, there appears little interest in the utopian dreams of a primitivist restoration. (4–5)

89. Ezra Pound, [Review of *Responsibilities*] *Poetry* (Chicago, 1914), 65–68.

90. W. H. Auden, "Yeats as an Example," in *Kenyon Review* 10.2 (1948), 189. Auden's more famous, and more sympathetic, assessment of Yeats's eccentric quaintness appears in his encomium, "In Memory of W. B. Yeats": "You were silly like us; your gift survived it all; The parish of rich women, physical decay, / Yourself. Mad Ireland hurt you into poetry. / Now Ireland has her madness and her weather still, / For poetry makes nothing happen: it survives / In the valley of its making where executives / Would never want to tamper, flows on south / From ranches of isolation and the busy griefs / Raw towns that we believe and die in; it survives, / A way of happening, a mouth." W. H. Auden, "In Memory of W. B. Yeats, d. January 1939," in *Selected Poems* (New York: Vintage, 2007), 89.

91. The next day I called on him at the Portland Hotel where he was staying with his wife. I went there to congratulate him on his first lecture, but in a tête-à-tête we discussed many subjects related to literature. This so exceeded my expectations and I was so deeply impressed by his cordiality that I decided to reciprocate this poet's friendliness and understanding by presenting him with something which I treasured very highly. You doubtless know what a prominent position the sword occupies in the mind of the Japanese. I had brought with me from Japan three swords which I treasured most. I made a present of one of these and I was rewarded by his sincere appreciation of my modest gift. Later on, he sent me nearly all the poems thus far published and expressed to me how pleased he was with my gift.

> . . . The name of the sword-smith is incorrectly spelt in his poems; it should be MOTOSHIGE and not Montashigi. Motoshige was a swordsmith who lived at Osafune, in the province of Bizen, the famous center of the sword industry of the Japan of about six hundred years ago. Strictly speaking he is Motoshige the Second whose father was Motoshige the Elder, or Ko-Motoshige, Ko meaning old. As for the embroidered silken cloth in which the sword was wrapped, this was made from one of the garments worn in feudal times by ladies of the Daimyos.

Funzo Sato, NLI MS.27,023 (acc. 4011, accessed 04/08/11).

92. Yeats is writing in the introduction to Pound's own *Certain Noble Plays of Japan*. W. B. Yeats, "Introduction to *Certain Noble Plays of Japan*," in Ezra Pound and Ernest Fenollosa, *The Classic Noh Theater of Japan* (New York: New Directions, 1959), 153.

93. The embarrassment is tinged with regret; among the Yeats material, one encounters a nameless manuscript for an introductory essay, written for a Japanese translation of the plays of J. M. Synge:

> When I read the plays and essays of John Synge I go back at moments to our Middle Ages and even further back, but as I go back, though I find much beauty at the journey's end, I am all the time among poor unlucky people, who live in thatched cottages among stony fields by the side of a bare ocean, or on the slopes of bare wind-swept mountains. In your Noh plays or in that diary of one of your court ladies of the eleventh century that I was reading yesterday, I find beliefs and attitudes of mind not very different but I find them among happy cultivated people. Once or twice when I have read some Japanese poem or play I have wished that Synge were living.

W. B. Yeats, untitled, MS 30,101, *National Library of Ireland.*

94. W. B. Yeats, "Imitated from the Japanese," [*New Poems*], *Yeats's Poetry, Drama, and Plays* (New York: Norton, 2000), 116.

95. Ibid.

96. W. B. Yeats, "[Introductory Rhymes]," [*Responsibilties*], ibid., 42; and W. B. Yeats, "Among School Children," [*The Tower*], ibid., 97–98.

Chapter Four. Loving John Ruskin

1. The passage is cited by Gary Genoshko, who attributes it to Guattari on the basis of the recollections of the Japanese economist Asada Akira (1989)—so, somewhat loosely—but the work Genoshko does to recover a "Japanese singularity" in Guattari's already fragmentary corpus is remarkable. See "*Japanese singularity,*" in Gary Genoshko, *Félix Guattari: An Aberrant Introduction* (London: Continuum, 2002), 122–54.

2. Sigmund Freud, *Beyond the Pleasure Principle,* trans. and ed. by James Strachey (New York, London: Norton, 1961), 8–10; Melanie Klein, "Notes on Some Schizoid Mechanisms," *The Collected Works of Melanie Klein,* 3 (London: Hogarth, 1975), 14.

3. Eve Kosofsky Sedgwick, "Paranoid Reading and Reparative Reading, or, You're So Paranoid,You Probably Think This Essay Is about You," in *Touching Feeling: Affect, Pedagogy, Performativity* (Durham and London: Duke University Press, 2003), 123–51.

4. Caroline Levine, *The Serious Pleasures of Suspense: Victorian Realism and Narrative Doubt* (Charlottesville: University of Virginia Press, 2003), 23.

5. See especially Levine, *The Serious Pleasures of Suspense,* and Jonah Siegel, "Black Arts, Ruined Cathedrals, and the Grave in Engineering: Ruskin and the Fatal Excess of Art," *Victorian Literature and Culture* 27.2 (1999), 395–417.

6. John Ruskin, *On the Nature of Gothic Architecture, and Herein of the True Functions of the Workman in Art* (London: Smith, Elder, 1854), 10.

7. Hugh Walker, *The Age of Tennyson* (London: George Bell and Sons, 1904), 199.

8. Raymond Williams, *Culture and Society, 1780–1950* (New York: Columbia University Press, 1958), 133.

9. John Ruskin, *The Political Economy of Art; or, "A Joy Forever" (and Its Price in the Market)* (New York: John Wiley and Sons, 1886), vii–viii.

10. Mikimoto Ryuzo, "Ruskin's Views of Economic Art," in *What Is Ruskin in Japan?* (privately printed, 1930), Ruskin Library of Tokyo, L1.17a.

11. Carolyn Dinshaw, *Getting Medieval: Sexualities and Communities, Pre- and Postmodern* (Durham, NC: Duke University Press, 1999), 21.

12. M. K. Gandhi, *Unto This Last: A Paraphrase,* trans. Valji Govindji Desai (Ahmedabad: Navajivan Publishing House, 1956), 2.

13. M. K. Gandhi, *An Autobiography: The Story of My Experiments with Truth* (Auckland: Floating Press, 2009), 476.

14. Georg Lukács, "What Is Orthodox Marxism?," in *History and Class Consciousness: Studies in Marxist Dialectics,* trans. Rodney Livingstone (London: Merlin Press, 1971), 1.

15. Lukács, "What Is Orthodox Marxism?," 1.

16. Lukács, "What Is Orthodox Marxism?," 1.

17. Benedetto Croce, *Historical Materialism and the Economics of Karl Marx* (New York: Russell and Russell, 1966), 25.

18. Avital Ronell, *Stupidity* (Urbana-Champaign: University of Illinois Press, 2002), 43.

19. For a more detailed account of Kawakami's biography, see Gail Lee Bernstein, *Japanese Marxist: Kawakami Hajime, 1879–1946* (Cambridge, MA: Harvard University Press, 1976).

20. C.F.G. Masterman, "Ruskin the Prophet," in *Ruskin the Prophet, and Other Centenary Essays*, ed. J. Howard Whitehouse (London: George Allen, 1920), 52.

21. W.D.P. Bliss, ed., *The Communism of John Ruskin* (New York: Humboldt, 1891); John Ruskin, *Fors Clavigera: Letters to the Workmen and Labourers of Great Britain*, 8 vols. (New York: Bryan, Taylor, 1894), 7:1.

22. Ruskin, *Fors Clavigera*, 10:2.

23. See Soseki Natsume, *Theory of Literature*, ed. Michael Bourdaghs, Atsuko Ueda, and Joseph Murphy (New York: Columbia University Press, 2010).

24. John Ruskin, *Munera Pulveris: Six Essays on the Elements of Political Economy* (London: Smith, Elder, 1872), v.

25. J.A.M. Whistler, "Mr. Whistler's Ten O'Clock," in *The Gentle Art of Making Enemies* (London: Heinemann, 1890), 152.

26. J.A.M. Whistler, "Whistler v. Ruskin: Art and Art-Critics," in *The Gentle Art of Making Enemies*, 26.

27. Ruskin, *The Works of John Ruskin*, vol. 20: *Fors Clavigera* (Orpington: George Allen, 1872) 282.

28. Howard Hull to author, Nov. 29, 2011.

29. The paintings cannot be identified. Howard Hull, the director of Brantwood, tells me that until about 1920, the "death room" contained a large number of Turner paintings, a still life by William Hunt, and a painting of Conwy Castle by John James Ruskin, the writer's father. But none of those paintings resembles anything in this photograph. Mr. Hull points out that by 1920, Arthur had made the decision to sell none of the Turners at Brantwood. Hull's immensely helpful letter (Nov. 16, 2011), which I gratefully acknowledge here, offers no speculations about who might have painted the works exhibited in this photograph.

30. John Pincher Faunthorpe, *Index to Fors Clavigera* (Orpington, UK: George Allen, 1887), 142, 249.

31. John Ruskin, *Time and Tide, by Weare and Tyne: Twenty-Five Letters to a Working Man of Sunderland on the Laws of Work* (New York: John Wiley and Son, 1869), 143.

32. Soseki Natsume, *And Then*, trans. Norma Moore Field (Tokyo: Tuttle, 2011).

33. Soseki Natsume, *The Miner*, trans. Jay Rubin (Tokyo: Tuttle, 1988), 161.

34. Ibid., 142.

35. Ibid., 142–43.

36. Ibid., 143.

37. Soseki, *Theory of Literature*, 49.

38. John Ruskin, "On the Present State of Modern Art, with Reference to the Advisable Arrangement of a National Gallery," in *The Works of John Ruskin*, ed. E. T. Cook and Alexander Wedderburn (London: George Allen, 1905), 209.

39. John Ruskin, *The Two Paths: Being Lectures on Art, and Its Application to Decoration and Manufacturing* (New York: John Wiley and Sons, 1876), 11–12.

40. See Williams, *Culture and Society* (New York: Columbia University Press, 1958); Ian Baucom, *Out of Place: Englishness, Empire, and the Locations of Identity* (Princeton, NJ: Princeton University Press, 1999); and Paul Gilroy, *The Black Atlantic: Modernity and Double Consciousness* (Cambridge, MA: Harvard University Press, 1993).

41. John Ruskin to William Michael Rossetti, June 15, 1863, qtd. in Julie L'Enfant, *William Rossetti's Art Criticism* (Lanham, MD: University Press of America, 1999), 192.

42. Marcus Huish, "England's Appreciation of Japanese Art," in *Transactions and Proceedings of the Japan Society of London*, vol. 7 (London: Kegan Paul, Trench, Trübner, 1908), 138.

43. Ann Cvetkovich, *An Archive of Feelings: Trauma, Sexuality, and Lesbian Public Cultures* (Durham and London: Duke University Press, 2003), 269.

44. Cvetkovich, *An Archive of Feelings*, 268.

45. J. B. Bullen, review of *Ruskin's Letters in the Mikimoto Collection: A Facsimile Edition*, ed. Masoa Simura, *Review of English Studies* 47.187 (1996), 459.

Chapter Five. The Sword and the Chrysanthemum

1. René Girard, *A Theater of Envy: William Shakespeare* (Oxford: Oxford University Press 1991), 279.

2. *Princess Mononoke*, dir. Miyazaki Hayao, Toho [Miramax], 1997.

3. Judith Butler, *Bodies That Matter: On the Discursive Limits of "Sex"* (London and New York: Routledge, 1993), 42.

4. Freud, "Fetishism," 154; Sigmund Freud, *Three Essays on the Theory of Sexuality*, trans. J. Strachey (New York: Basic Books, 2000), 24.

5. See Gilles Deleuze, *Coldness and Cruelty*, trans. Jean McNeil (Boston: MIT Press, 1971), 95–96.

6. Inazo Nitobe, *Bushido: The Soul of Japan* (Tokyo: IBC, 2003), 129–30.

7. Edwin Arnold, *Japonica* (New York: Charles Scribner's Sons, 1892), 113. Arnold was not the only Orientalist to publish on the Japanese swords. The geologist and Japanophile Benjamin Smith Lyman delivered a lecture on Japanese swords at the Numismatic and Antiquarian Society of Philadelphia published as "Metallurgical and Other Features of Japanese Swords" in the *Journal of the Franklin Institute*, vol. 161, no. 13. The descriptions of the Orientalists, like Nitobe's, delight in the formal elegance of the sword, and drift into reveries when contemplating the exquisite violence the sword performs. See also Countess Annie de Montaigu, "The Sword of Japan and Its Ornaments," *Monthly Illustrator* 4.13 (May 1895), 245–50; Ethel Watts Mumford, "The Japanese Book of the Ancient Sword," *Journal of the American Oriental Society*, vol. 26 (1905), 334–410. Meanwhile, the sword-themed poetry collection compiled by Noguchi and Miller, *Japan of Sword and Love* (1905), was followed by Shotaro Kimura and Charlotte M. A. Peake, *Sword and Blossom Poems from the Japanese* (Tokyo: T. Hasegawa, 1907) [Bancroft Z239.2.H302].

8. Benedict, *The Chrysanthemum and the Sword*, 224.

9. Negishi Yoshitaro, "The Japanese Sword," in *The Far East: An English Edition of the Kokumin-no-Tomo*, 1.1 (Feb. 1896), 32.

10. Christopher Reed, *The Chrysanthème Papers: The Pink Notebook of Madame Chrysanthème and Other Documents of French Japonisme* (Honolulu: University of Hawai'i Press, 2010).

11. Lauren Berlant, *The Female Complaint: The Unfinished Business of Sentimentality in American Life* (Durham: Duke University Press, 2008), 4.

12. See Reed, *The Chysanthème Papers*, 1–11.

13. Loti was, famously, a boor. B. H. Chamberlain and Lafcadio Hearn sent each other letters disparaging Loti's character and writing, and the hackneyed repetitiveness of his later works:

"To me Loti seems for a space," Hearn wrote in 1893, "to have looked into Nature's whole splendid burning fulgurant soul, and to have written under her very deepest and strongest inspiration. He was young. Then the colour and the light faded, and only the worn-out blasé nerves remained; and the poet became—a little morbid modern affected Frenchman." Lafcadio Hearn, "Letter to Basil Hall Chamberlain, February 18, 1893," in *The Life and Letters of Lafcadio Hearn*, ed. Elizabeth Bisland (Boston: Houghton Mifflin, 1922), 383.

14. John Luther Long, *Madame Butterfly* (New York: Century, 1903). For a textual history, see Reed, *The Chrysanthème Papers*, 12–13.

15. Mari Yoshihara, *White Women and American Orientalism* (Oxford: Oxford University Press, 2003), 4.

16. Charlotte Perkins Gilman [as "Charlotte Perkins Stetson"], *New England Magazine: An Illustrated Monthly*, vol. 5 [vol. 11], Sept. 1891–Feb. 1892, 647–756.

17. John Luther Long, *Miss Cherry-Blossom of Tokyo* (Philadelphia: Lippincott, 1895).

18. Long, *Madame Butterfly*, xiii

19. "The Rambler," *Book Buyer: A Monthly Review of American and Foreign Literature*, vol. 17 (Aug. 1898–Jan. 1899), 283; "Among the Newest Books," *Delineator: A Journal of Fashion, Culture and Fine Arts*, vol. 53 (New York: Butterick, 1899), 256.

20. "Madame Butterfly, by John Luther Long," in *Critic*, vol. 33, p. 526.

21. Onoto Watanna, "A Contract," in *A Half Caste and Other Writings*, ed. Linda Trinh Moser and Elizabeth Rooney (Champaign: University of Illinois Press, 2003), 50–59.

22. David Henry Hwang, *M. Butterfly* (New York: Dramatists Play Service, 1998).

23. Diana Birchall, *Onoto Watanna: The Story of Winnifred Eaton* (Urbana and Chicago: University of Illinois Press).

24. "General Gossip of Authors and Writers," in *Current Literature*, vol. 24 (July–Dec. 1898), 306.

25. Artaud's "brimbulkdriquant" and "rouarghambde" do not, to French readers, feel like real words, he argues, whereas the easy adoption of "chortle" and "galumphing" into standard English suggests that while Carroll was clearly generating new words, he was doing so in conformity to unwritten, but commonly understood, principles about what words could be and sound like.

> The easiest way to deal with the text [of "Jabberwockey"] is to engage in a systematic linguistic reading, based on the two operations of analysis and synthesis, i.e. on the order of Saussure's *langue*. This impels us to read the text on four levels: phonetics, morphology, syntax, and semantics. On the *phonetic* level, we shall note that the text is eminently readable, an excellent choice for public reading. All the words can be pronounced, even the coined ones, because they all conform to the phonotactics of English, i.e. to the licit ways of combining phonemes. "Hjckrrh!," the Gryphon's exclamation, is an unpronounceable illicit combination of phonemes: not so "slithy toves" or "borogroves." In technical parlance, Carroll's coined language is neither *lanternois*, the compulsive repetition of obsessional sounds which have nothing to do with a real tongue, and which one hears, for instance, in glossolalia, nor *baragouin*, the imitation of the sounds of another language, but *charabia*, the imitation of one's own language.

Jean-Jacques Lecercle, *Philosophy of Nonsense: The Intuitions of Victorian Nonsense Literature* (London: Routledge, 1994), 21.

26. Yuko Matsukawa, "Cross-Dressing and Cross-Naming: Decoding Onoto Watanna," in *Tricksterism in Turn-of-the-Century American Literature: A Multicultural Perspective,* ed. Elizabeth Ammons and Annette White Parks (Hanover, NH: University Press of New England, 1994), 109, 123–24.

27. Winnifred Eaton, *Me: A Book of Remembrance,* ed. Linda Trinh Moser (Jackson: University Press of Mississippi, 1997).

28. Winnifred Eaton, *Marion: The Story of an Artist's Model* (Montreal: McGill-Queen's University Press, 2012).

29. Miike, *Audition.*

30. https://www.theguardian.com/film/2001/mar/16/1.

31. For a note on torture porn, see: http://nymag.com/movies/features/15622/.

32. https://web.archive.org/web/20160325070923/ http://www.avclub.com/article/24-hours-of-horror-with-eli-roth-2066.

33. Miike quoted in Handke, p. 56; Martin, *Extreme Asia: The Rise of Cult Cinema from the Far East* (Edinburgh: Edinburgh University Press, 2015).

34. https://web.archive.org/web/20121111150310/ http://articles.latimes.com/2009/oct/04/entertainment/ca-secondlook4.

35. An especially creative deployment of this formal pattern opens the American horror movie *Ghost Ship,* https://www.youtube.com/watch?v=22XdYRbFHoE.

36. Robin Wood, "Revenge Is Sweet: The Bitterness of *Audition,*" *Film International* 2.7 (2004), published online, January 27, 2011, http://filmint.nu/?p=42.

37. The textbook in question being Julia Kristeva, "Approaching Abjection," *Powers of Horror: An Essay on Abjection* (New York: Columbia University Press, 1982), 1–31.

38. Quentin Tarantino, dir., *Reservoir Dogs* (Miramax, 1992).

39. Quentin Tarantino, *Reservoir Dogs,* screenplay, October 22, 1990.

40. Derek Malcolm, "Reservoir Dogs," Thursday, January 7, 1993.

41. *The Godfather,* dir. Francis Ford Coppola (Paramount, 1972).

42. *Mean Streets,* dir. Martin Scorsese (Warner Bros, 1973); *Dillinger,* dir. Max Nosseck (Monogram, 1945); Tarantino, *Reservoir Dogs,* screenplay.

43. *Pulp Fiction,* dir. Quentin Tarantino (Miramax, 1994).

44. See Laura Mulvey, "Visual Pleasure and Narrative Cinema," *Film Theory and Criticism: Introductory Readings,* ed. Leo Braudy and Marshall Cohen (New York: Oxford University Press, 1999), 833–44; Mary Ann Doane, *Femmes Fatales: Feminism, Film Theory, Psychoanalysis* (London: Routledge, 1991); Sigmund Freud, "Fetishism," trans. James Strachey, *The Complete Psychological Works of Sigmund Freud,* vol. 21 (London: Hogarth and the Institute of Psychoanalysis, 1961), 154.

45. *The Cutting Edge: The Magic of Movie Editing,* dir. Wendy Apple (A.C.E., 2004).

46. Tarantino's editor, Sally Menke, passed away in 2010; *Django Unchained* (Weinstein, 2012) and *The Hateful Eight* (Weinstein, 2015) were both edited by Fred Raskin.

47. Carolyn Dinshaw, *Getting Medieval: Sexualities and Communities, Pre- and Postmodern* (Durham: Duke University Press, 1999), 185.

48. bell hooks, "Cool Cynicism: Pulp Fiction," in *Reel to Real: Race, Class, and Sex at the Movies* (London: Routledge, 1996), 60.

49. *Kill Bill: Volume 2,* dir. Quentin Tarantino (Miramax, 2004).

50. Roger Ebert, "Kill Bill, Volume 1: October 10th, 2003," *RogerEbert.com*; Peter Bradshaw, "Kill Bill: Vol 2," *Guardian*, Friday, April 23, 2004.

51. Xavier Morales, "Kill Bill: Beauty and Violence," *Harvard Law Record*, October 2003.

52. See Herman Melville, *Billy Budd, Sailor* (London: Constable, 1924); Herman Melville, "Benito Cereno," in *The Piazza Tales* (New York: Dix and Edwards, 1856), 109–270; Herman Melville, "Bartleby," in *The Piazza Tales* (New York: Dix and Edwards, 1856), 31–108.

53. Richard Chase, cited in Barbara Johnson, "Melville's Fist: The Execution of *Billy Budd*," in *The Critical Difference: Essays in the Contemporary Rhetoric of Reading* (Baltimore: Johns Hopkins University Press, 1980), 89.

54. This particular citation comes from Anna Greer, " 'Isle of Dogs' creates beautiful world of doggos, but leaves good girls behind," on *bust.com*: https://bust.com/movies/194358-isle-of-dogs-good-but-problematic.html.

55. Adam Phillips, *Promises, Promises: Essays on Psychoanalysis and Literature* (New York: Basic Books, 2001), xviii.

INDEX

ILLUSTRATION CREDITS

Figure 0.1. Still from "Viewing Party," *The Office*, NBC Universal. Originally aired November 11, 2010. Image used in accordance with fair use.

Figure 0.2. Reproduced from *Narrative of the Expedition of an American Squadron*, Francis L. Hawks (1856).

Figure 2.1. Reproduced from "A Suggestion," *The Gentle Art of Making Enemies*, James Abbott McNeill Whistler (1890).

Figure 2.2. *Symphony in White, No. 2: The Little White Girl*, James Abbott McNeill Whistler © Tate, London 2018.

Figure 2.3. *Caprice in Purple and Gold: The Golden Screen*, James Abbott McNeill Whistler © Freer Sackler Museum (Smithsonian Institution) 2018.

Figure 2.4. Courtesy of the Bookplate Society. Identical *ex libris* card for Dennis Wheatley, illustrated by Frank C. Papé, found also in Wheatley's copy of *The Trial of Oscar Wilde* (1906).

Figure 3.1. Reproduced from *The Book Buyer*, Volume 12 (1895), p. 286.

Figure 3.2. Courtesy of Eric K. Carr.

Figure 4.1. Mikimoto Ruskin Library, Tokyo.

Figure 4.2. Mikimoto Ruskin Library, Tokyo.

Figure 4.3. Mikimoto Ruskin Library, Tokyo.

Figure 5.1. Reproduced from John Luther Long, *Madame Butterfly*, illustrated by C. Yarnall Abbott. Century Co. (1903), p. 84.

Figure 5.2:1–10. Stills from *Audition*, dir. Takashi Miike, Adness Entertainment (1999). Images used in accordance with fair use.

Figures 5.3:1–10. Stills from *Pulp Fiction*, dir. Quentin Tarantino, Miramax (1994). Images used in accordance with fair use.

Figures 5.4:1–1.: Stills from *Kill Bill (Vol. 1)*, dir. Quentin Tarantino, Miramax (2003). Images used in accordance with fair use.

A NOTE ON THE TYPE

This book has been composed in Arno, an Old-style serif typeface in the classic Venetian tradition, designed by Robert Slimbach at Adobe.